Fred Trueman

CHRIS WATERS was born in Sutton-in-Ashfield, Nottinghamshire, in 1973 and raised and educated in Lincoln. He entered journalism in 1995 at *Berrow's Worcester Journal* before returning home to start his sports writing career on the *Lincoln Chronicle*. In 1999 he became cricket correspondent of the *Nottingham Evening Post* and, since 2004, he has been cricket correspondent of the *Yorkshire Post*.

Fred Trueman

The Authorised Biography

Chris Waters

First published
2011 by Aurum Press Limited
7 Greenland Street
London NW1 0ND
www.aurumpress.co.uk

This paperback edition published in 2012 by Aurum Press

A catalogue record for this book is available from the British Library.

Picture on p. x courtesy of www.greatnorthernbooks.co.uk

ISBN 978 1 84513 746 5

1 3 5 7 9 10 8 6 4 2
2012 2014 2016 2015 2013

Typeset in Dante MT by SX Composing DTP, Rayleigh, Essex

Printed and bound by CPI Group (UK) Ltd, Croydon, CR0 4YY

To my dear parents, June and Francis
No words can express how much you mean to me

Contents

REMEMBERING FRED

By Ian McMillan

Remember the hair
Flopping over the face
Before the long run-up.
Remember the action,
Remember the man.

Remember the wickets;
Three hundred and seven.
In black and white photos
The big face is smiling
Or the big face is scowling.
Remember the bowling,
Remember the man.

Remember the legend, the thirties in Maltby,
Times harder than willow, times harder than leather
And cricket the chance to escape the pit's clutches,
Times colder than Headingley late April weather.

And remember the big man
The larger-than-life
Man who ran up like thunder
And bowled up a storm;
The man they called Fiery
Who burned with a passion
For cricket, and Yorkshire, and England
And Time has caught up with the man
And the innings is over
And the man has departed
But the legend lives on

The voice like a rumble of a slow moving coal train,
The face like a map that's been folded too long
And the action, the bowling, the run up, the wickets
Remember Fred Trueman
Now the over is done.

For BBC Radio 4's *Last Word*, July 2006

I

The Last Supper

A reunion of the former Yorkshire and England cricketers
Fred Trueman, Brian Close, Ray Illingworth and Geoffrey Boycott

Sawley, North Yorkshire, 2005

'Bloody hell,' groaned Geoffrey Boycott as he stared at his watch, a scowl across his face. 'Where's Fred? He was meant to be here half an hour ago. It's his local pub and he manages to be late.' Brian Close lit yet another cigarette – his third in twenty minutes – and then nonchalantly reassured Boycott: 'Fred's always late. He'll turn up soon.' Ray Illingworth nodded and remembered out loud: 'Fred took me to Edgbaston to play in a Test match. We had to be there at two o'clock and he said he'd pick me up at midday. At twenty past twelve I rang his wife and she said, "Don't worry, Fred is setting off shortly. He's just popped into the local garage to have a couple of tyres fitted."'

Close asked: 'So what time did you get to Edgbaston?'

'About three o'clock,' replied Illingworth.

'Bloody hell,' laughed Close. 'Were you bollocked?'

'Oh aye, Gubby Allen gave us the biggest dressing down you've heard, but it was Fred he was angry with. For some reason, Fred's always had problems with time-keeping.'

'Problems,' interjected Boycott. 'That's an understatement. Is he going to turn up or will we have to send out a search party?'

Another fifteen minutes went by before Fred Trueman charged through the entrance of the Sawley Arms pub. He was like a cowboy bursting through the swing doors of a saloon. His face was covered in sweat. He was muttering to himself in exasperated fashion, as if – to paraphrase his oft-repeated lament on *Test Match Special* – he couldn't believe what had just gone off. 'Sorry lads,' he spluttered in booming baritone. 'Got stuck behind a caravan for three miles and then a flock of sheep at Grassington. Bloody sheep, couldn't get past them. Even when you sound the horn they take no notice.' Boycott motioned to say something but decided not to. Illingworth wore a weary expression. An uneasy silence was broken by Close. 'Let's get this show on the bloody road . . .'

It was 6 July 2005. Trueman, Close, Illingworth and Boycott – four of Yorkshire and England's greatest cricketers – had come together for a special reunion. It was the first time they had all met up in thirty years after a history of fall-outs and bitter disagreements. Trueman suggested the event after an earlier reconciliation between him and Boycott; when Boycott got throat cancer in 2002, Trueman rang him to end two decades of silence between them. After taking a minute to collect himself, Trueman led the players into the picturesque pub garden. To mark the occasion, he had asked his friend John Blakey, a Leeds-born artist, to capture the former team-mates on canvas. The group portrait would be sold as a limited edition through Blakey's publisher, Great Northern Books, which had invited me to shadow the quartet in my capacity as *Yorkshire Post* cricket correspondent. It was the only time I met Fred Trueman.

Beneath a sunwashed sky, I watched Blakey arrange the 'Four Greatest Living Yorkshiremen' in front of a rowan tree. He immediately put Trueman at the heart of the painting, reflecting his seniority. At seventy-four years and five months exactly, Trueman was the eldest – eighteen days older than Close, with Illingworth seventy-three and Boycott sixty-four. Although Trueman had greying hair and a prominent paunch, he still cut a physically powerful figure. Boycott sat to Trueman's left; Illingworth to

Trueman's right. Both turned to face the former fast bowler as – ball in hand – he demonstrated the grip for his trademark outswinger. Close stood directly behind Trueman, his spidery fingers resting on his chair. The emphasis of the portrait was on Trueman, dapper in a white shirt and dark blue blazer.

As a handful of pub-goers observed from a distance, some seemed surprised by the natural camaraderie. During the seventies and eighties, the cricketers were often at each other's throats as Yorkshire County Cricket Club tore itself apart, but as they posed in the sleepy, Miss Marple-ish village of Sawley – about five miles from the market town of Ripon – one would never have guessed at their turbulent history. One onlooker even said the hallowed scene put him in mind of da Vinci's *The Last Supper*, with Christ at the centre of a mural flanked by the disciples. 'Well, I don't think Fred would quibble with that comparison,' chuckled his companion, 'but I don't think the good Lord would be too impressed.'

The cricketers were pictured in pensive mood – broad grins might have exaggerated the entente cordiale – but there was a light-hearted moment when Trueman bemoaned the ball he'd been given to hold. 'Call this a cricket ball?' he scoffed, examining it with contempt. 'This is a kid's ball – the sort they use in junior games.'

The comment tickled Close. 'I shouldn't worry about it, Fred. No one's saying you've got to bowl twenty overs with it.'

Trueman looked at the ball and pursed his lips. 'I could still do some damage with it,' he whispered. 'I could still take some wickets with this little bugger.'

Once Blakey had completed the preliminary sketches, the cricketers headed for a private meal in the pub conservatory. I trailed behind them like an equerry at the rear of a royal procession. En route they passed through a busy bar area where Trueman instantly became the centre of attention, the one the pub-goers seemed most interested to talk to and shake by the hand. There was a warmth and humanity about him as he moved through the company of admirers, a friendly touch to which the drinkers related. Described by former Prime Minister Harold Wilson as the 'Greatest Living Yorkshireman' (the comment inspired a querying correspondence from J.B. Priestley), Trueman had a spring in his step as the compliments and greetings came thick and fast. 'Fred, I'd just like to say it's an honour to see you,' said one old-timer with a lump in his throat. Another declared, 'Fred, you've been my hero since I was a lad in short trousers. Thank you so much for the pleasure you've given me.' An elderly lady called out, 'Aye up, our Fred, shouldn't you be at Headingley? We all reckon you could still do better than that Yorkshire lot.'

The words 'our Fred' seemed significant, while the look on Trueman's face suggested he agreed. 'Very nice of you to say so,' he said with a smile. Then, as a dark cloud suddenly fell over his ruddy complexion, he added, 'but I've washed my hands of Yorkshire County Cricket Club. I've no time any more for that club and its members.'

Trueman strode into the sunlit conservatory and took his place at the head of the dinner table. Boycott and Illingworth sat to his right, Close to his left, and also present were Blakey and Boycott's wife, Rachael. I sat opposite Trueman, who regarded me with a welcoming nod. Close, Illingworth and Boycott seemed oblivious to my presence as I tried to make notes as discreetly as possible. I was in my early thirties and new to Yorkshire and felt privileged and daunted to be in such company. Trueman ordered wine for everyone except Geoffrey Boycott, who preferred bottled water, and no sooner did a nervous-looking waitress arrive with a quantity of bread rolls than the 'Four Greatest Living Yorkshiremen' snatched them like kids seizing chocolate biscuits.

And then they were off . . .

Trueman conducted the arbitrary exchanges.

Trueman: I'll say one thing, I'm fed up of hearing about this reverse-swing business as though it's some sort of innovation. There's nothing new about it at all. It's just they never called it reverse-swing in our day. In our day, it was simply called swing. Are we saying the bowlers these days can do things we couldn't?

Close (*casually flicking cigarette ash into a plant pot behind his chair*): Couldn't agree more, Fred. These Pakistanis reckon they invented reverse-swing, but they never did.

Illingworth: I know for a fact the bloody Pakistanis never invented it. Donald Waterhouse was showing me how to wet one side of the ball in 1947. Fine bowler, Donald Waterhouse. Took a thousand Bradford League wickets.

Trueman: To hear some people talk, you'd think these modern bowlers were bloody magicians.

The appetisers arrived and the cricketers dived in, as though they hadn't eaten for weeks. Attention turned to the forthcoming Ashes series, which would start at Lord's in fifteen days' time. Trueman suggested it could prove close, despite Australia being expected to retain the urn. Michael Vaughan's England would beat Ricky Ponting's Australia 2–1 in arguably the greatest Test series ever played.

Trueman: If we can do the Aussies, I'll be the first to congratulate England and say 'well done'. I think Michael Vaughan has done a magnificent job and we could be in for an interesting few weeks.

Close: Yes, but who have we been playing? Bloody Bangladesh. I doubt our lot can bowl the Aussies out twice.

Trueman: I hear what you're saying, but we've got to go into this Test series with a positive attitude. We've got to believe we can beat these bastards. If you're playing a Test side and thinking they're invincible, why bother turning up? You've got to think positive.

Close (*laughing*): We can only hope.

Trueman: How good are these bloody Australians? I get fed up of people saying they're the greatest of all time. How can they be? There's no all-rounder. There's no Keith Miller, no Ray Lindwall, no Don Bradman, no Neil Harvey, no Bill O'Reilly, so how can they be the best ever? They're a good side, but it's ridiculous to say they're the best.

Close: I'd like to have seen our Yorkshire side of the sixties take them on. We were as good in the field as anyone and we beat the Aussies at Bramall Lane.

Trueman: We beat all the bloody touring sides. Look, the beauty of our Yorkshire side of the sixties was that we didn't have to hide anyone in the field. There were some outstanding fielders in that line-up – even you, Closey.

Close: You could come right up to the wicket and catch. We had bowlers who could land the ball on a sixpence – and we also had Fred.

Trueman pretended not to hear. Boycott and Illingworth suppressed giggles. Close topped up the plant pot behind his chair.

Boycott: Fred's right, this could be a fascinating series. What do you think, Ray, an England win?

Illingworth: If Harmison and Flintoff don't perform, we won't win, and I'm worried about Harmison.

Trueman: I tell you what, I'd like to see Steve Harmison or any of that England lot bowling on the f***ing flat pitches of the West Indies in the 1950s. I'd like to see them bowling on the wickets I bowled on. When I went to the West Indies, there was one thing I learned, and it was a great lesson. I learned to bowl one side of the wicket; otherwise, I got hammered. I remember one Test I played and they were bloody kind to us, the West Indies. They declared on 681 for 8 – and one of them was a run-out.

Close: You mean bowling against the likes of Frankie Worrell and Everton Weekes?

Trueman: And don't forget that fella Kanhai coming in at no. 7. And didn't the West Indies have some bloke called Sobers? These England lads don't know they're born.

The main courses arrived and were hastily demolished, Trueman making fast work of a large helping of steak pie and vegetables. I looked on spellbound, as though witnessing a stage play.

Illingworth: Thinking back to the Windies, Fred, do you remember when we played them in Barbados in 1960? We had them three down for not many and didn't get another wicket for two days. Frankie Worrell and Sobers got 200.

Trueman: Frankie Worrell got 197 not out and Sobers 226. If you got the ball past the bat in that match, you ordered a round of drinks.

Close: Since when have you ordered a round of drinks?

Trueman: Look it up when you get home, Raymond. Frankie Worrell and Sobers put on 399.

Illingworth: Is that all?

Trueman: Look it up, Raymond. They got very close to the 411 Peter May/Colin Cowdrey partnership at Edgbaston in 1957. Peter got 285 not out.

Boycott: How do you remember these stats, Fred?

Illingworth: Fred's always had a good memory.

Close (*grinning*): Particularly when it comes to his own wickets.

Trueman: I did take enough of the bastards. More than any other fast bowler in the history of the game.

Boycott: How many, Fred? Two thousand?

Trueman (*proudly puffing out his chest*): I took 2304 first-class wickets at 18.29.

Boycott: And how many Test wickets?

Trueman: Three hundred and seven at 21.57 – and it would have been 500 Test wickets if I'd played all the bloody Tests I should have played. The selectors seemed more interested in picking decent blokes than decent bowlers. It was un-be-liev-able (*emphasising each syllable*).

The conversation turned to fast bowling, a topic Trueman professed to know 'a thing or two about'.

Illingworth: Who do you rate fast bowling-wise, Fred? Who were the special fast bowlers in your view?

Trueman: The best in my book was the great Australian Ray

Lindwall. Nowadays, there's no one to hold a candle to Ray. What you tend to find these days are people who think they're fast bowlers but in actual fact are fast-medium bowlers.

Boycott: Don't you rate any of the current mob?

Trueman (*after a long pause*): There have been a couple of good ones, I suppose, and there's no doubt the two most successful bowlers with the new ball over the last fifteen years have been Glenn McGrath and Shaun Pollock. Both have one thing in common, and it sticks out like a sore thumb.

Illingworth: What's that?

Trueman: They bowl wicket-to-wicket. That's where their success comes from. If you look at the current England bunch, they're always too wide of the stumps. You only have to look at Steve Harmison to see what I'm talking about. He's very wide of the crease, you know, very wide.

Close: Harmison's bloody front arm faces third man. You only have to think back to your bloody action, Fred. You always had your arm straight and all the rest of it, but if you look at them nowadays, they're all over the shop.

Trueman: I've said it before and I'll say it again, the game of cricket is sideways on. It always has been and it always will be.

Close: All the long-striding pace bowlers in our day were sideways on. That's how you got control of how far your front foot went. The cricketers in our era worked it out. Nowadays, they're all chest on.

Trueman: You don't have to tell me.

Close: And another thing, I'd make all our batsmen bat with one hand in the nets to sort out their technique.

Trueman: They'd take no notice of you, you're wasting your time.

Close: Bloody crackers they are. The top hand in batting is the main hand, the hand that takes bat to ball. The bottom hand just supports.

Trueman: I've told you, you're wasting your time. The modern players don't listen to us. They're so daft they think we're bloody crackers.

The desserts came and went, followed by cheese and biscuits, and the dialogue grew increasingly bizarre, as though Trueman and co. had turned into the Marx Brothers.

Trueman: I hear people going on about Ant and Dec and comparing them to Morecambe and Wise. Ant and Dec? They're not comedians. Now Eric Morecambe was one of the greatest comedians that ever lived, and Ernie Wise was brilliant as well, but Ant and Dec? Ant and f***ing Dec? They're not fit to lick the boots of Morecambe and Wise.

Illingworth: Ant and Dec are presenters, not funny comedians.

Boycott: It's a different kettle of fish altogether.

Trueman: Totally bloody different.

Close: Look, I'm no fan of this Ant and Dec business, but it was Eric Morecambe who made the Morecambe and Wise double act what it was. It was Eric who was the brains behind the operation. In my opinion, Ernie Wise was too dependent on Eric Morecambe.

Trueman: Too dependent on Eric Morecambe? I'll have you know Ernie Wise delivered his lines at exactly the right time, and that's very important. He was top drawer, Ernie, and he never got the credit he deserved. Look, I'm very sorry, Brian, but Ernie Wise never got the praise he should have got.

The dinner drew to a close and the cricketers talked about meeting again, with Trueman especially keen on a reunion rerun, but it would be the last time they got together, chewed the fat and concluded cricket and life were not what they used to be. Almost exactly one year later, on Saturday 1 July 2006, Fred Trueman would pass away at Airedale General Hospital in Keighley, North Yorkshire, following a short battle with lung cancer; the reunion would be a poignant ending between the Yorkshire legends.

As they walked back through the bar and out towards the car park, exchanging smiles and handshakes before heading home, I took the chance to talk to Trueman having previously failed to get a word in.

He apologised for not having properly said hello and offered a handshake that felt surprisingly gentle. Trueman seemed wearied by the day's exertions – his cheeks were flushed and he sounded out of breath – but he was not too tired to press for information as to how 'my lads' (the current Yorkshire players) were getting on, while at the same time insisting he would 'never set foot inside Headingley again'. 'The way they have treated me over the years has been disgraceful,' he said, 'but I always want my lads to do well.'

When I enquired what Yorkshire had done to upset him, he fired back: 'How bloody long have you got?' Then, without hesitation, he reeled off a list as if well rehearsed. 'Er, they never gave me a second benefit when I was entitled to one at the end of my career – despite the fact the likes of Closey got one. They made me pay towards my own farewell present after I'd given them twenty years' service. They were the only – and I mean *the only* – county who did not send me a telegram of congratulation when I beat Brian Statham's world record for the most number of Test wickets against New Zealand at Christchurch in 1963. And all that civil war at Yorkshire in the 1980s involving Geoffrey, God bless him, led to me being voted off the Yorkshire committee and replaced by some bloke with a deaf aid from Keighley.'

Trueman paused briefly to dab his brow. The day was hot and his hackles were up. 'And then it's all the little things,' he continued, 'like the car park attendants at Headingley who won't let you park at the ground even if you point out you took 1745 first-class wickets for the club at 17.12. I mean, Yorkshire are charging their former players to watch Test matches at Headingley now, even though I could think of a few good reasons why I personally should be given complimentary tickets. It is unbelievable what Yorkshire have done to me over the years when you think of the blood, sweat and tears I've given for them. Absolutely un-be-liev-able.'

I tried to lighten the mood by telling Trueman I grew up listening to his work on *Test Match Special* but this seemed only to darken his demeanour.

'That BBC are just as bad. I gave them twenty-five years' service and they sacked me and Trevor Bailey and didn't even give us the chance to say goodbye. Would it have hurt them to have given us one last programme, a chance to thank everyone who'd tuned in? It's the sort of heartless attitude you'd expect from Yorkshire.'

'Why were you sacked?' I asked.

'Er, my BBC departure was very badly handled. I got a phone call at the end of the 1999 season from the head of sport, and that was it – they finished me on the spot. "I'm not sure how to speak to a sporting icon," this guy said, before telling me I was out. The BBC reckoned they wanted a younger audience, implying people like me were out of touch. Out of touch? I just told it as I saw it.'

I accompanied Trueman to his car, where he offered a firmer handshake and an invitation to ring him if I needed any quotes.

'Call whenever you want,' he said, 'but don't go asking questions about that Twenty20 rubbish. Twenty20? What sort of cricket is that?' Then, turning to Close, Illingworth and Boycott, he said, 'What do you think of this Twenty20 garbage?'

'Can't say I'm a huge fan,' replied Boycott.

'Nor me,' said Illingworth with a sardonic smile.

'Twenty20?' sneered Close. 'I think it's bollocks.'

'Right, I'm off,' said Trueman, 'Brian, Raymond, Geoffrey, it's been smashing to see you. Thanks so much for coming here today.'

And with that, Frederick Sewards Trueman waved a regal goodbye, cast a startled look at his watch and hurried behind the wheel of a dark blue Mercedes Coupe – registration FST 1X.

'Watch out for those sheep at Grassington,' cautioned Close.

'Oh aye,' groaned Trueman, countenance thunderous. 'Well, the little buggers had better not be blocking the road this time because my lovely wife will be wondering where I've got to. Oh, bloody hell, lads, is that the time? I've really got to dash, I'm running rather late . . .'

2

Curse of the Truemans

I can be blunt, but I've never said or done half the things attributed to me. And I was in the third division in the Yorkshire team when it came to drinking. Most of them could drink me under the table, yet I was the one who got the bad reputation. Lurid headlines haunted me all my career. The stories that I had said or done something outrageous became part of cricket's folklore. Stories like when I was supposed to have said to an Indian diplomat at a reception, 'Pass the salt, Gunga Din' were pure fiction. It was said that I wasn't taken on the tour of South Africa in 1964–65 because of my attitude to colour, yet I never knew I had one. Ridiculous stories were ten-a-penny. I called it the 'Curse of the Truemans'. Much of my time as a player I was more sinned-against than sinning, I can tell you. I used to go to bed at 9 p.m. knackered because that's the effect of bowling over 1000 overs a season – that's something for the present county bowlers to think about – and my team-mates would be out having a drink somewhere. Yet it was assumed that I must be attending an even bigger orgy somewhere else. In some hotels, chambermaids refused to bring breakfast to my room.

So proclaimed Fred Trueman in 1990 – comments that captured his colourful image. Widely perceived as a riotous figure, a sort of Attila the Hun in whites, anecdotes and allegations clung to him in the way moss clings to a stone wall. So engulfed was his career in rumour and tittle-tattle, gossip and hearsay, that no one was sure which stories were true and which were false – perhaps not even himself. As *Wisden* put it, 'every cricket story ever told somehow attached itself to Fred', while his friend and *Test Match Special* colleague Don Mosey reckoned Trueman must have accounted for 'something like 50 or 60 per cent of the game's folklore'.

The legend was born in 1949 when Trueman arrived on the cricketing scene. His first match was for Yorkshire at Cambridge University and during a team dinner the eighteen-year-old was alarmed to discover the menu was in French. Not wanting to embarrass himself, Trueman indicated he would have what a colleague had ordered before being asked whether he, unlike his colleague, would like dessert. 'I suppose I'd better,' said the peckish newcomer. Trueman studied the menu with exaggerated care before pointing innocently to the words at the bottom of the page – *Jeudi le douzième mai* (Thursday 12 May). 'I think I'll have that,' he announced, to howls of hilarity.

Brian Close, who also debuted in that game, remembers Trueman dropped a catch off his bowling and apologised with the first in a canon of one-liners. 'Fred shouted from mid-off, "Sorry, Closey, but the ball was going so bloody fast that bugger must be using a bloody steel bat."'

The wisecracks did the rounds of the county circuit. The young man was gauche and uncommonly outspoken and the game had encountered no one quite like him. Exceptionally quick and prodigiously talented, three years later he was playing for England, annihilating India in his maiden Test series. When the Indians sought refuge behind the square-leg umpire, finding Trueman's thunderbolts too hot to handle, the legend acquired a life of its own, eventually spiralling higher than Jack's magic Beanstalk.

To every cricket-loving schoolboy of the fifties and sixties – and quite possibly a few wrinkled observers too – Fred Trueman might well have been plucked from the pages of folktale. He was the absolute embodiment of the fearsome fast bowler: bristling with menace as he charged to his mark, black hair flopping, unbuttoned right sleeve rolled up afresh as though preparing for a fight. Then came an angled run culminating in a side-on delivery that mixed beauty and brutality as rarely before. Trueman expected a wicket every ball and considered it a slight if he failed to take one; he was a fast bowler to the very core of his being. 'He was always a promise and frequently a presenter of the dramatic,' observed former *Yorkshire Post* cricket correspondent J.M. Kilburn. 'He alerted spectators as he alerted opening batsmen. Bumper and yorker and magnetic away-swinger mingled like electric shocks to make both batting and watching a continuous adventure that began with a toss of the head as preliminary to a long, accelerating run-up leading to a wide delivery stride, a beautiful sideways presentation and a flowing follow-through. Culmination was often enough a stare, or glare, of disbelief in the batsman's survival and sometimes an uninhibited comment on the luck of the enemy. Trueman always had breath to spare for an expression of opinion.'

A natural showman and born entertainer, Trueman had more theatrics than a repertory company. He lapped up the attention of the stands as an actor laps up the roar of the auditorium. Charismatic, handsome – in a rugged, Heathcliffian way – and a bit of a novelty, he was the definition of 'box office'. His appeal was central to the growth of his legend. Bob Platt, one of his closest friends and a former new-ball partner at Yorkshire, said, 'Spectators in those days didn't just go to watch Yorkshire play, or to see England in action, they went along to see Fred bowl. He was one of the biggest draws in world cricket and whenever he came back to play for Yorkshire after a Test match he invariably put several thousand on the gate. But it wasn't just the crowds who loved him – his team-mates, the umpires, even opposition players revelled in the drama he brought to the game. Fred was blessed with wonderful humour and his brilliant one-liners had everyone in stitches.' The Truemanisms echo down the years:

To batsmen wearing a public school cap . . . '*I'll have that bugger off for starters.*' Or, after he'd dismissed them . . . '*'Ardly worth dressing up for, were it?*'

To batsmen who committed the cardinal offence of edging him

through the slips . . . *'Tha's got more edges than a broken piss pot.'* Or *'Tha's nicking me out the bloody averages.'*

To hapless players dismissed by a venomous delivery . . . *'That ball were wasted on thee.'*

To batsmen walking out to bat if he happened to be fielding near the boundary . . . *'Leave the gate open, sunshine, tha won't be stopping.'*

To practically every batsman he came across . . . *'I'll pin thee t'bloody sightscreen.'*

Geoffrey Boycott, who broke into the Yorkshire first team in 1962, used to rush to mid-on to hear Trueman's chuntering. 'Fred was by far the funniest man I played with and I used to want to field as close to him as possible because he would always come out with something that would have you rolling about with laughter. In my experience, Fred never swore directly at batsmen or umpires; he never went in for the sledging that goes on today. Fred would swear – of course he would. All the f***ing time, as it happens. But it was never directed as it is nowadays. Fred would just use swear words in his funny speech, which, to me, was very acceptable because it's not a playground out there and there aren't any women or children around. It was our shop floor, and many was the time Fred enlivened a long day's cricket.'

Fred Trueman, however, was more than a comedian and charismatic fast bowler. He was a symbolic figure in post-war Britain, an era that enhanced his Jack-the-lad image. During the 1950s – a decade that began with food rationing and ended with Harold Macmillan's 'you've never had it so good' election – many old values began to disappear. In their place emerged youth culture, rock and roll, Teddy Boys and a new word – teenagers. After Queen Elizabeth's coronation in 1953, television became widespread, beaming cricketers such as Trueman into people's homes. Television screened the work of the 'Angry Young Men' – playwrights and novelists such as John Osborne and Kingsley Amis, who railed against traditional society – and conveyed news of the stirring exploits of Edmund

Hillary and Sherpa Tensing, who conquered Mount Everest. Amid a growing sense that anything was possible, the closed world of the British establishment found itself on a collision course with the cocky new Britain growing up around it. Fred Trueman – cockier than most – was a role model for those who refused to kowtow.

In a tribute to his friend in the 2007 *Wisden*, the broadcaster Michael Parkinson observed: 'Fred didn't set out to change the world and would have dismissed any suggestion he was a revolutionary as nonsense. But there is little doubt that what his critics would term his boorish behaviour towards authority during the 1950s was part of the kindling for a drastic change in British society in the years that followed. Certainly people of my background and generation saw Fred not simply as a great cricketer but as an emblematic figure; outspoken, bloody-minded, Jack-as-good-as-his-master. We some-times forget how class-ridden Britain was forty and more years ago and how cricket represented the status quo. The game was run by a private members' club. It was Gentlemen and Players, with the England team picked by the President of MCC and the cricket correspondent of the *Daily Telegraph*. Or so Fred believed. And he wasn't the only one. But radical changes were afoot. The Butler Education Act had given bright working-class children the right to free education. A new generation began to question the old order. Fred – bolshie, outspoken and anti-authoritarian from the start – was a figurehead.'

Trueman's rebelliousness boiled over on his first England tour in 1953–54. In the volatile, pre-independence West Indies, he was accused of misconduct on and off the field. 'Terrible Trueman'-style headlines made a lasting impact as he gained a reputation for being a handful. After that tour, he played just three of England's next twenty-six Tests, and, by spring 1957, had played only seven Tests since his debut against India five years earlier. Had Trueman taken part in the fixtures he missed, he would probably have been the first man not only to 300 Test wickets but also 400 – if not the 500 he'd talked of at the Sawley Arms in 2005. Trueman's treatment at the hands of the selectors after the 53–54 tour – he was bypassed for

Australia in 54–55 and South Africa in 56–57 – remained a grievance for the rest of his life. 'Irrespective of the fact I was at the top of my game for Yorkshire and frequently topped the county bowling averages, I was often overlooked for England. To my mind, the reason for this was personal. Quite simply, some of the selection committee did not like my forthright attitude, which they misinterpreted as being "bolshy". Rather than pick the best eleven players for the job, the selection committee would often choose someone because he was, in their eyes, a gentleman and a decent chap. Such attributes often took precedence over someone's ability to play international cricket. For this reason, I was selected for far fewer Tests than I believe I should have been.'

As the fifties wore on, the 'Curse of the Truemans' went into overdrive. In extreme cases the public believed him capable of downing several pints a night, getting his leg over at the same rate and still bowling his boots off for Yorkshire and England. Although no saint in the bedroom or stranger to the bar-room, Trueman's exploits – like reports of Mark Twain's death – were exaggerated. To a man, Trueman's former team-mates, family and friends insist the public image was substantially false.

'Fred wasn't a candidate for canonisation and there were times he fell foul of the eleventh commandment – thou shalt not get caught,' said Platt. 'But even in the Yorkshire team there were a lot worse boozers and party animals than Fred. Our former captain, Vic Wilson, for instance, used to disappear regularly at the weekends with his toothbrush in his top pocket, telling us all in the team hotel he was off to visit some cousin or other. As Fred used to say, "He's got a lot of f***ing cousins, that one", and yet no one batted an eyelid at Vic. Fred had the odd bird along the way – of course he did. He made no secret of it, and there's plenty who aren't whiter than white in that regard. But I can honestly say I only saw Fred worse for wear through drink on a couple of occasions: not absolutely arseholed – just fresh. Yes, he liked a few beers in his younger days and had a few nights out as most players do, but his image was blown out of all proportion.'

In reality, Trueman couldn't drink to save his life. It was the biggest myth that built around him. 'Fred was a useless drinker,' said former Yorkshire and England all-rounder Richard Hutton. 'He couldn't take alcohol in serious quantity. But folk always wanted to buy him a drink if he happened to be in the bar after a day's play and, of course, he never said no, so you'd find all these pint pots lining up at his elbow that he was never touching and myself and the rest of the players would drink them instead. Fred was a talker – not a drinker. He'd talk all night given half the chance because he loved telling stories and was a great raconteur. Fred kept very late hours and burnt the candle at both ends, but he was up talking to all hours – not drinking.'

The impression Trueman drank for England – as well as played cricket for them – was furthered by his work on *Indoor League*. He presented the 1970s pub game show on Yorkshire Television with a pint in one hand and a pipe in the other. His widow Veronica recalled: 'Fred used to say, "Why do people always offer me beer whenever we go out?" And I would say, "Well, Fred, you do spend half your life standing in front of a television camera with a foaming tankard in your hand mouthing the catchphrase 'Ah'll si'thee', so of course people are going to think you drink beer." Fred could never understand this. He also advertised Webster's bitter on television and yet the irony was he was never a boozer. Fred liked the occasional gin and tonic or glass of red wine, but that was about it.'

Of the myriad stories that stuck to Trueman, one in particular drove him round the twist. During a dinner in honour of the 1952 Indian tourists, he was allegedly sitting at the top table when he purportedly nudged a high-ranking official in the ribs and demanded: 'Pass the salt, Gunga Din' – a derogatory term for an Indian. 'That story has one fatal flaw in placing me at the top table because they would never have seated England's most junior cap in such an exalted position,' he wrote. 'I did attend that dinner, but there was no incident, and I didn't even hear the story myself until I came back from that unfortunate tour of the West Indies, which may be more than a coincidence.'

Of course, it was exactly the sort of thing you could imagine Trueman saying, which was the point. So constant and carefree were his stream of one-liners, no one believed him when he protested his innocence. The 'Pass the salt, Gunga Din' story was never corroborated and can be added to the sundry cases of mistaken identity that litter the annals of Trueman legend. A man associated with as many tales as Beatrix Potter was the subject of as many false sightings as the Loch Ness Monster – although not even 'Nessie' could claim to have been spotted in two places at once, as Trueman was on numerous occasions.

In 1963 he was hauled before the Yorkshire committee to account for his 'bad language and disgusting behaviour' at a Bristol hotel. The hotel management demanded an apology from the club – otherwise Trueman would never be allowed there again. Trueman listened patiently while the committee read out the charges before insisting he could not possibly have been guilty.

'Have you any witnesses to that effect?' enquired a committee member.

'About 20,000,' declared Trueman.

'What the blazes do you mean?' came the reply.

'Well, when Yorkshire were staying in Bristol, I was playing for England against the West Indies at Lord's, and if someone had only taken the trouble to check the fixture list, this pantomime could have been avoided.'

The Test was the one in which Brian Close was beaten black and blue by pace bowlers Wes Hall and Charlie Griffith before Colin Cowdrey helped England to a draw with his arm in plaster. Trueman took eleven wickets in one of his greatest performances. The hotel withdrew its complaint and apologised.

Another time, the manageress of a Worksop hotel complained to Yorkshire about Trueman's 'disgusting behaviour'. A few weeks later, Trueman passed the scene of his supposed misdemeanour, popped in and ordered a drink at the bar. He was served by the manageress and asked her if she knew who he was. The woman said she didn't know. Trueman said he thought that odd; after all, she'd barred him from her hotel and complained to his employers. The barman, standing nearby, said, 'Don't you know who this is? This is Freddie Trueman.' The woman was dumbstruck. Having made his point, Trueman stormed off, leaving his drink untouched. The story was verified by writer and broadcaster Mosey, with whom Trueman had been staying in a different hotel.

'Apart from taking holy orders and entering a monastery, I could think of no effective way of stopping all this rubbish,' wrote Trueman. 'In fact, I did act like a monk on many occasions – avoiding crowds, even going my own way on tour with the Yorkshire and England teams.' Platt says Trueman made a conscious effort to avoid the limelight at the height of his fame. 'Fred used to say any publicity was good publicity, but he used to get pissed off with all those people who thought he was up partying to all hours. That was clearly impossible when you consider he was bowling over 1000 overs a season and hardly missed a game in twenty years. Quite often, if Yorkshire were playing away, Fred would go out on his own or he'd stay in his hotel room while the rest of the boys were having a drink. As he became more famous, he developed a wide circle of friends and acquaintances outside the game and would often go out with them or visit their homes.

'I've been there when people he'd never met have come up to him in bars and said things like, "I see you're out boozing again," or some such rubbish, and I know there were times it got him down. Fred resented the way people seemed to think they had a divine right to say or do whatever they liked, whereas nowadays they wouldn't be able to get near to someone like that because of all the agents, personal minders and God knows who else who protect celebrities. But there were no bodyguards or posh houses to escape to in Fred's day. He couldn't just hide in a country mansion.'

Trueman believed he was a public figure only during the hours of play and that his leisure time was private unless he chose otherwise. 'You don't get doctors taking pulses at cocktail parties,' he would say. His stance was understandable, if palpably naïve, and at times he let his frustration get the better of him. Trueman complained people would jostle him in restaurants or bars in the hope of eliciting a response and that he would never dream of going up to the likes of footballer Stanley Matthews if he happened to see him in a restaurant, or the actress Elizabeth Taylor if he chanced to see her walking down the street.

Trueman also disliked the 'chore' of signing autographs and being hounded by those who not so much requested his signature as demanded it. Youngsters and adults were often sent packing with a brusque 'bugger off' or something stronger if they approached him in the wrong way, at the wrong time or in the wrong place – particularly if they assumed intimacy by addressing him as 'Fred' or 'Freddie' instead of 'Mr Trueman'. Throughout his life, Trueman was a stickler for being addressed in what he considered the right and proper way, which basically meant 'Fred' or 'Freddie' to anyone who knew him or 'Mr Trueman' to those who did not. Anyone who called him 'Trueman' – as happened often during the class-conscious fifties – ran the risk of receiving the standard retort: 'I have a dog at home which comes to my side when I call its name. I'm not anybody's dog to beck and call by shouting "Trueman".' Only once did he relax his stance – during National Service.

'The paradox of Fred Trueman was that the instinctive and charismatic entertainer on the field of play could be insecure and awkward off it,' observed Michael Parkinson. 'Sometimes he found it difficult to be a public figure, unable to understand that the blokey image he projected on the field might persuade his fans he was a laugh-a-minute in his private moments . . . What he developed was the ability George Best had (when sober) to be at the centre of attention and yet detached from it. Again, like Best, I suspect that for all he liked to be considered gregarious, Fred Trueman was, by nature, a loner.'

If Trueman struggled with the stresses of fame, he had reason to resent their effect on his private life. His first marriage to Enid Chapman, the strong-minded daughter of a former Mayor of Scarborough, was stormy at the best of times but rendered twice as tempestuous by the stories she'd heard of him living it up with some floozy or other. 'I always remember someone claiming they'd seen Fred picking up this bird at Marks & Spencer in Scarborough and word getting back to Enid,' said Geoffrey Boycott. 'Now this sort of thing used to happen all the time and on this occasion Fred went spare. "How the f***ing hell could I have been in Scarborough?" he protested. "We were playing Northants down at their place. How the f***ing hell could I have got up to Scarborough before the store shut at half past five to take a bird out?" But people would say these things and it was because the stories sounded better with his name attached. It was just a part of his incredible legend.'

And yet the 'Curse of the Truemans' could also be a blessing . . .

Trueman's image in part furnished a fame that stretched far beyond the confines of cricket, boosting his celebrity and bolstering his esteem. During the fifties and sixties it would have been difficult to find an English woman, let alone an English man, who did not recognise the distinctive mop of jet-black hair and well-chiselled features – manageresses of Worksop hotels excepted. Trueman was rarely out the newspapers and regularly appeared on television chat shows. He was the most talked-about figure in English cricket until Ian Botham and remains instantly recognisable by the syllable 'Fred'. Trueman also profited from the stories about him – real or imagined. In later years, he undertook numerous speaking engagements and theatre tours before sell-out audiences, commanding in excess of £1000 a night. Trueman stories formed an integral part of after-dinner repertoires up and down the land, enhancing his reputation and embellishing his legend. As Gordon Ross observed in *Cricket's Great Characters*: 'After-dinner speakers from Wick to Plymouth regard a "Trueman" story as much a part of the evening as the Loyal Toast or white wine with the fish; their authenticity is immaterial. I have heard stories told about Trueman which I have known happened as far back as Harold Larwood – one was even attributed originally to Wilfred Rhodes, but still they keep coming as Truemanisms. This, surely, is the mirror of his popularity.'

Trueman's image gave him a degree of positive notoriety. Many Yorkshiremen saw him as the sort of Yorkshireman they wanted to be: one who said what he bloody well liked and liked what he bloody well said. Trueman – a working-class man victimised but never vanquished by the establishment – symbolised a certain kind of Yorkshireness. As former *Manchester Guardian* cricket correspondent Neville Cardus observed: 'Trueman through and through tells you he is a Yorkshireman. I cannot see him as, say, a member of the Kent eleven. He is honest and outspoken to the point of becoming an embarrassment. If he uses strong words now and then it is because ordinary language sometimes fails him. Freddie once bowled a university cricketer with a great ball which swung from leg to off. "That was an incredible ball," said the overwhelmed batsman. "It was bloody incredible," retorted Freddie, not liking understatement . . . If he exhibits himself, well, hasn't he something to show of Yorkshire nature, Yorkshire independence, Yorkshire relish? In a single rush of blood to the head he has the power to win a match for Yorkshire or England in half an hour.'

Just as others were inclined to inflate his behaviour, so Trueman was guilty of fanning his legend. He basked in the kudos of his militant image and macho status on the county circuit. Trueman boasted of his sexual conquests in the company of team-mates – exploits that were invariably pure imagination – and liked to be considered a cricketing Don Juan. He then spent his retirement trying to distance himself from stories and situations he'd personally trumpeted. 'We used to have a saying in the Yorkshire dressing room that you took everything Fred said and divided it by ten,' laughed Platt. 'He wasn't averse to laying it on thick. Many was the time Fred would turn up before a day's cricket and tell us he'd been shagging this bird or that bird and we'd say, "Look, f*** off, Fred, you wouldn't be able to bowl if you were shagging like that." He was rather prone to exaggeration of his bedroom activities. There were lots of times I used to say, "Fred, why don't you deny some of the things that are said and written about you?" and his reply was always the same. "Why the f***ing hell should I? As long as I'm making brass out of it, let them say what they like." Quite often, Fred would point to the example of George [Brian Statham, his England pace bowling partner] and say, "Now George is as clean as a bloody whistle and he doesn't earn the spin-off brass I get." You see, a lot of the time Fred encouraged the myths and stories because he recognised their commercial value. The trouble is, he only encouraged *some* of them – not *all* – and I suppose he wanted to have his cake and eat it.'

Trueman's larger-than-life persona was compounded by improbable stories he told about himself. He recalled touring India for the Bengal Cricket Association's silver jubilee celebrations and a torturous rail journey in which the train made an unscheduled stop in the middle of nowhere. Trueman claimed to have got off the train and asked the stationmaster for the whereabouts of a toilet – a request that left the stationmaster flushed with excitement. Trueman said he was led into a room where the stationmaster drew back a red velvet curtain to reveal a Victorian chamber pot on a plinth with 'F.S. Trueman' painted on it. When friends challenged him how the toilet came to be there, what became of it, how it was known he would pass by and, just as importantly, be in need of a pee, Trueman replied: 'How could I possibly have made it up?'

In 2002, Trueman purported to have been involved in a similarly implausible incident at a sportsmen's dinner. 'I was signing autographs when someone told me that in the fifties his father ran a pub across the road from Bramall Lane. "My father told me that as soon as the lunch interval came in a game, you'd run across the road and into his pub," said the diner. "You'd spend the lunch interval downing eight pints. And when you went back to play in the afternoon, my dad had to ensure you had a constant supply of pints. You used to mark your run-up with the pint glass and take a drink from it before every delivery."

'"I've never heard such a load of bloody rubbish in my life," I told the diner, much to his astonishment. "For heaven's sake, I was a professional sportsman who played cricket at international level."

'The diner looked somewhat disappointed. "So, it isn't true, then?"

'"Of course it's not true!" I told him.

'I signed for this chap and asked for the next autograph hunter in the queue to come forward. "I heard what tha telt that bloke," said diner number two. "I knows all that about you 'n' that pub were rubbish."

'"Thank you," I said as I signed his menu.

'"I knows it were rubbish," diner two continued, "'cos I know you used t'spend t'lunch interval having three women on t'go in different rooms in t'pavilion!"'

In telling that story, which seems utterly far-fetched, Trueman blurred the line between fact and fiction, which is exactly what he accused others of doing.

The most infamous story attached to his name was a classic example of image control – not to mention a graphic illustration of what Platt calls 'the odd bird along the way'. In July 1962, Trueman was sent home from Taunton by Yorkshire captain Vic Wilson in the greatest controversy of his county career. Trueman reported late for duty at 11 a.m. on the opening day – half an hour before start of play – after oversleeping at the team hotel. The previous day he'd captained the Players in the last ever Gentlemen versus Players fixture at Lord's and did not set off for the West Country until early evening along with Yorkshire team-mates Philip Sharpe and Don Wilson. Trueman claimed to have overslept because the trio didn't arrive in Taunton until 2.30 a.m. as the route west was choked with holidaymakers and because he'd accidentally taken a wrong turning to Exeter. This is not Don Wilson's recollection, who remembers a different reason for Trueman's tiredness. 'We travelled over from London in Fred's Bentley, and the hotel had Fred and I down to share a room. His marriage to Enid had completely broken down and he had this bird with him – I think she was something out the D'Oyly Carte opera company. Fred said, "Wilse, it's comfortable in this Bentley of mine, so why don't you sleep in my car and me and the bird will take the double room."

'In the morning, I tried to wake Fred but there was this "Do Not Disturb" sign on the door and I couldn't rouse him. I shouted, "Fred, we've got to get to the f***ing ground else we're in trouble," but he didn't hear me. I went to the ground and Vic Wilson said, "Where's Fred?"

'I replied, "I think he's slept in. He was captaining the Gents– Players yesterday and I think he's tired out."

'Vic said, "I know he's not tired out. I know he's got a bird with him." And all hell broke loose. Eventually, Fred turned up at the ground with this bird in tow, and Vic sent him home. But Fred further disobeyed Vic because he didn't leave the ground. There were pressmen everywhere and it was a right old situation.'

Instead of heeding Wilson's command, Trueman sought out Don Mosey, who was covering the match for the *Daily Mail*. He proceeded to pour out his heart for a full six hours, complaining he'd been badly treated after bowling more than 600 overs since the start of the season. Mosey listened, sympathised and even spared Trueman further embarrassment by keeping him away from the dressing room where, at various points, he threatened further showdowns with 'that bastard Wilson'.

When Trueman appeared before a Yorkshire committee comprising club president Sir William Worsley, cricket chairman Brian Sellers and club secretary John Nash, they supported Wilson's decision to send him home but sympathised with Trueman, who claimed he'd gone to the wrong room and not received a wake-up call. To Trueman's delight, the committee – apparently unaware of the full story – agreed to pay his travel expenses, gave him ten bob for his lunch en route and even paid his match fee. 'I left that disciplinary committee meeting very pleased with the fact I had been vindicated, and not a little satisfied that I had stuffed someone who seemingly had been out to get me,' he wrote. 'The press made a real meal of the incident and publicity like that was exactly what I wanted to avoid in my benefit year. I was so livid I very nearly quit Yorkshire for another county.'

Shortly before he died, Vic Wilson gave his version of events. 'I'd warned Fred about his time-keeping on several occasions and only the previous Saturday we were playing at Sheffield and he'd arrived late then. He said he'd been up all night because his daughter had toothache. All the other players had to toe the line to be there on time, and Brian Sellers had instilled in me that players had to be there at 10.30 a.m. – not 10.31 a.m., and certainly not 11 a.m. Fred overstepped the mark on several occasions before the inevitable happened. You can't have one rule for the rich and one for the poor. Fred broke the rules and so had to pay the price.'

Although the consensus among the Yorkshire players was that Wilson acted fairly, Trueman never forgave him. He refused to contribute to Wilson's retirement present at the end of the season, telling anyone who cared to listen: 'What? Give money to that bastard who sent me home from Taunton? Not bloody likely.' In the end, Ronnie Burnet – Wilson's successor as captain – diplomatically persuaded Enid Trueman to contribute to the retirement fund: a laughable irony.

Trueman's life became an endless merry-go-round of anecdotes and one-liners. It would be possible to produce an entire volume of Trueman stories – followed by a sequel. As John Arlott put it, 'Many of the stories about Fred Trueman are apocryphal; many are not; but even those referring to situations that never existed are ingredients of him, for he is partly a myth – indeed, he accepted a place in mythology with some eagerness. His life is recorded in gossip as well as in *Wisden*.'

One story encapsulates the Trueman saga. In 1968, while playing a charity match in India, Trueman was sitting in the lounge of a Bombay hotel when the Australian batsman Norman O'Neill whispered, 'Fred, I do believe those two Indians at the next table are talking about you.'

Trueman's reply was instant and matter-of-fact. 'Aye, they talk about me all over t'world, Norm, lad.'

3

Shadow of the Pit

There is something profoundly affecting about Fred Trueman's birthplace. Its location in South Yorkshire is remote and depressing, reflecting a man who rose up from nothing. The skyline is dominated by Maltby Main Colliery, one of the few pits to survive the Thatcherite purge, and the surrounding countryside is stark and sombre, as though fashioned in keeping with the forbidding coal works. To stand in this area and breathe in its ambience is to contemplate Trueman in the environment that shaped him. The earthy setting is raw and unvarnished, as if the character was formed in that desolate soil.

The birthplace, technically, no longer exists, for bulldozers demolished 5 Scotch Springs. One of twelve miners' cottages next to the pit yard, it was buried beneath landfill in the 1970s when Maltby tip pressed up on its doorstep. There is no trace now of these isolated houses, just a slurry pit near to the mounds of landfill. The scene is filled with a hopeless air and impossible to equate with the origins of greatness. 'When you think of where Fred came from to where he reached, it brings a tear to the eye,' said Bob Platt. 'Fred didn't just hail from a humble background. He hailed from practically nothing. He might have been hewn from the rock of that South Yorkshire countryside.'

What was once Scotch Springs is now unmarked wasteland off the appositely named Scotch Spring Lane. Motorists pass by oblivious to its significance as they head up towards Stainton village, about half a mile north-west, or down towards the A60, which runs into north Nottinghamshire. The location is roughly eight miles south of Doncaster and eight miles east of Rotherham, and had Trueman been born approximately four miles further south – not the 300 yards of popular myth – he would have been a Nottinghamshire citizen and never been able to represent Yorkshire. So lost to the landscape is Scotch Springs that Ron Buck, a childhood friend, was invaluable in identifying where it stood. A former coal face worker at Maltby Main, Buck's voice shook with pride and emotion as he surveyed once more the scenes of their boyhood. 'That was where Fred came from – *that*,' Buck trembled, jabbing an index finger in the direction of the wasteland. 'People don't realise what a climb it was, how far he came in life, as well as in cricket.'

Fred Trueman was born on 6 February 1931. Legend has it the momentous event took place in the outside toilet backing on to the pit yard as Trueman sprang an appropriately fast surprise on his mother, Ethel. In a scene that might have been borrowed from a Hollywood movie, Trueman's father, Alan, known as Dick Trueman, braved a snowstorm and sub-zero temperatures to dash to Stainton to fetch the doctor. By the time he returned, Ethel was cradling the fourth of their seven children – a brother for Stella (aged seven), Phyllis (three) and Arthur (two). The baby weighed an improbable 14lb 1oz and was delivered by his grandmother, Elizabeth Stimpson, in whose honour the boy was christened Frederick Sewards – the latter her maiden name. According to Flo Halifax, one of Fred's three sisters, the new addition was too big for his cot. 'Mum and Dad had to keep Freddie in a drawer pulled out from the sideboard because they couldn't afford a bigger cot. But it didn't seem to bother Freddie – Mum always said he was a well-behaved baby and didn't cry very much.'

Although the Truemans lived in the countryside, the shadow of the pit loomed over Scotch Springs. From their modest property about a mile from the tip, the whaleback of the mine was clearly visible. To the right of the house sat clusters of slag heaps, while black water swirled in filthy slurry pits. The area was strewn with debris from the tip and even the trees were coated in smuts. Ron Buck, a regular visitor, remembers well the grim conditions. 'I used to walk to Fred's house through a tunnel that took you right under the tip and brought you out at Scotch Springs, and the sights and sounds of the colliery were all around. At Fred's place, you'd hear buzzers sounding the miners' shifts, wagons bumping along in the coal yard, that sort of thing, and there was no escaping the hustle and bustle. There was a railway line just along from where the Truemans lived, where all the coal was loaded on trains, and there were times you wondered how Fred and his family got any sleep, such was all the activity in the area. It must have been very hard for the family to cope.'

The colliery-owned property was impossibly cramped. There were three tiny bedrooms: the boys occupied one, the girls another, the parents another, while the grandmother slept in the living room. By the time Fred Trueman was six, Flo and John had arrived to lift the head count to nine. The family also kept a dog, although there was barely enough room to swing a cat. 'They were packed in like sardines,' said one Maltby resident. 'And there wasn't what you'd call much etiquette in the house. There were very poor circumstances inside the home and I felt extremely sorry for the family. Scotch Springs was cut-off and incredibly bleak.'

According to another Maltby resident, the family was perceived in unflattering terms. 'I think some folk in Maltby perhaps looked down on them in those days. They were a bit grubby in appearance and rough around the edges, and Fred was different to the other kids at school; scruffy is putting it mildly. They were gypsies really – albeit stationary ones. Fred's mother had a strong gypsy air and was very much like those gypsies who came round your house peddling their pegs and bits and pieces and telling your fortune and so on. Fred's mother didn't do any of that to my knowledge, but she was of the same swarthy appearance.'

David Frith, the cricket writer and historian, says John Arlott told him Trueman's mother 'was a gypsy – or probably a gypsy' – something Arlott did not refer to in his biography of Trueman, *Fred:*

Portrait of a Fast Bowler, published in 1971, which devoted only a few paragraphs to the family history/background. 'That's how John described her to me, but he'd never have written it,' said Frith, one of the writer and broadcaster's closest friends. 'With John, the real stories were away from the microphone, away from the typewriter.' Fred's widow Veronica says she's long suspected a gypsy link. 'I remember one night Fred was going back down memory lane and he was talking about when the fair used to come up to Maltby and how his grandmother, Elizabeth Stimpson, used to make dresses for the gypsies. Now that struck me as very interesting because gypsies tend to deal with their own; it's a bit of a closed shop. It makes you wonder why Fred's grandmother was making clothes for the gypsies when they came to the fair, and whether the family perhaps had gypsy connections. Fred didn't say any more about it and I kept my opinions to myself, but it's possible there was some sort of relationship there.'

Nothing in the grandmother's roots is suggestive of gypsies. Elizabeth Stimpson was born in Islington, London, the daughter of a railway platelayer from Boston, Lincolnshire, and married Arthur Stimpson, a colliery platelayer. Maltby residents recall her as 'a lady' – friendly, petite, and with long plaited hair. They say she was rarely seen without a hat and that she made dresses for a variety of families and friends. The consensus in Maltby is that Elizabeth Stimpson neither looked nor dressed like a gypsy and that it was Trueman's mother who had the gypsy appearance. 'Fred's mother was a total show girl,' added Veronica. 'It was in her veins; it was natural. It was where Fred got it from really. He was the male version of his mother. I never met Fred's father, but Fred always said he was a very slight man – only about five foot six with an angular face and wiry build. His mother was several inches taller and physically more powerful. His parents were different in terms of appearance.'

The lineage on Dick Trueman's side is unremarkable, although there is a strong connection with horses and an outdoor lifestyle. Dick Trueman was a steeplechase and point-to-point jockey in his early teens, riding in the colours of Earl Fitzwilliam at Wentworth

Woodhouse, a country house near Wentworth in South Yorkshire. When his weight counted against him, Dick Trueman went into mining and worked at Maltby Main Colliery for over forty years. Although he kept his hand in with horses as a part-time groom for a local racehorse owner named Captain Adcock, Trueman senior spent most of his life at the coal face. Dick Trueman's father, Albert, was a horse dealer and cattle breaker who shipped horses to the Western Front on behalf of the army during the First World War, while his grandfather, Thomas, was a gardener. His great-grandfather, also Thomas, was a gamekeeper. There is nothing to indicate any branch of the family moved around, with Dick Trueman's relations firmly rooted in Lincolnshire and South Yorkshire.

Fred Trueman's siblings refute the idea of a gypsy link. 'I suppose some people in Maltby might have thought we were gypsies because we had fairly dark complexions and because Dad had connections with horses in his younger days,' said Flo. 'But we were a poor family – not a gypsy one. Personally, I think people will always say things about famous families and famous people and put two and two together and make five.'

In 1993, Fred Trueman claimed his mother was Jewish. He said she was adopted at birth and that her natural mother was the daughter of a Jewish couple named Bennett who'd lived in Leeds. Trueman said his grandmother worked as a dressmaker for the Bennetts in the early 1900s and that she adopted Ethel because the family wanted to avoid a scandal. He said his mother revealed the secret shortly before her death in 1992, saying he and his siblings had a right to know. However, records show the Bennetts were an unremarkable family from Winterton, North Lincolnshire. There were no Jewish connections in their family line. Trueman even purported to have aristocratic blood, claiming Lord Scales of Rawmarsh was his great-grandfather. But there was no such person as Lord Scales of Rawmarsh, suggesting a desire to invent stories and inhabit a fantasy world that was possibly something of a family trait.

Although the Truemans faced significant hardship beside Maltby pit, they were not as poor as some British families. Unemployment was rife in the 1930s, with street corners littered with jobless men. When Fred Trueman was two, unemployment soared to 2.5 million – some twenty-five per cent of the workforce – and queuing at soup kitchens was a way of life. Northern England bore the brunt of the depression, with coal, steel and shipbuilding heavily hit. The Truemans scraped by on the thirty-seven shillings Dick Trueman earned each week at the pit and were, to some extent, self-sufficient. Trueman senior kept first one, then two, and eventually four allotments on which he reared hens, cockerels and pigs, while Captain Adcock allowed him to shoot across his land and bag 'luxuries' such as pheasant and quail. The family income was supported by seasonal pea-picking and potato-lifting in which the young Fred played an active part. The Truemans received the miner's allowance of free coal and even had electricity, which the colliery installed at a time when most local homes still ran on gas.

Life, however, was a perpetual struggle for Fred Trueman's parents. While Ethel looked after the children, working so hard the young Fred felt sorry for her, Dick toiled in the bowels of the earth to put bread on the table and heat in the hearth. Most mornings he rose at four o'clock before swapping the darkness of night for the darkness underground. Day after day he worked the cramped, narrow tunnels, chipping away at the coal seams in suffocating heat before shovelling up the dirt in readiness for mining. Danger was a constant companion and twice Dick Trueman was lucky to survive. In 1923, he avoided the Maltby Pit Disaster in extraordinary circumstances when Elizabeth Stimpson begged him not to go to work as she'd dreamt that something terrible would happen. Later that day, a huge underground explosion killed twenty-seven men.

The second incident took place in 1948 when Dick Trueman suffered a serious accident. 'They used to have family stalls at the pit,' said Flo. 'There'd be a Smith stall, a Trueman stall, that sort of thing, and on this particular day a wagon broke free and Dad couldn't shout to my cousin, Tony, to get out the way in time, so Dad ran and pushed him and the wagon crushed Dad. Dad managed to save

Tony, but the wagon crushed Dad's left arm and he could have been killed. Dad had to have a steel girder in his arm and was off work several months. After that, he used to have a little purse with a piece of string attached to it that Grandma made because he couldn't fit his hand into his pocket properly.

'We used to have school dinners in those days, which were fivepence a time, and when the teachers heard Dad had had this accident they said we were entitled to free dinners. Anyway, when Dad found out he went ballistic. "I don't accept charity off nobody," he said, and told us to go back and tell the teachers we weren't to have these free dinners, even though he'd only got a pittance in compensation from the colliery. But the teachers insisted – and it knocked Dad for six. As soon as he was able to go back to work, the first thing he did was write out a note saying his children would be coming home for their dinner from now on.'

The accident ended Dick Trueman's career on the coal face and he became a training officer for recruits. When he retired on his sixty-fifth birthday, he burnt his pit clothes in the back garden, at the same time vowing none of his sons would follow him down the mine. It saddened him deeply when Arthur, too, became a coal face worker.

Fred Trueman saw fleeting service at Maltby Main. After leaving school at fourteen he worked for several months as a haulage hand, pulling tubs of coal. He returned to the pit in the winter of 1948–49 after Yorkshire asked him to find a job in a reserved occupation to avoid National Service. Trueman worked in the tally office, issuing miners with tickets that kept a check of how many men were underground. He went back to the tally office in the winter of 1950–51 to supplement his income as an uncapped player. Despite his oft-repeated insistence he never worked down the pit, Trueman never missed a chance to seek out his father and help shovel coal while Dick Trueman – then in his fifties – took a well-earned breather.

Fred Trueman always maintained his father was forced out of the horse trade and into mining by the economic slump of the 1930s.

But records show Dick Trueman went underground in 1911 – the year Maltby pit officially opened. He stayed there six years before joining the York and Lancaster Regiment of the British Army. Dick Trueman's war service has never been publicised and there was only a forty per cent chance of obtaining his official service record from the National Archives. More than half the seven million records of those who served in the Army during the Great War were destroyed when German bombers hit London in 1940, but Dick Trueman's is preserved in the Burnt Document series. Although riddled with scorch marks and illegible in places, it shows he served at home from March to August 1917 before receiving his solitary overseas posting to France/Belgium. Dick Trueman arrived on the Continent on 23 August and returned home on 30 October after suffering a gunshot wound to his left shoulder while serving with the 1/5 (Territorial) Battalion. During his sixty-eight days on mainland Europe, 41056 Private Trueman was embroiled in one of history's most sickening battles.

The Battle of Passchendaele – the Third Battle of Ypres, or simply Third Ypres – was an umbrella term for a series of operations that took place between July and November 1917. The struggle for control of the village of Passchendaele, near the town of Ypres in west Flanders, formed part of the Allied campaign to drive a hole through German lines, advance to the Belgian coast and recapture German submarine bases. Although Canadian forces eventually captured Passchendaele, the campaign was an operational disaster for the Allies, who advanced just five miles in a little over three months and lost thousands of men. Casualty figures remain contentious but most experts put the death toll in excess of 600,000, with most of those being British servicemen – including former Kent and England left-arm spin bowler Colin Blythe. The British campaign – spearheaded by Field Marshal Douglas Haig – began with a massive bombardment that failed to soften German defences and destroyed the drainage system of the low-lying land. With Flanders hit by some of the heaviest rains to fall in Europe during the twentieth century, the terrain degenerated into an impassable quagmire of mud. In a

desperate attempt to gain freedom of movement, Allied soldiers laid
duckboards across the swamps – wooden ladders designed to act as
walkways. But they were precarious and slippery and if a soldier lost
his footing, or came under attack, he ran a serious risk of falling off
and disappearing slowly – limb by limb – into the stinking mud.
These horrendous scenes – witnessed by Dick Trueman – were
captured by Siegfried Sassoon in 'Memorial Tablet':

> I died in Hell – (They called it Passchendaele).
> My wound was slight,
> And I was hobbling back; and then a shell
> Burst slick upon the duckboards: so I fell
> Into the bottomless mud, and lost the light.

Another who conveyed the misery of Passchendaele was English
war artist Paul Nash. 'I have seen the most frightful nightmare of a
country more conceived by Dante or Poe than by nature . . . Sunset
and sunrise are blasphemous, they are mockeries to man, only the
black rain out of the bruised and swollen clouds all through the bitter
black of night is fit atmosphere in such a land. The rain drives on,
the stinking mud becomes more evilly yellow, the shell holes fill up
with green-white water, the roads and tracks are covered in inches
of slime, the black dying trees ooze sweat and the shells never cease.
They alone plunge overhead, tearing away the rotting tree stumps,
breaking the plank roads, striking down horses and mules,
annihilating, maiming, maddening, they plunge into the grave which
is this land; one huge grave, and cast up upon it the poor dead. It is
unspeakable, godless, hopeless.'

Dick Trueman's service record reveals nothing of his battalion's
activities during the Passchendaele operations or how he came to be
wounded – only that he was injured on 22 October 1917. But the
battalion's war diary for that month survives. It shows he fought at
the Battle of Poelcappelle, which occurred three days before the First
Battle of Passchendaele and was a disaster for the Allies, who made
only minor advances and lost 13,000 men. The battle took place on

9 October 1917 and the diary entry makes desperate reading:

> *The march up to the assembly position was rendered extremely difficult and exhausting owing to the state of the ground. Very wet weather for a week previous had produced mud of great depth, whilst the whole area of operations consisted of shell holes, mostly containing two or three feet of water . . . At Zero hour (5.20 a.m.), the battalion moved forward to the attack, the men keeping very close up to the barrage. In crossing the Ravenbeek, where the mud was anything up to waist-deep, the barrage was lost for a time, but it was caught up again later. Hostile pillboxes were encountered and captured near Fleet Cottage, a machine gun captured in one of them being used effectively against the enemy. In the advance from the Ravenbeek up the slope towards Meetcheele, the battalion came under heavy artillery fire from the Comines group of hostile artillery and was also exposed to cross fire from machine guns in Wolf Copse on the left and Snipe Hall on the right.*

The diary matter-of-factly records the casualties:

	Killed	Wounded	Wounded & Missing	Missing	Missing Believed Killed
Officers	6	1	2	–	1
Other ranks	58	249	2	49	–

The failure of Poelcappelle was not communicated to British commanders, with the result that the next attack – the First Battle of Passchendaele – was poorly planned. When Dick Trueman was wounded on 22 October, 1/5 (Territorial) Battalion was back on the front line at nearby Zonnebeke, the only clue what happened coming from a brief entry in the war diary:

> *A line of posts was established 200 yards in front of our front line, and a trench to join these was taped out by the company commandos. This trench, which was to serve as a 'jumping off' place for the Canadians, was dug the same night our line heavily bombarded.*

After returning to Britain, Dick Trueman served at home until war ended in November 1918. He was placed on the reserve list before being discharged in March 1919 as 'surplus to military requirements as a result of wounds received in action'. He went back to Maltby pit and kept much of his war service hidden from his family. Fred's brother John remembered: 'All he said to me was, "It's a war I want to forget, son. A generation of youth died unnecessarily. We had bad generals who were sat back, drinking whisky and giving orders. There were men going over the top getting killed every day. There were men being shot as cowards."

'He said they weren't cowards, and I can understand how he felt. When those heavy guns were going, and when a soldier gets shell-shocked, his mind's gone and he doesn't know what he's doing. To be lined up against a wall and shot for that, my father hated that. He never bought a poppy after the war because he was disgusted at the way those lads had been treated. Dad said none of them should have been shot – not one. Can you imagine the hell they lived in? It's like my dad said, in the trenches, what could you do? There were dead bodies and rats running all over the place because you couldn't bury the lads. There were men blown to pieces, arms missing, heads blown off, legs lying everywhere. The stench of death was all around and the soldiers were living in infested rat-holes.'

As to his father's injury, John added: 'My father said that after he'd been shot, another German soldier was about to bayonet him when one of his friends stepped in and killed the German. The bullet stayed in my father's shoulder until 1938, the year I was born, and despite the awful circumstances surrounding the injury there was a funny story regarding its removal. Dad had to have a skin graft and the skin came off a lady's bottom. He used to joke there's not many men who can look over their shoulder and say they can see a lady's bum.'

Fred Trueman and his siblings held their father in high esteem. 'He fought in one of the worst wars that's ever been fought and then he worked down that black hole for the rest of his life,' said John. 'To look at him, you wouldn't have believed it possible because he was only a tiny fellow – nowhere near as strong and powerful as

Fred. But he had a massive heart and incredible bravery, and I never once heard him moan or complain.' Dick Trueman belonged to the stiff-upper-lip generation – a generation that simply accepted its lot. In stark contrast to Fred Trueman, who was highly sensitive and sentimental, he rarely showed his emotions and kept them to himself. Even when Fred Trueman rose to great heights as a cricketer, his father never basked in his son's achievements and was more likely to talk them down than up. In many ways he was a stereotypical Yorkshireman: a man who dispensed praise as frequently as a stereotypical Scotsman dispenses loose change.

Walter Smith, a former teacher at Trueman's secondary school in Maltby, recalls an incident that encapsulated Dick Trueman's character. 'Yorkshire were playing at Bramall Lane and Fred took an absolutely blinding catch – the sort you'd see once in a blue moon. Dick Trueman was sitting in the pavilion and, as I walked past, I said, "Well, that was an absolutely brilliant catch, wasn't it." Dick looked at me and said, "Brilliant? It was straight down his bloody throat." He completely made light of a brilliant catch. Dick was a very bluff Yorkshireman, the type who didn't call a spade a shovel. He was a typical miner, a rough diamond, and Fred was exactly like him in that regard.'

Flo said there were never any sides to her father; what you saw was what you got. 'There were never any airs and graces with Dad. He didn't try and pretend to be something he wasn't. The only time he had his teeth in and his trilby on was when he went to a cricket match. Otherwise, he'd keep his teeth in a glass in the bathroom and Mum would say, "They'll stop there until there's another match at the Lane or at Chesterfield." But in many ways he was a Victorian man – very protective of his children and a stickler for discipline. He'd only let you go so far, and then when you saw the pipe start to go in his mouth, you knew you daren't go no further. But his discipline was verbal, not physical. He only smacked us once, and it hurt him more than it did us.'

Despite his taciturn nature, Dick Trueman possessed a dry sense of humour. He shared his son's fondness for quick repartee and never let mickey-takers have the last laugh. Once, when Fred Trueman experienced a poor run of form, Dick Trueman was ribbed by his mining colleagues. 'Tha didn't tell us tha lad had turned slow bowler,' joked one. 'Aye, we thought lad were fast bowler,' chuckled another. But Dick's retort stopped them dead in their tracks. 'Did tha notice Queen t'other day when teams were presented at Lord's? Queen spoke to our Fred, moved on and came back. I'll tell tha what she said. She said, "I forgot to ask tha – how's tha father?"'

Dick Trueman provided an early audience for Fred Trueman's jokes. The technique that evolved into a polished after-dinner routine first materialised in the family home, where the young Trueman displayed a penchant for story-telling. 'When Freddie got a bit older he used to tell Dad these jokes and to start off with Dad would be all stern-faced,' said Flo. 'Then you'd suddenly see the pipe start to twitch in Dad's mouth as Freddie told his stories and Freddie would say, "Go on, Dad, let it go", and although Dad tried his utmost not to smile, he always did. Other times, Freddie would come home and say, "I've got a right tale to tell you today, Dad", and Dad would say, "I don't want to hear it, son. I don't want to hear it." We'd be in the other room and after Freddie had told his tale we'd invariably hear Dad say, "Now I don't want to hear you telling your mother and sisters this", and Dad would be chuckling away to himself. But it was too late – Freddie had already tried it out on us.'

Flo said they could not have wished for better parents. 'They gave up everything for us. We came first in every respect – even though they'd nothing to give except their love. We used to say to them, "When we're working, we'll pay you back", and the reply was always the same – "We don't want paying back. We had you because we wanted you – not for what we could make out of you." Even when Freddie offered to buy them a bungalow when he got established, they wouldn't accept it. Dad said, "Son, you're not buying me or your mum anything. The money you've earned from cricket is yours and I don't want to hear no more on the subject." Freddie was very close to them and could confide in them about anything.'

Dick Trueman initiated his son's interest in cricket. The father of one of the world's fastest bowlers was himself a left-arm spin bowler for Stainton village, serving as captain for a number of years and doubling up as a useful batsman. Dick Trueman learned the game from his own father, who'd been good enough to receive an offer to play for Yorkshire in the 1880s. But he turned it down because he earned more in one day selling horses than Yorkshire were prepared to pay for a week. Encouraged by his father, Fred Trueman took up bowling at the age of four. He practised against a dustbin lid propped up by two bricks in a narrow lane at the back of Scotch Springs. Trueman spent many carefree hours pretending to be Harold Larwood or Bill Voce while his friends imagined themselves to be Len Hutton or Maurice Leyland. The youngsters played from dawn until dusk, improvising with a wooden pit prop as a bat – half-inched from the pit yard – and a tennis ball.

'Quite a few of us played cricket, boys and girls, and if Freddie was bowling we were always out quickly,' said Flo. 'He bowled as fast at his sisters as he did at anyone else and we'd be in tears because we never got a chance to bat properly. We'd ask Dad to tell Freddie not to bowl as fast at us but it didn't do any good. Freddie was just so stubborn. He said that if the girls wanted to play they had to accept the same conditions as the boys. Even from a very young age he always wanted to win, and if he didn't, he'd go away and try to work out where he'd gone wrong.'

Trueman played cricket at the village school in Stainton, bowling at three chalk marks on the playground wall. One day he overheard his favourite teacher, Miss Nelson, reprimand a senior boy for his lacklustre attitude during a school match. 'Go and watch young Freddie Trueman playing cricket if you want to know what the right attitude and determination are all about,' she told him. It was the first time he'd been complimented on his cricketing ability.

The young boy accompanied his father to Stainton's games, bowling to the men as they waited to bat. Once, Stainton found themselves a man short and the eight-year-old was pressed into action. When he walked out to bat, the opposing captain instructed his bowler, 'Take it easy – he's only a young boy.' Dick Trueman overheard and demanded, 'Tha'll bowl proper – or don't bother.'

Fred Trueman's fondest memory of playing for Stainton was when his father reached a hundred while he was batting at the other end. Typically, Dick Trueman didn't punch the air or high-five his son but simply settled over his bat to face the next ball. Dick Trueman gave up playing after his accident at the coal face and swapped his flannels for an umpire's coat. He was said to have been a scrupulous official.

Despite his family's impoverished circumstances, Trueman enjoyed a happy childhood. He spent much of his time in Stainton village, where the countryside contrasted with the grime of Scotch Springs and fostered a lifelong love of nature. Trueman went bird-nesting with friends and enjoyed jotting down registrations of passing cars. On rare occasions he was home, he liked nothing better than to prop his leg over an armchair and read the *Dandy* and *Beano*. Along with his parents, brothers and sisters, Trueman attended Stainton parish church three times each Sunday – an obligation rendered less onerous by the fact the sermons of Archdeacon Folliott Sandford rarely lasted more than ten minutes. Trueman sang in the choir as the venerable archdeacon – always one bar ahead of the congregation – played the organ in slipshod fashion. The highlight of Trueman's year – and the closest he got to a holiday – was the annual Sunday school outing to Cleethorpes or Skegness. He remembered it felt 'like travelling to the other side of the world'.

One of Trueman's fondest childhood memories was of his father returning home with a wireless. Before that, the family's only contact with the outside world had been through a crystal set and the *Yorkshire Post*. Trueman recalled hearing on the wireless Len Hutton's world record Test score of 364 against Australia at the Oval in 1938. Never for one minute did he imagine Hutton would become his captain and team-mate.

Trueman had less happy recollections of the Second World War, when he watched frequent bombings of Sheffield from the sanctuary of Scotch Springs. Once, a Nazi bomber was shot down over the city and crash-landed a few miles from the house, becoming an instant magnet to Trueman and companions. He also accompanied his father to meetings of the local Home Guard, where volunteers discussed how they would combat the Nazis if they landed in the area. As it turned out, Stainton and Maltby got off lightly as the Germans decided they had bigger fish to fry.

The greatest danger to Trueman's young life came not from the Luftwaffe but German measles. No sooner had he recovered from that episode than he almost hanged himself trying to pinch apples from a farmer's field. Trueman was halfway up a tree when he slipped and a branch tore through the back of his shirt, jerking the collar tight against his windpipe. His friends pulled him down and when he woke up later in his mother's arms, he said he'd been talking to Jesus – suggesting it had been a close-run thing. Trueman had another accident up a tree shortly afterwards when he grabbed hold of a rope and pretended to be Tarzan. It was the era of the Johnny Weissmuller films and the rope snapped under the weight of Tarzan Trueman, who plunged into a brook in his Sunday best.

The Truemans left Scotch Springs in 1942 and moved to Maltby in an effort to make life easier for Ethel. 'Nineteen forty-two was a very bad winter and one day Mum got stuck in the snow on her way back from Maltby,' recalled Flo. 'She was stranded on a hill that went down towards the pit yard and was pregnant at the time with my youngest brother, Dennis. Dad was very concerned and had to go looking for her. Afterwards, he said, "We can't have this, Ethel. We've got a seventh child on the way, the others are growing up fast and need more space, and you're having to walk two miles just to fetch a loaf of bread. I'm going to apply to the colliery for a bigger house."'

The Truemans lived at 10 Tennyson Road – part of a concentrated group of miners' homes. Convenient for the colliery and shops, it was near the Grand Cinema, where Ethel Trueman was a regular visitor. 'Mum loved the pictures,' said Flo. 'She saw all the big films that came to Maltby. In fact, she liked entertainment of all descriptions. We used to have a battered old piano at home and we'd sit around it during the winter while Mum played tunes. None of us could sing, but we could all make a noise; that's how we entertained ourselves.' Placid and fun loving, Ethel was spry and sprightly for her size. 'There used to be a sports day in Maltby and, when Mum was fifty, someone dared her to run the 100 metres,' added Flo. 'She accepted the challenge and ran against the young crop and left them all standing. Not only that, but she ran in her bare feet. She was very athletic, was Mum.'

Although the new house was better for Ethel and an improvement on Scotch Springs, it was hardly palatial. There was nothing glamorous about life at Tennyson Road. 'It wasn't as cramped as Scotch Springs but it would still be me, Fred and Arthur in one bed and the girls in another,' said John Trueman. 'Dennis was the only one who had any privacy – and that's because he slept in a cot. But I don't think Fred was ever that fond of Maltby. He preferred the countryside round about Stainton.' Flo's abiding recollection of Tennyson Road is that the toilets didn't work. 'The flaming chains were always on the blink. If you were in the toilet and they went to theirs next door, and they flushed their chain first, you got showered. It used to come through the cistern and the water dropped all over you. Old Mrs Martin next door would shout through the wall, "Ethel, we're using the toilet," so we knew not to use ours when they used theirs.'

Fred Trueman practised his bowling against Mrs Martin's outside wall – the end wall on the street. Games took place most evenings and Mrs Martin's patience was sorely tested. 'She used to come round our house and say, "Oh, Ethel, they're at it again – bang, bang, bang against the wall,"' said Flo. 'I think she got fed up with Freddie and his friends.' Terry Hunt, who also lived on Tennyson Road, recalled: 'A good number of us used to play and we'd be out there in all weathers. Fred was fast, but he wasn't very accurate. He could be quite erratic, but he frightened us to death. No matter who he was playing against, he always wanted to knock their block off.'

When not playing cricket and practising his bowling, Trueman got up to his share of mischief. Hunt recalls an occasion they got in trouble with the local police. Don Mosey mentioned the incident in his biography of Trueman, *Fred: Then and Now*, published in 1991. 'The first recorded instance we have of Fred being wrongfully accused of a crime came in those earliest days. He was charged with cutting a neighbour's clotheslines. In vain he protested his innocence, but his reputation as a lively sort of lad damned him and he was actually fined.' Trueman, however, was guilty as sin. 'It were me and him,' laughed Hunt. 'It were VE night, May 1945, and a group of us lads were celebrating in a wood. We'd got a big bonfire going but we ran out of wood and needed some more to chuck on the fire. Me and Fred nipped off and stole a wooden clothes post that was holding up somebody's clothes line – about seven or eight foot long, it was – and chucked it on the bonfire. The family who lived in the house got the police involved and we were fined five shillings each. We were a bit rough and ready in those days, and Fred was a little bit rougher than most. He was quite an uncouth sort of lad, if truth be told, and his language was always a little bit fruity. Fred was different to the rest of his family. They were mostly calm and laid-back people.'

John Gibson, another childhood friend, recalls a further stunt the young Trueman pulled. 'On Mischievous Night, if there was somebody you didn't like, you'd collect dog dirt, wrap it up in paper, put it on the person's doorstep, set fire to the paper, knock on the door and then do a runner. Inevitably, the person would come out their house and stamp the fire out with their shoe – at the same time treading in the dog dirt. Freddie and the rest of us would laugh ourselves silly.'

Trueman and friends frequently visited Maltby fair, playing on the coconut shies. 'We'd club our money together – three wooden balls for a penny – and every now and then Fred would deliberately throw a ball over the back of the stall,' said Ron Buck. 'The rest of us would be waiting to pick it up and make off with it. Fred used to do this quite often when the fair was in town and it made sure we had enough balls to last us the cricket season.'

After leaving school at Stainton, Trueman attended Maltby Hall
secondary. He claimed he was bright enough to have gone to
grammar school but said his parents couldn't afford the uniform and
books. The records of those who attended Maltby Hall in Trueman's
day have been destroyed by fire, so there is no way of verifying his
academic prowess. But Frank Anderton, who was in the same year,
retains a different impression. 'Fred wasn't all that bright at school
and was in what they called the lowest stream. He wasn't the
sharpest knife in the drawer but it never seemed to bother him. The
only thing he bothered about was his sport and he was a genius with
his bowling. Even at the age of eleven or twelve he was something
special.'

Two teachers shared his passion for cricket – Dickie Harrison and
Tommy Stubbs. They wasted no time putting Trueman in the school
team – even though he often played with and against boys three
years older. Harrison gave up his free time after lessons to encourage
his charges, sometimes placing a penny on off stump and a two-
shilling piece on middle stump and allowing them to keep any coins
they knocked off. Trueman – a talented all-round sportsman who
also played football and rugby – pocketed more than most.

While playing for the school, Trueman suffered the worst injury
of his cricketing life. Story goes he was batting without a box during
a match at Wickersley, near Rotherham, when he was struck in the
privates by what passed for a fast bowler in schoolboy cricket. In
reality, Trueman dismissed a batsman before sending him on his way
with a few choice words. The batsman hurled the ball back in a rage,
striking Trueman an agonising blow. Flo recalls the panic that swept
through her household. 'The doctors said the injury could have
crippled Freddie and he had to have an emergency operation. They
feared he might not be able to have any children when he grew up.
Freddie was confined to home for several months and had to have his
school lessons there. It was a very depressing period but Tommy
Stubbs kept his spirits up, and when Freddie was able to walk again,
Mr Stubbs let him score or umpire the school games.'

Trueman did not play again for Maltby Hall School, leaving two years later to work for a newsagent. He rose at dawn to deliver papers to two hundred homes, going around again during the evening. The regular walking restored his fitness and he'd fully recovered by 1946. Just as his thoughts turned again to cricket, however, the family was dealt a shattering blow. Stella, his eldest sister, was diagnosed with stomach cancer and tragically died at the age of twenty-two. Tall and attractive with a cheerful nature, Stella worked at the Royal Ordnance Factory in Maltby during the war and had recently married when illness struck. She doted on Fred, whom she regarded with a motherly eye. 'Stella couldn't have any children of her own and was very close to Freddie,' said Flo. 'They spent a lot of time together and she was very fond of him. It hit Freddie hard when Stella passed away.'

A talented writer, Stella liked to pen verse in her spare time and Flo retains her last-ever poem. Entitled 'The Night Nurse', and written as she lay very ill in Jessop's Annexe, Graves Park, Sheffield, in March 1946, it has never been seen outside the family.

How young she is, how patient and how kind
To watch her moving with such tireless grace
Is like a falling fountain on the mind
Is like a flower found in a desert place

She moves so quietly through the world at night
And pauses there beside some sleepless bed
Or sits before the lamp-lit desk to write
A halo of spun gold about her head

She is the light when all the world is dark
She is the shelter from the pain in the storm
And in her youthful heart there lays the spark
Of love and life to keep the future warm

4

Hit 'em First, Ask Questions Later

Fred Trueman's cricketing hero wasn't a fast bowler. He wasn't even a county or international player. He was Arthur Trueman, his eldest brother, a talented right-hand opening batsman. Whenever they played at Scotch Springs or on the back streets of Maltby, Arthur dominated their fraternal rivalry. Fred always struggled to get him out – and it used to drive him mad with frustration. The faster he bowled in an effort to succeed, the faster the ball sped off Arthur's bat. The more he provoked him with a cheeky remark, the more Arthur smiled at his younger brother. The age difference between them was only two years, but they were light years apart in cricketing terms.

If Fred's love of cricket was sparked by his father, it was Arthur who stirred his competitive juices. While the young Fred made mincemeat of his other friends and siblings, scaring them to death with his pace and aggression, he found Arthur a totally different challenge, a source of annoyance as well as admiration. Tall and lean with a muscular build, Arthur was a stylish and powerful driver. He not so much crashed as caressed the ball, his grace and elegance belying his physique. 'Arthur used to hit Freddie's bowling all over the place,' said their sister Flo. 'Freddie would get all upset and Dad would say, "Look, you'll just have to try harder next time, Freddie." So it became Freddie's mission to get Arthur out. Arthur's skill spurred Freddie on and was his biggest motivation in his younger days.'

Ron Buck played cricket with the Trueman brothers and said Arthur was the better teenage prospect. 'The feeling in Maltby was that if anyone was going to be the professional, it would be Arthur. As good as Fred was, it was Arthur who seemed a cut above. But Arthur was different to Fred in that, first and foremost, he played cricket for fun.'

According to Dennis Trueman, Fred's youngest brother, what distinguished Fred was his fierce determination. 'If Arthur had had Fred's determination, I think he'd have been a fantastic cricketer. I'm not saying he'd have been better than Fred and played for England necessarily, but I certainly think he'd have played for Yorkshire. Arthur got picked to play for the Yorkshire second team at Middlesbrough once but didn't turn up. He went to Doncaster races with his drinking mates.'

In contrast to Fred, Arthur loved beer and could drink for England. He thought nothing of downing fifteen pints after a colliery shift. Arthur entered ale-drinking competitions on holiday and won his fair share. His appetite was matched by his prodigious physique. 'Arthur was a very quiet, gentle man unless someone upset him – and then they'd usually wish they hadn't,' said his brother John. 'Fred could look after himself in a scrap, but Arthur was the strongest; his hands were like a JCB. Arthur would never go looking for trouble but he'd never run away from it either. He used to say, "Hit 'em first, ask questions later." That was his motto.'

Flo recalls an incident that encapsulated his outlook. 'Arthur once went into the club in Maltby for a drink and was minding his own business when a group of men came in and started to get rowdy. Freddie was famous by then and one of these men started shouting and swearing and saying things like, "Oh, so this is Trueman country, is it?" and "There isn't a good Trueman in this town." Well, they say they'd never seen anything so quick. Arthur got up, tapped this man on the shoulder and said, "My name's Trueman" – and laid him straight out. Then he calmly finished his pint and walked out the door.'

Fred Trueman hero-worshipped his elder brother. If they weren't playing cricket in their younger days, they were out and about living life to the full. The boys helped out on their father's allotments, plucking chickens and collecting eggs. Everywhere they travelled on Arthur's bike, with Arthur on the saddle and Fred on the crossbar. 'Wherever Arthur went, Freddie went,' said Flo. 'In fact, Arthur couldn't lose Freddie. When Arthur started courting he used to say, "Dad, would you tell our Freddie I've got a girlfriend", and Dad would say, "Freddie, you can't go out, your brother's got a girlfriend", but Freddie always followed them. Arthur used to come home and protest to Dad, "I've seen him. I've seen him." But it never did any good. Freddie was not the sort to be shaken off lightly.'

Such was their bond, Fred was devastated when Arthur got married. The supposedly tough-as-boots fast bowler – nineteen at the time and playing for Yorkshire – couldn't face going to the wedding. 'Freddie was heartbroken,' said Flo. 'He thought he'd lost him. I think he thought that, deep down, Arthur would never leave him. He realised that was the end of him and Arthur, the end of their partnership. They were just so close, almost like twins.'

Although Fred didn't attend the wedding, the brothers stayed close until Arthur died in 1991. The esteem in which Fred held him was illustrated during a television interview when he recalled handing Arthur a bail as a souvenir after taking his best Test figures of 8 for 31 against India at Manchester in 1952. 'I said, "Here you are, there's a present for you."' Then, as a look of profound, almost childlike pride swept across his face, he added, 'Wild horses couldn't drag that bail off him today.'

Once Trueman had recovered from his serious groin injury, it was with Arthur's club that he resumed his career. Roche Abbey were a small village side that played at the foot of Maltby Craggs on a ground with a prominent sideways slope. One of their players, John Skelding, counselled the young quick bowler: 'If tha can pitch it outside t'off stick, it'll come back down t'hill.' Aided by Skelding's advice and the ground's topography, Trueman captured twenty-five wickets in his first four games. 'Roche Abbey's ground was perfect for Fred,' recalled Ron Buck. 'Not only did it slope dramatically but it was bumpy and uneven, and I felt sorry for our opponents because Fred's pace was intensified in those conditions. In fact, trying to get anyone to keep wicket to him was a problem because people were afraid of losing their teeth. Basically, the person who kept wicket was the lad who drew the shortest straw.'

Buck's wife, Betty, made teas for Roche Abbey and said Trueman's success often caused her problems. 'Fred could be a pain in the bum sometimes because he'd bowl the opposition out well before tea and then I'd have to rush round getting all the sandwiches ready. For that reason, I was always happy when Roche Abbey batted first. Fred was a funny character in those days – a little bit braggy – and the thing that stood out was his incredible deter-mination. All the little teams we played against were frightened to death of him, but he was never the type to think, "Oh well, I'll ease up on them a bit." He always bowled as fast as he could.'

Although Arthur represented Roche Abbey, the club wasn't Fred's first-choice destination. At the start of 1946 he'd applied to join Maltby CC – only to be told they already had enough pace bowlers. Later that summer, Roche Abbey were drawn against Maltby in a cup competition and Trueman returned match-winning figures of 6 for 9, prompting a delegation of Maltby officials to travel to Dick Trueman's allotments to enquire whether the youngster would join them after all. Dick Trueman – never one to back down on a point of pride – puffed on his pipe and told them to get lost.

In every rise to stardom there is invariably a pivotal moment, some fairytale feat that sets the ball rolling. For Fred Trueman it came when Roche Abbey were drawn against the might of a Sheffield League XI in a cup game at the Craggs. Roche Abbey batted first and were shot out for 43, Arthur Trueman top-scoring with 20. So confident were the visiting team of knocking off the runs that eight of their number got changed in the break between innings. Dick Trueman, who was umpiring, asked what they were playing at. He

was told both openers had scored centuries the previous week and
that they didn't expect problems against a little village side. 'I'd be a
bit careful if I were you,' he advised. 'There's a fifteen-year-old who
can bowl a bit here and you might find yourself "lad-licked".' Half an
hour later, the Sheffield side had been routed for 11 and Trueman
had figures of 6 for 1. Arthur chipped in with a couple of wickets and
Fred was shouldered from the field by his jubilant team-mates. The
visiting captain knew Cyril Turner, the former Yorkshire all-rounder
and then professional at Sheffield United Cricket Club. He advised
Turner to look at the teenage tearaway, and, a few weeks later, the
membership of the Sheffield club – closed for the season – was
dramatically reopened. Dick Trueman, however, was not convinced.
'T'lad's too young,' he protested. 'I'll not have him rushed.' But
Turner was adamant – and put his foot down.

Throughout his childhood, and even into adulthood, Trueman
had no more demanding critic than his father. After each game for
Roche Abbey he'd pore over his son's performance with a fine-tooth
comb, pointing out where he'd gone wrong and what he needed to
put right. 'If I'd done well I could tell he was very proud and happy,
but he never admitted it to me,' said Trueman. 'Many's the time I
knocked down five or six wickets and he'd tell me I'd been lucky to
get more than two because the others came from bad deliveries.
Then he would analyse my game, saying I would have got more
wickets but I didn't put my left foot down properly, or my left arm
was in the wrong position, or my chest was opening too early, or
my run-up was too fast for accuracy. I used to sit there and take it all
in, saying nowt.'

Motivated by a desire to be better than Arthur, so Trueman
equally craved his father's approval. When such recognition wasn't
forthcoming – at least not verbally – it only made him more
determined. No matter how much he might have *detected* pride and
happiness in his father's demeanour, Trueman longed for
unequivocal proof. Before long he'd resort to telling others how
good he was in a palpable attempt to convince himself. Dick
Trueman accompanied his son to his first day of net practice at

Bramall Lane. They made an indelible impression on Charlie Lee, the Sheffield United batting coach and future Derbyshire captain. 'Old Dick Trueman was a typical miner of the period in his dark suit, cloth cap and heavy boots, and, like all miners, he had a habit of spitting all over the place. Fred was in ordinary clothes. He had no whites and wore a pair of plimsolls. You couldn't imagine the scene was set for a significant moment in Yorkshire cricket.'

Lee strapped on his pads and put the youngster through his paces. 'There wasn't room for much of a run-up in the nets at the Lane, but nevertheless Fred got some pace into his first ball, which pitched and shot right over the top of the net and wall behind me and just missed a tram going down Shoreham Street. Those first few deliveries were all over the place. Then, suddenly, Fred got one on line. I played at it, was a bit surprised not to connect, and when I turned round there were two stumps sticking out of the net like herrings on a Grimsby trawler.' That night, Lee travelled home to Rotherham on the tramcar with Cyril Turner. 'We sat quiet for some time, then suddenly Cyril began to chuckle, and I knew what he was going to say. "He'll play for Yorkshire this lad, tha knows," he said. "He just needs to find a bit of control. There's nowt needs doing to that action."'

For all he loved playing cricket and terrorising batsmen, Trueman had no aspiration to turn professional. When he joined Sheffield United he hadn't even seen a first-class match; his only knowledge of leading players came from reading newspapers or listening to the wireless. Trueman's background offered him little in the way of expectation; most men went down the mine or joined the Forces and simply accepted they'd do such work for the rest of their lives. As far as Trueman was concerned, cricketers might as well have been mythical figures. Such was the romantic picture he built in his mind of the first-class environment, he confessed to feeling distinctly underwhelmed when he first set foot inside Bramall Lane. 'There was not a single tree to be seen,' he lamented, 'and rather than the chirping of birds or the distant drone of a mower or chug of a tractor, there was the constant sight and sound of the heavy industries on which the city had built its name.' Bramall Lane, in fact, epitomised everything grim and unglamorous about Yorkshire cricket. R.C. Robertson-Glasgow, the former Somerset pace bowler, captured its mood when he wrote of Yorkshire's Maurice Leyland: 'His element was foul weather. He would disappear into the haze of Bramall Lane, where a sterner sort of game was being played under the name of cricket, and entrench himself among the sawdust and smoke and off-breaks and appeals, and do his raw, tough work in silence.'

When Trueman left school, his ambition wasn't to be a cricketer, but a bricklayer – a target he achieved in 1946. Encouraged by his parents to find a trade, he quit delivering newspapers and became an apprentice bricklayer for a Maltby firm. His job was to wheel barrow loads of bricks – a task as mentally stultifying as physically shattering. When the foreman told him he was expected to load the barrows as well, Trueman complained he had enough to do and a heated argument ensued. In one of his first recorded brushes with authority, Trueman told the foreman to 'bugger off' – and was sacked.

Employment in those days was plentiful, however, and Trueman walked straight into a job at Tinsley Wire Works in Sheffield, making wall tiles on a machine. The work was equally monotonous and the pay measly, and in an effort to alleviate the boredom Trueman and his colleagues indulged in horseplay. 'We had some great laughs,' recalled Terry Hunt, the friend from Maltby who also worked at the factory. 'One day, Fred and a few others decided to play a prank on the boss. They filled a bucket with water and balanced it on top of a door. As soon as the boss walked in, he got drowned. Needless to say, the gaffer didn't see the funny side.'

Trueman quit soon afterwards and got a job making bottles at a glass factory in Rotherham. This was another mind-numbing occupation and cricket began to hold increasing appeal. With growing anticipation, Trueman looked forward to the nets at Bramall Lane, where Turner took him under his wing and taught him the mechanics of fast bowling.

A useful all-rounder in Brian Sellers's all-conquering Yorkshire team of the 1930s, Turner was a popular figure who hailed from the South Yorkshire town of Wombwell. J.M. Kilburn described him as 'self-effacing and made of modesty', while Len Hutton – whom he took under his wing when Hutton broke into the first XI in 1934 – considered him 'a second father'. With his kindly manner and caring nature, Turner inspired similar respect and devotion from Trueman. The boy warmed easily to his gentle encouragement and was anxious to repay his faith in his ability.

For his part, Turner had excellent raw materials to work with. Trueman's action was near-perfect – a gift from God – and he generated a surprising amount of pace, despite standing only 5ft 4in and weighing less than ten stone (the 14lb 1oz baby had yet to reach physical maturity). But the teenager often lost control in his quest for speed and his delivery sometimes became a sling. Trueman also dragged his back foot too far, making him prone to bowling no-balls. Under the no-ball law in force back then, a bowler had to deliver the ball with his back foot behind the bowling crease, the line on which the stumps are positioned. However, some pace bowlers dragged their back foot before releasing the ball, meaning they could get much closer to the batsman than modern bowlers. Trueman also held the ball incorrectly with his fingers across the seam. Turner showed him the proper outswinger's grip – with fingers straddling the seam – and encouraged him to follow through properly; hitherto, Trueman stopped suddenly as though he'd just seen a ghost.

Eric Burgin, the Sheffield United bowling coach, says Trueman was blessed with the glimmer of greatness. 'In those days, Freddie used to bowl off about eighteen yards and run in as fast as he could. He was bloody quick, but wayward – one down the off side, one down the leg, all mixed in with a couple of good 'uns. But right away the potential was there. It was obvious the lad had something special.'

Despite Trueman's lively disposition, Burgin recalls him as a pleasure to coach. 'Freddie was very easy to handle at Sheffield

United. Everything was new to him and he wasn't as outspoken as he later became. If you told him something he'd listen to it and try to put it into practice. He had a tremendous attitude and was eager to learn.' So impressed were United's coaching staff, they pitched him straight into the second team. He took 6 for 11 on debut against the Steel Corporation. Trueman turned up for the game without any cricket boots and sporting a pair of white bell-bottomed naval trousers. One United official was heard to remark, 'For God's sake, someone find this lad some decent gear.' Trueman couldn't afford any kit of his own.

Word of his potential soon spread to Headingley, where he was invited to the nets before Yorkshire chose their Federation squad for a southern tour in 1948. Just as Dick Trueman expressed reservations about his son making the jump to play for Sheffield United, so Turner urged Yorkshire to wait another year so he could 'polish the diamond'. This time Yorkshire were adamant – and put their foot down.

Trueman travelled to Leeds with his father, who took a day off from the pit, and Cyril Turner to begin the next big chapter in his cricketing development. It was the first time he'd been to Headingley and he admitted feeling overawed – 'the only field of that size I'd seen before had been full of turnips'. The colt bowled eleven balls and hit the stumps three times, one of his victims being Brian Close. The trial was cut short by an elderly man who wandered into the net to speak to Trueman. 'A little man in a trilby came up to me and asked me my name. He asked if I was with anybody and I said, "Yes, my dad", who was sitting behind the nets. "Let me talk to him," he said, and I thought, I can't introduce him, I don't know who he is. So we walked up to Dad and he stood up and said, "Hello, Mr Hirst." The great George Hirst, and I didn't even know who he was. That's how much I knew about Yorkshire cricketers.'

Hirst was one of cricket's immortals. Born near Huddersfield in 1871, he scored over 35,000 runs and captured over 2700 wickets during a first-class career that spanned thirty-eight years. Hirst performed the double of 1000 runs and 100 wickets in a season fourteen times and, in 1906, achieved the only instance of a player scoring 2000 runs and taking 200 wickets in a season. Lancashire and England captain Archie MacLaren called Hirst 'the most untiring and enthusiastic cricketer who ever wore flannels', while the Yorkshire potentate Lord Hawke labelled him 'the greatest county cricketer of all time'.

Hirst told Trueman to wait by the nets while he talked to his father and Cyril Turner. They were gone an hour and a half as the young boy wondered what he'd done wrong. Eventually, Dick Trueman reappeared and told his son they were going home. They travelled back to South Yorkshire in silence until their bus neared Doncaster, whereupon Dick Trueman piped up: 'It's going to cost me six pounds, but I don't care about that. You've been picked for the Federation tour – and you're going.'

The Federation was effectively Yorkshire's third team and an established breeding ground for under-18s. This particular squad included Trueman, Brian Close and Ray Illingworth – another all-rounder of immense potential. The boys were managed by Herbert Robinson, president of the Huddersfield Cricket League, whom one local newspaper described as 'endowed by nature with enough energy for two men, and enough ideas and enthusiasm for three or four'. The tour began on Monday 16 August 1948. Yorkshire arranged for the team coach to stop at Maltby to pick up Trueman, who was wearing a green sports jacket and grey flannels his father had bought especially for the trip. He was joining boys from more affluent backgrounds and knew only Close and Illingworth by sight, but he soon established himself as the life and soul of the party. Trueman led sing-songs as the coach headed south and drew great cheers when he dangled Illingworth out the window to be travel sick.

First stop was Harrow, where the seventeen-year-old Trueman spent his first night away from home in the unlikely setting of a public school. Eric Fisk, an all-rounder who played for the Yorkshire second team, remembers the accommodation as somewhat limited.

'We slept on what could only be called straw mattresses. It was a pretty rough night, but we survived it – just. Fred was very popular and we warmed to him quickly. He always seemed to be at the centre of what was going on.'

Herbert Robinson referred to that first night in a light-hearted account of the tour he subsequently sent to each player, a copy of which Fisk retains. Robinson entitled the narrative 'Tha Knows' – apparently Trueman's favourite saying on the tour. 'It will be a long time before I forget our first night,' wrote Robinson. 'It reminded me of the long night that I spent on patrol during the war trying to accustom myself to a camp bed and army blankets. In place of silence came the echoed expression, "Tha knows". I did not complain of the noise, for, like all of you, I was too uncomfortable to sleep. Like all of you I dozed in fitful spasms and, feeling half-baked, welcomed reveille.'

The first match was against Buckinghamshire Colts. Trueman picked up two wickets without reaching top form. The team travelled to Sussex, where, in addition to playing at Brighton, they took in a day of the Championship game against Somerset at Eastbourne. It was the first time Trueman had seen a county match and he watched transfixed as Harold Gimblett made 310, then the highest score in Somerset's history. In the Federation fixture, Close scored a hundred described by Robinson as 'sound, effortless and masterly'. Trueman took four wickets and caught the eye of the Sussex committee, who told Robinson that if Yorkshire weren't interested in the young prospect, Sussex most definitely were. Trueman also impressed the Middlesex hierarchy during a five-wicket win.

Fisk remembers the tour as largely uneventful – except for one incident involving Trueman. 'Freddie and this other lad came back from a Brighton nightspot and reckoned they'd got lucky with a couple of lasses. Anyway, Herbert Robinson got wind of it and said they'd better sit in a bath of disinfectant in that case because they couldn't be sure where these girls had been. So Freddie and this lad were made to sit in a bath of disinfectant when, in all honesty, I think it was just bravado on their part. I don't think either of them had been doing anything they shouldn't.'

At the end of a happy and successful tour, Trueman confessed to feeling a lump in his throat when the team coach dropped him back at Maltby. He'd had a glimpse of a vastly different life and sensed cricket could possibly become a way of life. He threw himself into practice with renewed vigour and began to read assiduously about the game. Trueman developed a phenomenal recall for records and statistics – many of which he'd later rewrite. He acquired a profound love of cricket's traditions and immersed himself in the game's rich heritage. For Fred Trueman not only played the sport with distinction, he revered it with the love of an armchair obsessive.

Towards the end of 1948, Trueman was promoted to Sheffield United's first team. He again made the transition look effortless, taking fifteen wickets in the last five games. The climb to the higher grade helped him financially: he earned £6 per week plus expenses and could earn another £6 from a collection if he bowled well; when he worked as a bricklayer, his weekly wage was 17s 6d. When the season ended, Trueman was summoned – all expenses paid – to the winter coaching classes at Headingley. There he came under the contrasting gaze of Bill Bowes and Arthur 'Ticker' Mitchell.

Team-mates at Yorkshire in the 1930s, Bowes and Mitchell had a wealth of experience. Bowes, veteran of fifteen Tests and a participant in the 1932–33 Bodyline tour, was one of the greatest fast-medium bowlers in England's history. In a first-class career of 372 games, he took more wickets (1639) than he scored runs (1531). Gangling and bespectacled, Bowes was one of cricket's unlikeliest figures, *Wisden* noting 'he looked far more like a university professor, and indeed batted and fielded like one.' Mitchell, a dour right-hand batsman, was the archetypal man for a crisis. A magnificent close catcher, especially in the gully, he played six Tests and toured India under Douglas Jardine in 1933–34. The events surrounding Mitchell's Test debut against South Africa at Headingley in 1935 are the stuff of legend. When Maurice Leyland withdrew through illness on the morning of the match, Brian Sellers drove the ten miles from Leeds to Baildon to fetch Mitchell, who was busy in his rose garden. Mitchell relented only after much protest. 'Oh, all right then. Just let me tidy mesen up a bit.'

This incident encapsulated Mitchell. Whereas Bowes was a gentle giant and avuncular coach, Mitchell was ferocious and forbidding, the sort of man who'd think nothing of reducing a young boy to tears and for whom the conferment of praise was anathema. As a player, Mitchell eschewed any form of frivolity or showmanship, once rebuking his Yorkshire team-mate Ellis Robinson after he'd taken a brilliant diving catch: 'Gerrup, tha's makkin an exhibition o'thisen.' Len Hutton described Mitchell as 'too hard for me', while fellow Yorkshire and England batsman Herbert Sutcliffe called him 'as grim as a piece of stone from Baildon Moor'. In later years, Fred Trueman said he couldn't recall Mitchell smiling, let alone laughing, and quipped he was 'the type of man who, if he went riding with the Four Horsemen of the Apocalypse, would not noticeably enliven the party'. Trueman once asked Mitchell's son what his father would think of modern Test players hugging and kissing. 'Put it this way,' he was told, 'I can't even remember him hugging and kissing my mother.' Mitchell could be impossibly short with boys who couldn't cut it and Trueman remembered him telling more than one lad not to come again. Nevertheless, he had the utmost respect for Mitchell and described him as 'one of the best coaches there has ever been'.

Bowes and Mitchell – good cop, bad cop – had different methods of man-management but were unanimous in regarding Trueman's talent. Although Trueman himself was an unlikely-looking cricketer (Ray Illingworth remembers 'a thin, pasty-faced, narrow-chested waif with hair falling over his right eye and ear'), Bowes and Mitchell were convinced the boy's bowling action was so fundamentally fine everything else could be built around it. They worked hard to instil greater accuracy during weekly sessions in the Winter Shed, where Trueman bowled on wooden boards at the Kirkstall Lane end. Echoing Eric Burgin's experience at Sheffield United, Bowes recalled Trueman as 'the ideal pupil' and 'unfailingly obedient'.

Trueman's trips to Leeds were torturous in the extreme. He caught a bus from Maltby to Doncaster, another from Doncaster to Leeds, followed by another from Leeds to Headingley. Once, he arrived in Doncaster too late to catch the last bus to Maltby and had no choice but to walk the thirteen miles home through a snowstorm that became a blizzard. He eventually arrived at Tennyson Road at 3.30 a.m., and at 5 a.m. got up to work at Maltby tally office. Yet he accepted such hardships with equanimity. In a short time, he'd impressed some fine judges – Cyril Turner, Bill Bowes, 'Ticker' Mitchell, George Hirst – and felt increasingly optimistic about turning professional. As the 1948–49 winter drew to a close, that optimism soared when one of Dick Trueman's friends called at Tennyson Road brandishing a copy of the *Sheffield Telegraph*. Inside was a report of an after-dinner speech by Herbert Sutcliffe, who predicted Trueman would 'play for Yorkshire before he was 19 and for England before he was 21'.

'Yon Sutcliffe knows what he's talking about,' enthused Dick Trueman's friend. 'If he says . . .'

'Aye,' said Dick Trueman, softly. 'If he says . . .'

Fred Trueman always remembered the moment. 'Dad's voice trailed away. He turned his head to look at me. That look I shall never forget. It appeared to me a mixture of absolute wonder and complete surprise. As if he had just laid eyes on me for the very first time.'

5

Do You F***?

It was a Friday morning in early May. The wild flowering trees of the surrounding countryside were at their best. The sky had softened into a sea of white islands. Gorse and broom broke the sequence of pink and white of crab apple and cherry blossom. The fields were dotted with the full floppy lushness of primrose and, in the woods, there was a smattering of the delicate blue of the first bluebells.

Fred Trueman painted a romantic picture of the day he was first selected for the Yorkshire first team. Weather reports show 6 May 1949 was actually a day of blustery winds and squally showers, but none of that mattered to the ecstatic eighteen-year-old. The postman had brought a telegram informing him he'd been chosen to play in a three-day game at Cambridge University. If it was raining outside, he could see only sunshine. 'All manner of feelings swept through my body,' he recalled. 'I was excited. Gloriously happy. Proud. Apparently, Mum shouted through from the kitchen, asking me who had been knocking at the door. I didn't hear her for the sound of angels singing. Dad didn't see the telegram until he came home from the pit. Typically, he didn't say anything and kept his emotions and thoughts to himself. Though the way he kept putting the telegram down only to pick it up minutes later and read it again suggested to me that he was very proud and wanted to savour and cherish the moment, relive it again and again, so that it would be imprinted in his memory for all time.'

Dick Trueman organised a day off work and took his son to Doncaster to buy him new clothes. He spent over £20 – almost three months' wages – emphasising how important he considered the Yorkshire call-up. Fred Trueman had no cricket gear of his own, so his father borrowed a bat from Maltby CC. A friend lent Trueman some pads and gloves, delighted his kit was to feature for Yorkshire.

As he prepared for his trip to Fenner's, a whirl of emotions running through his mind, Trueman thought he'd 'arrived' and was very much part of Yorkshire's plans. Nothing, however, was further from the truth. In those days, Yorkshire's youngsters were not under contract but employed on an ad hoc basis. It was the club's policy to arrange three or four friendlies at the start of each season against university teams, MCC and sometimes a touring side. These games served not only as preparation for the serious business of the County Championship but to blood youngsters who'd reached a certain level in the nets or club cricket. Such matches were used to eliminate borderline players as well as encourage potential stars.

Despite his own progress in the nets, Trueman was considered a borderline case. Traditionally, Yorkshire had never been enamoured with outright speed, preferring the control of the fast-medium bowler. Yorkshire's opening bowlers at the time – both fast-medium – were well established. Alec Coxon, thirty-three, had been part of England's Ashes team in 1948, while Ron Aspinall, thirty, had cemented his place the previous summer. They'd played in Yorkshire's two preceding games in 1949, against the New Zealanders and Somerset, taking twenty-seven wickets between them. Both were rested for Cambridge, hence the vacancy for Trueman. Two other bowlers were above him in the pecking order: Bill Foord, a bespectacled schoolteacher from Scarborough, and John Whitehead, an undergraduate at London University. Both were kept from regular cricket by their academic commitments and unavailable to Yorkshire in the month of May.

Such considerations were far from Trueman's mind as he joined the team coach bound for Fenner's. This time the only player he knew was Brian Close, who was also making his first-class debut along with twenty-three-year-old Frank Lowson, the man considered most likely to succeed Harry Halliday as Len Hutton's opening partner. Trueman confessed to feeling 'overawed and awkward' on the journey south and worried what his team-mates would think of him smoking a pipe. Trueman had taken up the habit two years earlier and kept it from his parents for several months. One day he came home smoking a pipe only to find his father sitting in his chair when he thought he'd be at work. 'It was too late to hide the thing, so I just sat back and waited for a belt in the ear hole,' he recalled. 'Eventually, Dad folded his paper, took off his glasses and said, "How long have you been smoking a pipe?" I told him the truth – "since I was sixteen." "Oh well," he said, "if you smoke a pipe you won't go far wrong." He always smoked one himself.' When Dick Trueman discovered that Fred's elder sister, Phyllis, was smoking cigarettes as a youngster, he wasn't so lenient. He made her smoke an entire packet – one after the other – in a failed attempt to put her off for life.

On a slow Fenner's pitch, Cambridge batted first and Trueman opened the bowling with Close. In an effort to combat unhelpful conditions, Trueman tried to bowl too quickly and lost rhythm and control. He was no-balled for dragging and made only the occasional ball talk. It was hardly the start he'd envisaged, although his maiden wicket settled his nerves when he had opening batsman Robert Morris caught at short leg off a bouncer. 'Regarding the history of Yorkshire cricket, what I'd achieved was a minute drop in the ocean, but I felt pride and satisfaction at having taken my first wicket,' he said. 'I had made an indelible mark on the county's statistics, however small. Strangely, that first wicket also served to give me a greater sense of my own being. I felt my life had real purpose. I knew what I was cut out to do. Play professional cricket and, in particular, take wickets.' Trueman claimed a second victim, Barry Pryer lbw for 0, to finish with 2 for 72 from twenty overs as Cambridge totalled 283. Next day, Halliday scored a hundred as Yorkshire replied with 317 for 6 declared. Cambridge followed up with 196, Trueman bowling with greater precision to return 1 for 22 from 16 overs. An unbeaten 78 from Lowson helped Yorkshire to a modest target and a nine-wicket win.

Trueman had begun his first-class career in satisfactory if unspectacular style. He hadn't disgraced himself, but nor had he made the impact he'd craved. He still had enough swaggering self-belief to tell Herbert Sutcliffe, an interested onlooker, that he intended to become 't'fastest bloody bowler in t'world'. Close, who marked his own debut with four wickets and an innings of 28, says Trueman had practically achieved that target. 'There was no messing – even at eighteen Fred was as fast as anyone in the game. In those days, he was trying to bowl as quick as he possibly could and at times it looked like he was hurling it rather than bowling it. In those days, I can remember that the ball used to go against his arm. In other words, because he was slinging it a little, trying to get that extra pace, he was cutting it and it was going against his arm rather than with his arm. But it didn't take him long to develop a natural action and start bowling outswingers, which was his strength.'

Captaining Cambridge University was Doug Insole, who later played for Essex and England. 'Fred didn't create a massive impression on debut but he was certainly rapid. As a character, though, he seemed rather subdued. He was probably overawed to be playing his first match and he wasn't the Fred Trueman he later became. The thing I remember most was the old wooden bat he carried around with him. It had the name of his colliery burnt into the back of it, which caused one or two laughs in both dressing rooms.' A postscript to Cambridge has gone down in history. *Wisden*, in the mistake of the millennium, noted: 'Yorkshire gave a trial to three young players: Lowson, an opening batsman, Close, an all-rounder, and Trueman, a spin bowler.' Trueman forgave the insult – but never forgot it.

Despite teething problems and first-match nerves, Trueman performed sufficiently well to be retained for Yorkshire's next game at Oxford University. The pitch was livelier and, with Coxon back to guide him at the other end, he found better rhythm to return first-innings figures of 4 for 31, his victims including Oxford captain Clive van Ryneveld, who played rugby for England and cricket for South Africa. Trueman took 2 for 41 in the second innings in a match to forget for Yorkshire, whose 69-run defeat was their first against Oxford since 1896. Trueman consoled himself with £40 wages from the university games – 'more cash than I'd ever seen in my life' – and paid back his father for buying his new clothes.

Whereas Close and Lowson kept their places for the next match at Somerset, with Close going on to play for England that summer as he became the youngest man to the double of 1000 runs and 100 wickets, Trueman was dropped as Ron Aspinall returned. With Close worthy of selection as a batsman alone, and with captain Norman Yardley a handy swing bowler, there wasn't a place for the burgeoning Trueman, whose wicket-taking potential was not then viewed above his tendency to be profligate. When Aspinall ruptured his Achilles at the end of May, which led to his retirement the following summer, Trueman presumed he'd be back in the side only for Yorkshire to turn to Frank McHugh, a tall inswing bowler. It wasn't until the Whitsun fixture against Lancashire at Old Trafford that Trueman finally played his third first-class match – and first in the Championship – which he failed to mark with a wicket. He was dropped once more and recalled a week later after Yorkshire rested seven first-team players for the fixture against Minor Counties at Lord's.

Trueman had never before visited cricket's headquarters. He'd only once been to London – passing through on the Federation tour bus the previous year. So excited was he to be playing at the home of cricket he travelled by train from Doncaster to King's Cross without a small but significant piece of information – where the Yorkshire team were staying. Following the time-honoured maxim 'when in doubt, ask a policeman', Trueman approached a London bobby, who had no idea where Yorkshire were booked in.

A taxi driver proved more helpful and ferried him to the Bonnington in Southampton Row. Trueman told the receptionist he was a member of the Yorkshire side and apologised for his late arrival. The startled woman told him Yorkshire hadn't stayed there since the 1930s. Trueman hailed another cab and cruised around WC2 enquiring at one hotel after another as the fare shot up at a rate of knots. Finally, he cut his losses and returned to the Bonnington with just enough cash to pay for a room. When he arrived at Lord's next morning, Norman Yardley regarded him with an air of exasperation and the pointed greeting, 'Oh, you've got here, have you?' To Trueman's frustration, it turned out Yorkshire were staying at the Great Western, just a stone's throw from the ground.

After a quick cup of tea to calm himself, Trueman strolled on to the pavilion balcony and drank in the scene. He almost had to pinch himself to believe where he was. 'Playing at Lord's was more than a dream come true,' he remembered. 'It was like going to heaven without all the bother and problem of dying.' The match started poorly for Trueman and Yorkshire. Trueman was dismissed for a duck as Yardley's men totalled 231. Minor Counties replied with 210 (Trueman 1 for 58) before Yorkshire made 250 (Trueman contributing one run at no. 11). Left to score 272, Minor Counties were blown away by Trueman, who took 8 for 70 in his first great performance. *Wisden* was sufficiently impressed to upgrade its assessment of his bowling to 'fast-medium' – still something of a slur to its recipient – and his efforts attracted favourable comment. In his newspaper column, Middlesex and England batsman Bill Edrich observed: 'In young Fred Trueman, England might now have a new fast bowling prospect to nurture. However, looking at the young prospect, it appears to me this lean lad could benefit from a few helpings of roast beef and Yorkshire pudding.'

Yorkshire's reaction to Trueman's tour de force was to dwell not on the eight wickets taken but the seventy runs conceded. He was dropped for the next match at Worcester and found himself in and out of the side as Whitehead and Foord became available again. When the New Zealanders visited Sheffield in late July, Trueman was so anxious to impress he overstretched himself and wrenched a thigh muscle. He was carried from the field and missed the rest of the season. While he languished at home, Yorkshire won seven of their last eight games to share the Championship with Middlesex, but Trueman felt no part of the club's success. Incredibly, he received no message from Headingley, no get-well card or show of support. Instead, he felt 'tossed aside' and 'miserably forgotten', left to ponder what his future held.

Although outwardly brash and self-assertive, Trueman was highly vulnerable inside. Yorkshire's treatment of him at this time – thoughtless in the extreme – fostered a lifelong distrust of authority. Don Mosey, who first met Trueman during the 1949 season and recalled 'an entirely engaging openness about him, a readiness to laugh and enjoy life', said he was not the same from 1950 onwards. 'He became a great bowler but, in many ways, a less loveable human being,' wrote Mosey. In those lonely months in 1949, when he had nothing but his father's encouragement to sustain him, Trueman grew harder and worldly-wise. Much of that engaging openness was knocked out and replaced by simmering bitterness and brooding suspicion. He had not enjoyed a great summer – thirty-one wickets in eight games – but nor had he endured a poor one. He felt deserving of support and recognition.

Trueman's discontent was magnified by his unhappiness in the dressing room. There were cliques in the camp and an 'us and them' atmosphere. Senior players like Yardley and Hutton occasionally stayed in different hotels to the rest of the players, while the young pros shared less salubrious digs. The atmosphere was thick with rancour and it was difficult for youngsters to hold their own. In the early 1950s, Yorkshire possessed arguably as great a side as any in their history, yet won nothing. They had batsmen of the calibre of Hutton, Lowson, Willie Watson, Vic Wilson, Yardley and Ted Lester; world-class all-rounders in Close and Ray Illingworth; a top-drawer wicketkeeper in Don Brennan and great bowlers in Coxon, Johnny Wardle, Bob Appleyard and Trueman. Yet this motley crew of multi-talented, strong-minded individuals failed to gel into a trophy-winning unit. Instead, Surrey – moulded by the man-management skills of Stuart Surridge – dominated county cricket during the 1950s, with Yorkshire perennial and bickering bridesmaids.

In stark contrast to Surridge, who himself took charge of a side *Wisden* said 'needed to feel the smack of firm government to do itself real justice', Yardley struggled to control the dominant personalities. A Cambridge Blue at cricket, squash, rugby fives and hockey, Yardley was an affable, laid-back character whose approach was more arm-around-the-shoulder than rod of iron. He'd entered county cricket during the mid-1930s when Brian Sellers's Yorkshire players would have died for the cause. A gentleman at heart, Yardley simply wasn't cut out to handle players who rocked the boat. Trueman – who needed more handling that most – said Yardley 'seemed to lack the authority to control and influence the senior men, and youngsters like me suffered as a result'. Another Yorkshire player described Yardley as 'too nice a chap to be the skipper', while another complained the team had 'too many captains'. Trueman believed dressing-room disharmony shortened Yardley's career and that of Hutton, who might otherwise have continued beyond 1955. Trueman said Yorkshire didn't realise their potential because there were 'too many arguments, too many jealousies'.

'It was a harsh place to be,' recalled Eric Burgin. 'One or two wanted to rule the dressing room and it was difficult for young players like Fred at that time. Johnny Wardle was a bit of a bully, as were one or two others, and the atmosphere could be pretty tense. There were some very talented players, but there wasn't much harmony.'

Wardle had a reputation for being especially difficult. One of the game's finest left-arm spin bowlers, he was a clown prince on the field and popular with crowds, but off the pitch was prone to disruptive behaviour. Ken Taylor, a Yorkshire team-mate, said Wardle 'looked after himself', while Illingworth blamed him for on-field divisions. 'I had an out-and-out go at Johnny one day,' he said. 'Youngsters were frightened to go for their catches. "Look," I said, "when I came into this side I was a bloody good fielder, and I'm still a good fielder. But buggers like you have destroyed all the confidence in everybody." After that, he was fine with me, but it was very unpleasant at the time.'

Appleyard was another prone to pig-headedness. One of England's greatest seam and spin bowlers, his skill was matched by his inherent stubbornness. Illingworth dropped a catch off him in one of his first games and received 'a rollicking like I'd never had in my life'. Appleyard also hogged the bowling, admitting: 'I've never understood why the laws prevent you bowling at both ends.' Illingworth remembers an incident at Bramall Lane when he was asked to take over at Appleyard's end. '"Pavilion end, next over, Ray," Norman Yardley said. I got there, took my sweater off, and there was Applecart.

'"What are you doing here? Skipper's told me to bowl."

'"Well, bugger off."And when I went back to Norman Yardley he said, "Oh, leave it for an over or two, then."

'Norman was a very nice man and a good captain technically, but Bob was an awkward bugger, and he wasn't the only one. Wardle was as bad. They'd argue about ends and all sorts, and then you'd get Fred who'd throw a bit of wood on the fire as well. And Norman wasn't strong enough to handle them.'

According to J.M. Kilburn, Yorkshire's failure to win the Championship in the early fifties was 'essentially an inability to take the last step, to crystallise individual talent, to create harmony from the varied instruments at their disposal'. Appleyard, however, feels the discord was exaggerated. 'We didn't fail to win the Championship because of dressing-room arguments. We failed to win it because Surrey were too good. They had one international bowler more than any other county have ever had. They had Alec Bedser, Peter Loader, Jim Laker and Tony Lock. And they were playing at the Oval, which was a result wicket in those days, whereas we had to trawl around Yorkshire and take the pitches we were given.'

Despite arguing like cats and dogs, Yorkshire presented a united front to opponents. 'They were always arguing, but when you tried to argue against them you came up against a brick wall,' said Leicestershire batsman Maurice Hallam. 'They were one clan – Yorkshire for Yorkshiremen.'

Trueman, however, felt no part of the clan. He didn't like

Appleyard, wasn't overly fond of Wardle and resented the policy of
'every man for himself'. What he wanted most was reassurance, for
others to tell him he was coming on well. Instead, all he heard were
comments along the lines of 'That John Whitehead's really got
something', or 'Alec Coxon is the greatest trier we've ever had'.
Trueman also felt Yardley had a low opinion of his ability. It was
Yardley who nicknamed him 'Fiery Fred', often putting him on to
bowl with the words, 'I think a spot of Fiery is called for'. But
Trueman sensed Yardley preferred Whitehead and Foord, who were
easier to manage and gave greater control. Trueman was bitterly
aggrieved when Yardley's autobiography described Whitehead as
'our new and most promising fast bowler' and didn't mention him.

Another factor contributed to Trueman's predicament – his
abrasiveness. Team-mates found him crude, unsophisticated and
impossibly loud. There was nothing malicious about him, but his
background had not equipped him with the necessary etiquette to
know his place. The likes of Yardley, Hutton and the 'gentlemen' of
the team didn't much care for his colourful patter, perceiving him
as an embarrassment. What they didn't realise – or perhaps failed to
appreciate – was that Trueman's brashness cloaked insecurity and
fears. Out of this insecurity stemmed an almost compulsive desire
to talk, to be at the centre of attention, to feel part of the group.
Consequently, Trueman became an easy target for dressing-room
banter as he said the wrong thing or acted the wrong way. To put it
bluntly, he had the piss taken out of him.

'Fred had a habit of putting his foot in it quite a lot,' said Ted
Lester. 'I remember one night he went to watch a film called *The
Snake Pit*, which is quite a harrowing film about a mental institution,
but Fred clearly expected a more literal interpretation. Next
morning, Norman Yardley asked him what he thought of the film
and Fred complained there hadn't been a single bloody snake in it. Of
course, everyone fell about laughing – but they were laughing at
Fred rather than with him. To be honest, Fred didn't get much joy
in the dressing room. Alec Coxon was a bit hard, Johnny Wardle was

a bit hard, and people like that kept Fred in his place. It wasn't a particularly happy ship, and Fred spent quite a lot of time on his own in the evenings. I don't think too many players wanted to be with him.'

Appleyard admits the players took the mickey. 'Fred was pretty wild back then. He was wild as a person as well as a bowler. He had his own views and was forever expressing them. As far as I was concerned, he was talking a lot of nonsense, and I used to tell him so. Normally, I'd get a fairly strong reaction. I admit there were times we used to get him going by taking the mick. If you wanted to liven things up a bit, all you had to do was say a few things to Fred.'

Trueman, in fact, could be painfully embarrassing – and liberal in his use of Anglo-Saxon. In social settings he was high explosive – liable to ignite at a moment's notice. One team-mate recalls the young Trueman occasionally approached women in bars with the chat-up line 'Do you f***?', leaving the rest of the players mortified. 'It was bloody embarrassing,' said the player, 'and the women, of course, just told him where to go. On one occasion, though, Fred got his comeuppance. He put the question to this bird and, quick as a flash, she said, "Aye, 'ow's about it, then?" Of course, it was all bluster on Fred's part and he scarpered.'

Trueman's dress sense courted derision. He wore garish jumpers and ill-fitting jackets, presenting a slovenly appearance in the company of team-mates. 'He used to turn up in a kind of royal blue suit and maroon-coloured pullover,' groaned Appleyard. 'We thought he needed to smarten himself up a bit, so Frank Lowson and I marched him into an outfitters in Maidstone one day and got him kitted out with a blue Air Force-coloured shirt, matching his suit, and a tie. To be fair, Fred did smarten up quite a lot after that. I'll never forget picking up the *Yorkshire Post* in 1952 after he'd taken a load of wickets against the Indians in his first Test series and there was a picture of him on the front page wearing a bow tie as he accepted an illuminated address from the people of Maltby.'

Bryan Stott, who broke into the Yorkshire first XI in 1952, believes Trueman would have received more sympathy had he come on the scene a decade later. 'There wasn't the same understanding in the Yorkshire side in the early fifties as there was in the late fifties and sixties. If Freddie had been given the same sort of respect and understanding we gave new players in the late fifties and sixties, gathering them into the family as it were, he'd have had a lot less trouble with authority, I'm absolutely sure of that. I'm very doubtful about the way Norman Yardley handled him; I'm very doubtful about the way Freddie was treated in his early years. There were quite a lot of mickey-takers in county cricket at that time – Closey had a lot of trouble on his first tour of Australia – and Fred got more than his share of stick.'

Trueman took his team-mates' ribbing to heart. Instead of withdrawing into himself, he became more outspoken and overbearing. But behind the bluster lurked a seed of self-doubt, a man who questioned his own ability. Eddie Leadbeater, another Yorkshire colleague, recalled a match against Middlesex that betrayed his unease. 'Freddie didn't do all that well at Lord's. We were in the hotel bedroom at night, and Frank Lowson came in. We were all going to go out. And Freddie said, "I don't think I'll go out." He was really upset, was Fred, almost in tears. "I don't think I'll ever make it," he said. And I said, "Oh, don't talk so silly, Fred. It's only one match."'

Perversely, England displayed more faith in Trueman. He was chosen for the Test trial in May 1950 to play for The Rest against the England first team. The selectors wanted to give their batsmen practice against pace before facing Ray Lindwall and Keith Miller in Australia that winter. They also reflected a national desire to find a fast bowler capable of giving Australia a taste of their own medicine. The game at Bradford, played on a turning pitch that didn't suit Trueman, was made famous by the performance of Surrey off-spinner Jim Laker, who took 8 for 2 in The Rest's first-innings 27. Trueman bowled only nine overs as England replied with 229, his one wicket that of his Yorkshire team-mate Hutton, bowled for a top score of 85. Trueman also had a hand in the dismissal of Yardley, whom he caught off Worcestershire leg-spinner Roly Jenkins. Warwickshire leg-spinner Eric Hollies took six wickets in The Rest's second-innings 113 as England won by an innings and 89 runs.

Following the highs of representative action, Trueman's fortunes suffered another low. He strained a side muscle against Nottinghamshire and was once more left to languish in Maltby. He returned for the last two Championship games and again finished the summer with thirty-one wickets. But he was still no more than a peripheral figure.

Increasingly determined to 'bloody well show 'em', Trueman stormed into the 1951 season with a point to prove. He had one less competitor to worry about following the retirement of Coxon, who'd enjoyed his best season in 1950 with 131 wickets. However, there were rumours Coxon's face didn't fit and that he'd punched Denis Compton during a festival match at Kingston. Trueman, however, wasn't guaranteed a game. Appleyard was flourishing at the age of twenty-six and would sweep all before him in 1951, heading the national charts with 200 wickets, while John Whitehead was available from mid-season after completing his degree course. Trueman still had to scrap to prove his worth.

There were encouraging signs in the season's early weeks. Trueman captured 5 for 19 against the touring South Africans and returned tidy figures in Championship cricket. When Nottinghamshire visited Sheffield in late June, he won the game with second-innings figures of 8 for 68, a new career best. But any thoughts he'd finally seen off Whitehead were immediately dashed. To his horror, Trueman was dropped for the next match against Glamorgan at Headingley and instead chosen for the second XI game against Lincolnshire at Grimsby – as twelfth man. Yardley offered the lame excuse the squad had already been picked prior to Trueman's destruction of Nottinghamshire in order to meet press deadlines – a damning indictment of how Yorkshire was run. To compound his misery, Trueman received a rollicking at Grimsby for falling asleep in a deckchair during play as Bill Foord pressed his own claims with 7 for 35.

When he returned to the first team the following month, Trueman again took out his frustration on Nottinghamshire, claiming the first hat-trick of his career during a nine-wicket win at Trent Bridge. He knocked back the off stumps of Reg Simpson and Alan Armitage and had Peter Harvey caught at the wicket, finishing with 8 for 53 – another career best. But Trueman's dissatisfaction with Yorkshire had hardened like cement. In late August, matters came to a head when he told Yardley he wasn't happy and was thinking of leaving. There'd been interest from Lancashire and Surrey and Trueman still hadn't received his county cap. Four days later, Yardley capped him at Bradford – along with Appleyard – and Trueman agreed to stay.

In those days, it was often said a Yorkshire cap meant more than an England cap. When Trueman arrived home in Maltby, he was surprised to see his father sitting in his chair when he knew he was due on night shift at the pit. Dick Trueman, however, had heard the news on the wireless and swapped shifts to make sure he was there when his son returned. 'When I walked into our lounge with a big, broad smile on my face, Dad's face puckered up,' said Trueman. 'I thought, "Good God. He's going to cry." Dad then pulled himself together. "Well, lad, on a night like this in a Yorkshireman's life, he doesn't go to work," said Dad. "Come on, then, lad, where is it?" I took my cap out of my kit bag and handed it to him. Again, I thought he was going to cry. Dad studied the cap and gently ran his coarse fingers over the material, pausing at the county's white rose emblem before emitting a sigh of satisfaction. I'll never be able to describe exactly what that cap meant to Dad. Only Yorkshire people of a certain age will know.'

Trueman never wore the cap again. He gave it to his father, who'd sacrificed everything for the good of his children. When Dick Trueman died in 1970, the cap was placed on top of his coffin – although not, as Fred Trueman claimed, by Fred himself. 'Fred asked me to put the cap on top of Dad's coffin,' said Dennis Trueman. 'Anything to do with illness and death and Fred didn't want to know.'

Shortly before Trueman received his cap, Yorkshire introduced a rule that capped players called up for National Service would be paid £5 a week. Although he didn't want to stop playing having fought so hard to secure his place, Trueman saw the sense in getting National Service out the way – particularly as his winter job at the pit was soon to be declassified. At the end of 1951, he was assigned to the Royal Air Force and posted to RAF Hemswell in Lincolnshire. The base, which had once been home to Wing Commander Guy Gibson of Dam Busters fame, was just thirty miles from Maltby. Trueman was handed a cushy job in the sports equipment store and given responsibility for maintaining the cricket and football pitches. He didn't much care for answering to authority, while the 7.30 a.m. breakfast parade came as a shock. But he found the people at RAF Hemswell friendly, while the fact he played professional sport gave him a certain kudos. He settled in quickly and made new friends. 'Freddie was a bit brusque but he was a very matey sort of chap,' recalled fellow serviceman Brian Smith. 'He was a lucky bugger, mind, because he didn't have a proper job. In fact, nobody could pin down what he did. Sometimes he drove a mower around the cricket ground, but that was about it.'

When he wasn't driving the mower, a pipe between his lips, Trueman often drove his car around the airfield perimeter as another serviceman, Peter Varley, taught him to drive. Trueman bought the car – a 1932 MG with a fabric body and bumblebee backside – for £70 from a father and son in Maltby despite never having set foot behind a wheel. 'I gave them their money, eased myself into the driver's seat and said, "Right, what do I do?"' recalled Trueman. 'Their jaws dropped on to their chins and the father said, "Bloody hell, are you telling me you can't drive?" I said I couldn't, and since they were canny Yorkshire folk and didn't want to give me my money back, they showed me what was what and how to work the clutch and the gears. And off I went, vaguely in the direction of the camp. I drove the car back to RAF Hemswell without trouble, incident or insurance. When I got back to camp, I was feeling pretty pleased with myself, but Peter Varley blew his top and gave me a right bollocking. In those days, you could drive unassisted as long as you displayed "L" plates, but I didn't even have those. So I went out and bought some "L" plates and Peter taught me to drive. Six weeks later, I passed my test first time.'

Trueman often drove to Maltby with his service mates in tow. 'He'd turn up unannounced at the weekend and there'd be four or five RAF lads with him,' said Flo. 'Freddie would say, "Oh, Mum, I've told them they can stop the weekend." Well, there used to be bodies all over the house. Mum would have to get blankets out and they'd all doss down in the front room, but no one was ever turned away. Sometimes it was hilarious on a Saturday night; I don't know how Dad ever put up with it. There'd be jokes and Dad would try to be all serious, but then his pipe would start twitching and he'd join in the fun.'

Although National Service prevented Trueman playing regularly for Yorkshire, it was understood he'd be given frequent time off. He had plenty of opportunity to play cricket at Hemswell, turning out for his unit, the RAF team and Combined Services. He also had a sympathetic group captain in Jim Warfield, a cricket fan who allowed him to practise on camp. John Whitehead, a radio technician, recalls Trueman bowled in an aircraft hangar. 'I don't know how he wangled it, but Freddie managed to get a net set up to practise his bowling. The rest of us thought it was brilliant because we all had this net to play in. I wasn't much of a cricketer myself, but I remember practising with Freddie on quite a few occasions. He bowled left-arm leg breaks because he said he didn't want to knock me out.'

Cricket wasn't the only sport Trueman played on camp. 'Freddie once hit a seventy break on the Naafi snooker table, which was unheard of,' said Whitehead. 'The table was decrepit to say the least, because the lads used to be on it every night, and it was only tended to once in a blue moon. Freddie also got invited to the Officers' Mess because they had a squash court. He beat them hands-down, and I don't think he'd ever played squash before.'

Trueman was good PR for RAF Hemswell. They liked him to play cricket as often as possible. He usually took it easy in RAF games, bowling off four or five paces, but he could still be inspired to give of his best. In a match against the Gentlemen of Lincolnshire at Woodhall Spa, he was angered by the attitude of an arrogant batsman. After facing a few gentle balls from Trueman, the bloke called out to his partner, 'You won't have any trouble with this lad. He's not very quick.' Trueman bowled him a bouncer and the batsman was carried off. 'You shouldn't have done that, Fred,' admonished one RAF officer. 'He's the son of our host for dinner tonight.'

Stanley Bayliss, who also served with Trueman, says most of the matches were light-hearted affairs. 'We had a wonderful team spirit and, needless to say, won most of our matches. The players were various ranks, from officers to junior ranks, and it was always difficult when referring to team-mates as "Sir" and saying things like, "Sir, would you mind moving there?" or "Sir, would you come in a little closer?" But Fred soon put that right. He insisted on Christian names, and there we were addressing squadron leaders and flight lieutenants as Bob or Bill or Charles or whatever. The feeling of rank disappeared and the players bonded really well.'

Although well-liked among his service mates, Trueman was less popular back in Maltby. As a capped Yorkshire player with plenty of money, he was perceived by some as a big-time Charlie. 'Fred had a bad habit of going into a pub, chucking his money on the bar and saying "Drinks all round",' recalled his contemporary John Gibson. 'That offended quite a few people. It was bragging, you see, showing everyone he had some money, whereas most of us didn't. Quite a few folk got fed up with that.' School acquaintance Frank Anderton says Trueman possessed an obnoxious attitude. 'Fred could be pretty ignorant sometimes. When he was in the Silver Dollar club in Maltby, he had an arrogant air about him. He knew he was good, and he let people know it, but you don't want it shoved down your throat all the time.'

Although Trueman never hid his light under a bushel, there was a pointed element to his showy behaviour. He and his family had been looked down on locally and now he relished that people looked up to him. For everyone who shied away from him back home, others wanted to shake his hand and buy him a drink. Folk who'd previously given him a wide berth were only too pleased to share his success, and before long he'd give them plenty more reason to crawl out the woodwork . . .

6

Bollocks To You, Mate

The telephone rang in the RAF sports store. Fred Trueman answered and was greeted with the words, 'How does it feel to have been picked to play for England?' Not recognising the voice, and sensing a wind-up, Trueman replied, 'Bollocks to you, mate,' and slammed down the phone. His fellow erks were always playing practical jokes.

A few seconds later, the phone rang again. 'Fred, how does it feel to have been picked to play for England?' Again he said 'Bollocks' and slammed down the phone. A few seconds later, the phone rang a third time. 'Fred, it's Bill Bowes. The chap who just called was John Bapty of the *Yorkshire Evening Post* and he's brought me to the phone to convince you it's true. Fred, you *have* been picked to play for England. Congratulations on your marvellous achievement.'

It was Friday 30 May 1952. Trueman had been chosen for the first of a four-match Test series against India at Headingley. He'd just returned from two weeks' leave to play in Yorkshire's opening four home games of the season, taking twenty-five wickets. Now he went back to Group Captain Warfield and asked for more leave, Warfield agreeing on one condition – Trueman arranged some tickets for him and his wife.

Trueman reported to the Prince of Wales Hotel in Harrogate for the traditional pre-match dinner and immediately felt ill at ease. 'The first thing I noticed was that there was a hierarchy in the England team similar to the one that existed in the Yorkshire dressing room. And being the young debutant I was at the bottom of the pecking order. I was made aware of that by the fact that Bill Edrich, Denis Compton and even my club team-mate Len Hutton kept themselves to themselves all evening, only recognising my presence by way of a nod of the head when I was initially introduced to them. I felt as if I had gained entry to a small and elitist club.' Trueman quietly sipped orange juice and looked around for someone to talk to. The experience did little to calm his nerves.

Hutton had his own worries: he'd just been appointed England's first professional captain to celebration in Yorkshire and a mixed response elsewhere. Lord Hawke's famous remark, 'Pray God no professional will ever captain the England side', reverberated loudly in Hutton's ears. As it turned out, Hutton could not have wished for a better series to slip into the role. The Indians were weak, despite having won their first ever Test against England in Madras the previous February, and particularly fragile away from home. India had lost five of their six matches on foreign soil since entering Test cricket in 1932, the other a rain-ruined draw against Australia in Sydney. Their 1952 side was young and inexperienced: Vijay Hazare's men had only fifty-seven caps between them going into the Headingley Test, in which Hutton was making his fifty-seventh appearance, against a combined England aggregate of 234.

On a typically benign Headingley pitch, Hazare won the toss and opted to bat. Alec Bedser opened at Trueman's favoured end, the Kirkstall Lane end, while the newcomer ran up the slope from the Rugby Stand end. When England took the field, Trueman strode up to Bedser, who was playing his thirty-ninth Test and had carried England's pace attack since the war. 'If you keep 'em quiet at one end,' he advised, 'I'll get the bastards out.' Trueman made little impression against openers Pankaj Roy and Datta Gaekwad, so Hutton quickly took him off. He wanted to save him for a crack at Polly Umrigar, a prolific scorer against lesser pace but known to be vulnerable against faster men.

After Bedser bowled Gaekwad, Trueman was recalled for a shot at India's no. 3. Sure enough, Umrigar jabbed unconvincingly at a short ball from Trueman and edged to wicketkeeper Godfrey Evans, handing Trueman his first Test wicket. After slipping to 42 for 3, India recovered through a splendid stand of 222 between Hazare and Vijay Manjrekar, the latter dominating Trueman as he swept to a maiden first-class hundred. But in the final hour of the opening day, England clawed back the initiative when the visitors lost three wickets on 264. Trueman claimed two of them: Manjrekar well caught low at second slip by Allan Watkins for 133 and Coimbatarao Gopinath bowled for a duck. Next morning, overnight rain came to the aid of Jim Laker, who took the last four wickets as India were dismissed for 293. Trueman finished with 3 for 89 from 26 overs – an encouraging but expensive start compared with Bedser's 2 for 38 from 33 overs. England replied with 334, the elegant Tom Graveney top-scoring with 71 and Evans contributing a jaunty 66. Then, at five minutes to three on Saturday 7 June 1952, and with more than 25,000 crammed into Headingley, India began their second innings. What happened next was straight out of *Boy's Own* . . .

Trueman – this time given the Kirkstall Lane end – purposefully marked out his twenty-two-yard run. A hush of expectation fell on the ground as he tugged up his sleeve and tore in to bowl. His first ball to Roy was well outside off stump and allowed to pass through harmlessly to Evans. The second was a rank long hop: Roy top-edged a hook and was caught at first slip by Denis Compton . . .

0 for 1.

India sent in Madhav Mantri, a solid defensive player who'd scored an unbeaten 13 in the first innings at no. 8. Mantri somehow survived the rest of the over – a wicket maiden – as Trueman worked up a fierce head of steam. From the fourth ball of the second over, Bedser got one to lift awkwardly off a length to Gaekwad – the only delivery of the day that behaved unpredictably. It took the splice of the bat and ballooned apologetically to Laker in the gully . . .

0 for 2.

Umrigar played out the remainder of the over – another wicket

maiden – before Trueman eagerly re-entered the fray. Inspired by
the growing excitement of the Leeds crowd, which seemed to infuse
him with an extra yard of pace, Trueman steamed in to bowl the
opening ball of his second over. It was arrow-straight, took Mantri by
surprise and sent his middle stump cartwheeling . . .

0 for 3.

As the stands erupted, a disconsolate Mantri trudged back to the
pavilion. To his astonishment, it wasn't Hazare – India's most
experienced batsman – who came in next, but Manjrekar, with the
captain having opted to drop down the order. Mantri considered it
a pusillanimous decision. 'I crossed Manjrekar on my way in and his
pale face is still vivid in my memory. He looked at me and muttered
in Marathi: *"Mala bakra banaola"* (I've been made the sacrificial goat).
Hazare wanted to avoid the intense pressure of going in at nought for
three and had asked Manjrekar to bat ahead of him. It was an act of
self-preservation that should never have been allowed to happen.'
Despite his first-innings century, Manjrekar was a twenty-year-old
playing only his third Test. Like most of his colleagues, he'd little
experience of dealing with pace, the pitches in his own land dis-
couraging speed. Unsettled by his team's situation, and momentarily
frozen, he aimed a loose cover drive at his first ball from Trueman
and lost his leg stump . . .

0 for 4.

In the space of fourteen balls, India's batting was in shreds,
Trueman had three wickets in eight balls and English cricket had
found a new hero – not to mention a long-awaited answer to
Lindwall and Miller.

'There was pandemonium in the stands,' recalled Trueman. 'I
couldn't believe what was happening to India, to England, to me. I
happened to glance across to Len Hutton. For a brief moment our
eyes met. Then Len's head fell, he sighed and shook his head from
side to side as if saying, "I don't believe it, Fred." I was having trouble
believing it myself . . . Dad was somewhere in that crowd. The man
who had sacrificed so that I could have the opportunities he was
denied. The man who had stuck by me when I had been injured and

Yorkshire had not given a thought to my welfare or well-being. I wondered how Dad was feeling.'

As England celebrated Manjrekar's wicket, Hutton pointed to the scoreboard. 'Take a good look at it,' he urged his players. 'You'll never see another like it in a Test.' Such were the feelings of disbelief that attended the most dramatic start to a Test innings, the sports editor of the *Yorkshire Evening Post* telephoned his reporter at the ground to check whether India, in actual fact, were 4 for 0.

Trueman was on a hat-trick. Hutton stationed eight men around the bat as Hazare – having finally appeared at no. 6 – tentatively took guard. Trueman raced in and produced a searing yorker that flew an inch past the outside edge and just missed off stump. The crowd let out a collective gasp. Caught up in the emotion, Trueman followed with an indifferent couple of overs and was rested by Hutton. He took his sweater to intense applause. Gaekwad recalls the mood of the Indians. 'We were shell-shocked. There's no other word for it. To be nought for four in a Test match was incredibly upsetting. We'd been very much in the game until then but Freddie changed all that. He was focusing totally on out-and-out speed. He didn't have the control of later years, but it didn't matter. As the wickets went down he was shouting and swearing because that's how he thought a fast bowler should be. He was making all sorts of elaborate gestures and loving every minute.'

Watching at the Kirkstall Lane end was eleven-year-old Geoffrey Boycott, who'd gone to the game with friends. 'We caught the train at 7.55 a.m. from Fitzwilliam and got the bus to Headingley and queued up there. Then we ran like hell to get behind the bowler's arm to make sure we got the best seats possible. When Fred got his first two wickets, this fella said to us, "If he gets another wicket this over, I'll buy you all an ice-cream." Well, he bloody well did get another wicket, so we all had an ice-cream on Fred.'

After the players trooped off for tea, Trueman sat on his own in a corner of the dressing room. 'I was acting as substitute fielder and I brought Freddie a sandwich and a drink,' said Bryan Stott. 'He was in a state of shock, quite frankly. He was mesmerised the way things had gone. He was temporarily lost for words, which, for Freddie, was quite amazing.' Stott recalls the fear in the Indians' eyes. 'I could see their batsmen on the balcony when Freddie was on the rampage. There was sheer panic among them. It was quite incredible. Most of them looked a bag of nerves.'

After tea, Hazare and Dattu Phadkar mounted a revival of sorts, lifting their side from 26 for 5 to 131 for 5. But ten minutes from the close, Hutton brought back Trueman, who clean bowled Hazare with another straight ball that effectively settled the contest. Trueman returned England's best figures of 4 for 27 and wasn't needed on day four as Roly Jenkins and Bedser mopped up the tail. Reg Simpson top-scored with 51 as England won by seven wickets. Pankaj Gupta, the India manager, admitted his players had been scared of Trueman. 'It is terrible, terrible,' he told the *Yorkshire Post*. 'I am very distressed. This Trueman has terrified them.'

There was no time for Trueman to bask in his triumph. Directly after the match he joined an RAF cricket tour of Holland and Germany, from which he was released for the second Test at Lord's. Trueman's journey back to England was impossibly laborious. He left Germany at 4 a.m., caught a bus, a train, a ferry, a taxi, followed by another train and taxi, eventually arriving at the team hotel in London at 8.15 p.m. Such a journey would be unthinkable now just two days before a Test. Trueman still managed four wickets in each innings but his performance was patchy. On another good pitch, he conceded 182 runs, which offended Hutton's sense of economy. England won by eight wickets on the back of a splendid 150 from Hutton and 104 by Evans in a first-innings total of 537. Trueman was back in action the following day for Combined Services against the Indians at Gillingham. He tried to bowl too quickly, turned his ankle, and wasn't fit again until the third Test at Old Trafford three weeks later.

Anyone who thought Trueman's display at Headingley a happy accident was emphatically disabused of the notion in Manchester. England batted first and made 347 for 9 declared, their innings extending into Saturday morning after rain delays on the first two days. With the pitch wet through and the light uncertain, India were clearly intimidated by Trueman. Operating from the Stretford end with a stiff wind blowing over his right shoulder, he made the ball spit and soar as Hutton attacked with three slips, three gullies, two short legs and a silly point. After Bedser had Vinoo Mankad caught at short leg, Trueman got to work. He had Roy and Hemu Adhikari caught in the slips as India plunged to 5 for 3.

In came Umrigar, who'd looked as scared and susceptible as any top-order batsman and whose arrival invariably prompted Hutton to call on Trueman. On his way to the middle, Umrigar stammered, 'B-b-bowling's not bad today, F-F-Fred.' Trueman looked him up and down with something approaching contempt and replied, 'It's not meant to be, Polly.' As Umrigar hopped around during his fifteen-ball innings, Tony Lock – fielding at backward square leg – taunted, 'I say, Polly, do you mind going back a bit, I can't see the bowler when you stand there.' Asked by the umpire where he wanted the sightscreen, Umrigar was said to have replied, 'Between me and that mad devil Trueman.' Tom Graveney says the only certainty is that Umrigar was petrified. 'Polly was bloody terrified of Fred. His first movement when Fred came running in was back towards square leg and he wasn't able to deal with his pace. Fred was a dragger, and his front foot pitched two or three feet beyond the popping crease. Apart from being quick anyhow, he was a yard closer than the modern bowler, and poor old Polly just couldn't cope.'

After softening up Umrigar with a salvo of short balls, Trueman shattered his stumps so spectacularly one of the bails broke (it was the bail he gave his brother Arthur). Such was his stranglehold over Umrigar, he dismissed him four times in the series as he scored just 43 runs at 6.14. When he left Test cricket in 1962, Umrigar had made 3631 runs at 42 and become one of India's all-time greats. But his failures in 1952 – and cat-on-a-hot-tin-roof antics at the crease – were largely responsible for propagating the image of Trueman as a bowler so devastating that batsmen bolted for cover behind the square-leg umpire.

Roared on by a packed and partisan crowd, Trueman followed Umrigar's wicket by having Phadkar caught in the gully off a wild slash to leave India 17 for 5. Hazare and Manjrekar added 28 for the sixth wicket – the highest stand of the innings – before Trueman bounced out Manjrekar, who fended to short leg trying to protect his face. Trueman bowled Ramesh Divecha, Bedser bowled Hazare, before Trueman rounded off the innings by having Gulabrai Ramchand and Khokhan Sen caught at the wicket. In 21.4 overs, India had been routed for 58 – their joint-lowest Test total – and Trueman had 8 for 31 from 8.4 overs: the best Test figures by a truly fast bowler. 'I was backed up by magnificent fielding from all my colleagues,' said Trueman. 'It gives you heart when you have people like that fielding to you. You can't do without luck and I certainly had my share. Another time I might have returned none for 131.'

With India on the ropes and his bowlers still fresh, Hutton enforced the follow-on. Trueman soon removed Roy for a duck and followed up by hitting Adhikari so violently in the mouth the batsman was carried off in some distress. But Trueman himself succumbed to injury as he suffered a sudden attack of stitch, managing only eight overs in the innings. Adhikari reappeared to top score with 27 as India staggered to 82, Bedser taking five wickets and Lock four as England won by an innings and 207 runs. Nineteen years later, Adhikari returned as manager of the first Indian team to win a Test series in England. John Hampshire, the former Yorkshire and England batsman and international umpire, recalls the moment Trueman encountered his adversary at Bradford Park Avenue. 'Yorkshire were playing the Indians and I missed the match with a broken thumb. I finished up in the bar with Fred at lunchtime and Fred saw Adhikari coming out the committee room. He said, "Nah then, sunshine. I'm glad to see you've got your colour back."'

No sooner had the Manchester Test finished than Trueman received a telegram from Captain Warfield. He assumed Warfield had taken the trouble to convey his congratulations. Instead, the telegram instructed: 'Report back to unit 8.00am Sunday.' Trueman had done himself out of two days' leave. A fortnight later, Trueman was released for the Roses match ahead of the fourth and final Test at the Oval. After Yorkshire scored 200 at Old Trafford, Trueman and Eric Burgin, his old Sheffield United coach, took advantage of a drying pitch to skittle Lancashire for 65, claiming five wickets each.

Yorkshire made 163 for 8 in their second innings to gain a lead of 298, but Trueman lost his head on the final day. He had a set-to with Lancashire captain Nigel Howard and was spoken to by the umpires. 'We were pressing hard for victory and Fred lost his temper when Howard took a few runs off the edge of the bat,' said Burgin. 'He started giving Howard some verbals and it got out of hand. Eventually, the umpire called Norman Yardley over and said, "I can't have this sort of language being directed at the opposing captain." Meanwhile, Fred had gone back to the start of his run-up and was casually sitting on the grass without a care in the world. Norman Yardley went over and said a few gentle words when he should have given him a right old rollicking.'

The game ended with the last pair of Frank Parr and Bob Berry hanging on for dear life as Lancashire closed on 166 for 9. 'Funnily enough, Fred was held up in some quarters as being responsible for us not winning the match,' added Burgin. 'Roy Tattersall came in towards the end and Fred was more about hurting him, I think, than bowling him out. He hit Tattersall on one occasion and he had to have physio. In those days, you didn't play so many overs because of the time factor. We lost about ten minutes while Tattersall was being treated and that made a big difference. Fred could get very upset if things didn't go his way.'

Although he'd matured as a bowler since debuting at Cambridge, Trueman had yet to mature as a thinking cricketer. Against county players he now expected to get out, and certainly against batsmen who played him as timorously as the Indians, he was prone to over-enthusiasm in his lust for speed. Like many a young fast bowler, Trueman didn't always use his loaf; he relished making batsmen jump about as much as he relished taking their wicket. He revelled in the terror and theatre of his pace, even asking the Yorkshire groundsman to water the stump holes so the stumps would go flying through the air when he hit them. But even when striving and straining for extra zip, his action remained a thing of great beauty. As R.C. Robertson-Glasgow wrote of Don Bradman, 'Poetry and murder lived in him together'. So they did in F.S. Trueman.

John Arlott captured the Trueman in motion of 1952. 'There was in his approach that majestic rhythm that emerges as a surprise in the Spanish fighting bull. It steps out of the toril, stands hesitant, cumbersome then, suddenly, sights the peon from the cuadrilla, pulls itself up and sets off towards him in a mounting glory of rhythm, power and majesty. Such was the run-up of the young Trueman as, body thrown forward, he moved first at a steady pad and gradually accelerated, hair flopping, and swept into the delivery process. Again the analogy of the bull holds good, for the peak of its charge is controlled violence, precisely applied in a movement of rippling speed. Trueman's body swung round so completely that the batsman saw his left shoulder blade: the broad left foot was, for an infinitesimal period of time, poised to hammer the ground. He was a cocked trigger, left arm pointed high, head steady, eyes glaring at the batsman as that great stride widened: the arm slashed down and as the ball was fired down the pitch, his body was thrown hungrily after it, the right toe raking the ground closely behind the wicket as he swept on.'

Rain decimated the Oval Test. Only ten hours, thirty-five minutes' play was possible as England made 326 for 6 declared before reducing India to 98 all out, Trueman capturing 5 for 48 and Bedser 5 for 41. At one stage, India were 6 for 5, echoing their cataclysmic collapse at Headingley. The weather denied Hutton the chance to enforce the follow-on and the overwhelming likelihood of a 4–0 whitewash. Trueman ended the series with 29 wickets at 13.13 – a record for an England bowler against India. It gave him 61 wickets for the season at 13.78, putting him second in the averages to Warwickshire's Roly Thompson (18 wickets at 12.72).

In a little over a year, Trueman had gone from twelfth man in a

Yorkshire second-team game against Lincolnshire at Grimsby to a
successful member of the England attack. He was voted Cricket
Writers' Club Outstanding Young Cricketer of the Year and, the
following spring, named one of *Wisden*'s Five Cricketers of the Year.
'Already Frederick Sewards Trueman gives promise of becoming a
second Harold Larwood,' proclaimed the almanack. 'His long run-up
to the bowling crease with a smooth gathering of momentum for
the delivery is reminiscent of Larwood. Like Larwood also, he is
stocky, strong in the back and very lively with the opening new ball
of the innings. He has the speed, too, and above all this forthright,
outspoken young man has the determination to succeed.'

Hutton, however, sounded a cautionary note. He felt the young
Trueman lacked stamina, predicted he wouldn't reach the top for
another five years and admitted he'd played Test cricket 'sooner
than I'd hoped'. Hutton said if England had not been short of great
fast bowlers, Trueman might have been 'left to mature in less
strenuous pastures'. He felt Trueman's 8 for 31 at Old Trafford 'too
good to be true', adding, 'the helpful pitches on which he bowled
in Tests that season, coupled with the vulnerability of the Indian
batsmen against fast bowling when the ball lifted abruptly or went
through quickly, made Freddie look to be a better fast bowler than
he was.'

At the end of the season, Trueman returned to RAF Hemswell to
start his second and last year of National Service. He kept himself fit
playing football for his unit and also turned out for a club side in
Maltby. While representing the RAF, Trueman was spotted by Ernie
Blackburn, manager of South Kelsey FC. Blackburn was a good
friend of Lincoln City manager Bill Anderson, who was sufficiently
impressed with the bustling centre forward to invite him to play for
City's third team.

In those days, Lincoln was a Second Division club – the old
equivalent of a Championship outfit. They'd won the Third
Division North the previous year – scoring a record 121 goals along
the way – but had found life tough at the higher level. Although

Anderson's move for Trueman was part publicity stunt, it was also with one eye on an injury crisis that had deprived him of Johnny Garvie, one of his leading strikers. With good results scarce and funds scarcer, Anderson was keen to boost his forward line in any way possible.

A genial Geordie who'd played left-back for Nottingham Forest, Sheffield United and Barnsley before a broken leg ended his career at twenty-two, Anderson was one of management's great characters. He'd been appointed Lincoln boss in 1947 at the age of thirty-four and, by the time he left Sincil Bank in 1965, had become the second longest-serving manager at a professional club behind Manchester United's Sir Matt Busby. Anderson smoked heavily, relished practical jokes and was accompanied everywhere by Sandy, his golden Labrador. Anderson was also a useful cricketer, playing one game for Lincolnshire as an opening batsman against Nottinghamshire seconds. During the fifties, Anderson worked miracles to keep Lincoln in Division Two and gained a reputation for turning bargain signings into handsome profits. The tabloids dubbed him 'Soccer's Mr Magic' and 'The Game's Shrewdest Manager', often referring to him as 'Bi££ Anderson'.

Andy Graver, star of Anderson's side and Lincoln's all-time record goalscorer, remembers Trueman's first day at Sincil Bank. 'I was walking up the High Street and I saw this bloke in front of me and thought, "Hello, that figure looks familiar." He looked a bit lost and told me he was looking for Lincoln City's ground. I said, "You just want to be down here and turn right, mate. I'll take you down if you like." I didn't tell him I was a Lincoln player. When we got to the ground, Bill Anderson walked towards us and said, "Hello, Fred, I see you've already met Andy, then." Fred looked blank because he didn't know who I was, and Bill said, "This is the man you've got to knock out the centre forward position."'

Graver remembers Trueman as down-to-earth and funny. 'He was a grand lad, Fred, and he fitted in well. If someone said something he found amusing, he'd laugh like hell and could be very jolly. But if someone said something that upset him, he'd say, "Just you shut your bloody mouth." My team-mates were forever pulling my leg, saying, "You'll have to watch yourself now, Andy. Fred'll take your place in the side." I used to say, "Well, if he takes my place at Lincoln, I'll just have to take his place at Yorkshire."'

Trueman's goalscoring prowess was immediately evident. In his first game for City A, he scored four times in a 5–0 win over Appleby Frodingham, the *Lincolnshire Chronicle* calling him 'a dashing and enthusiastic leader'. He followed up with two goals in a midweek practice match, prompting Anderson to promote him to the reserves. Trueman made his reserve team debut against Peterborough United at Sincil Bank on Saturday 15 November 1952. The game – which ended goalless and was ruined by fog – attracted a record Lincoln reserve crowd of 7328. The *Lincolnshire Echo* wrote of Trueman: 'In the first half he had the ball in the net once, but was given offside, and so disjointed was the City attack that he was rarely in the picture.' The *Lincolnshire Chronicle* noted: 'Trueman had little opportunity to show his worth as a centre forward as he had no support. When he did get the ball he could make little headway against a fine centre-half in Rigby.' The *Chronicle* added: 'Early in the second half many made their way home as the fog became so dense it was impossible to see across the pitch.'

Trueman kept his place for the reserves' next game, against Mansfield Town at Field Mill, but failed to score in a 4–2 defeat. The *Lincolnshire Echo* said City's display 'had the quality of a bottle of ginger pop – early effervescence followed by gradual subsidence'. The following week, City reserves were at home to Halifax, but Trueman didn't play. He opened a Christmas Fair at Horncastle Queen Elizabeth's Grammar School after Yorkshire voiced concerns about him getting injured playing football. In an interview with the *News Chronicle*, Norman Yardley outlined the club's position. 'I must be honest and say that Yorkshire don't like the idea of Trueman playing football. The matter has been discussed and a letter is going to Trueman from secretary John Nash suggesting that it might be in the best interests of everybody if he didn't play this football.'

The cricket–football debate intensified in December 1952 when

Brian Close suffered a serious knee injury playing for Bradford City against Port Vale. Close, who'd previously represented Leeds United and Arsenal, sustained torn cartilages, one of which had to be removed. His knee was still heavily swollen during the 1953 cricket season. Close's injury, allied to Trueman's involvement with Lincoln, prompted Yorkshire president T.L. Taylor to declare at the club's annual meeting in January 1953: 'The risk of injury that would adversely affect their bowling is so great that I feel sure they would be well advised to take the long view and concentrate upon their cricket.'

In response, Trueman told the *Daily Telegraph* he had opted to forgo his footballing ambitions. 'After playing in those three games (for Lincoln), I received so many letters advising me not to risk injury in big football that I had a long talk with my father. We came to the conclusion that if my future in cricket might be as big as many people seemed to think I would do well to concentrate only on the one game.' Trueman added he would in future confine himself to RAF matches.

Close, on the other hand, was in no mood to buckle. He told the *Telegraph*: 'Professional football is as much my life as professional cricket. As for the risks involved, I do not think professional soccer is as dangerous as a good deal of amateur soccer, particularly as we get the best possible treatment afterwards. The amateurs often have to look after their injuries themselves. In any case I do not want to be wrapped up in cotton wool.'

Close's knee injury ended his footballing career and he was fit to play only two first-team games for Yorkshire in 1953. In later life, he admitted: 'I was lucky to get myself right for 1954. It was touch and go whether I would be fit. I played for two-thirds of that season with Yorkshire with a pressure bandage on my knee.'

Although unhappy with Trueman and Close playing football, Taylor made no reference at the annual meeting to the case of Willie Watson, the Yorkshire and England batsman who played wing-half for Sunderland and who'd been a member of England's 1950 World Cup squad. Yorkshire deemed it acceptable for batsmen to play football but not bowlers – a classic case of one rule for one, one for another.

It didn't prevent Yorkshire's cricketers playing the odd game of football among themselves. Ken Taylor, who represented Huddersfield Town and Bradford Park Avenue, recalled: 'Fred wasn't a bad player in a rugged kind of way. He liked to play centre forward – but then so did Closey. And neither of them had any idea of passing the ball. We needed three footballs – one for Fred, one for Closey and one for the other twenty of us.'

During the 1960s, Yorkshire allowed Trueman to play local league football as a means of keeping fit in the winter. Ted Lester remembered: 'When Fred lived in Scarborough, I got him a few games of football for the Old Scarborians. He played a full season for us but he was a bloody nuisance in many ways. He got into the habit of turning up late. In amateur football, you didn't have a reserve and many times we had to play the first ten minutes without Fred. Once we were playing a cup-tie and, because it was a cup-tie, we happened to have a reserve. Fred hadn't turned up so I said, "Forget him." Just as we were about to kick off, someone said, "Fred's here", and I said, "Well, he can forget it. He's not playing now." Funnily enough, I didn't have any more trouble with him after that. Fred wasn't as good a footballer as he thought he was, though.'

Having abandoned hope of playing both sports professionally, Trueman turned his attention solely to cricket. Although still hampered by National Service, the 1953 season promised much for a man who, in his own words, 'had strafed those Indian wallahs' the previous year. The Australians were in town to contest the Ashes, having held the urn since 1934. As England's 'Great White Hope', Trueman expected to play a prominent role but his early season did not go to plan. Due to RAF commitments and an ankle injury, Trueman didn't play for Yorkshire until the end of May, denying him the chance to press his claims. Whereas 1952 had given him wet and lively wickets, perfect for pace bowling, 1953 presented only wet and lifeless ones. In five unfinished county matches, Trueman managed just seven wickets and failed to find form. Having started the previous year so well that Test selection was a formality, he was now unable to guarantee his place – an unthinkable concept nowadays when a bowler capturing twenty-nine wickets in his first four Tests would be an automatic shoo-in. Much to his frustration and the surprise of many, Trueman was left out of the first two Tests at Trent Bridge and Lord's as England gave the new ball to first Bedser and Trevor Bailey and then Bedser and Brian Statham.

From the outset the series was gloriously nip-and-tuck. England had the better of the match in Nottingham, Bedser taking fourteen wickets before rain ruined their victory hopes. Australia bossed the game in London only to be thwarted by a classic rearguard, Watson (109 in 346 minutes) and Bailey (71 in 257 minutes) saving England with a fifth-wicket stand of 163. Although Trueman was named in the squad for the third Test at Old Trafford, where Australia were saved by rain after plunging to 35 for 8 in their second innings, Hutton preferred the spin of Wardle and Laker. Trueman was overlooked completely for the fourth Test at Headingley, which Australia dominated before being thwarted again by 'Barnacle' Bailey, who scored 38 in four hours, twenty minutes to leave the series deadlocked.

While the Leeds match was in progress, England applied to the Air Ministry for Trueman's release so they could assess him playing for Yorkshire. Right on cue, he produced an outstanding display against Kent at Scarborough, taking ten wickets as Yorkshire won by 152 runs. During that match, Trueman was one of the first ten players named for the winter tour of West Indies, despite not having played a Test all summer. But after capturing six wickets in the Roses game at Bramall Lane, followed by another three against Leicestershire, he was chosen in a twelve-man squad for the decisive final Test at the Oval. At last he was to have a crack at the Australians.

After Hutton lost the toss for the fifth time in the series, the English public showed what it thought of Trueman's return by cheering wildly when he was summoned to bowl. Those cheers intensified when his second ball to Arthur Morris was a bouncer that echoed the hostility of Lindwall and Miller. From the last ball of the over, groans resounded when the normally reliable Denis Compton dropped Morris at leg slip to deny Trueman an instant success. He had to wait until his second spell before claiming his first wicket – that of Neil Harvey, which left Australia 107 for 4. Black-and-white footage survives of the dismissal. In Trueman's smooth, side-on approach, the mounting glory of rhythm and power is thrillingly evident. Harvey – compact and left-handed – is fractionally late on a pull stroke and top-edges to mid-wicket, where Hutton claims a good catch running back against the gas-holder background. Trueman followed up by having Jim de Courcy and Graeme Hole caught behind to leave Australia 160 for 6, which became 160 for 7 when Bedser caught and bowled Ron Archer. Australia's last three wickets added 115, Ray Lindwall top-scoring with 62 before Trueman had him caught behind to end the innings with England's best figures of 4 for 86. 'Erratic, yes; wild, most certainly; but full of fire and dynamic,' appraised former Australia batsman-turned-writer Jack Fingleton.

It wasn't just a good many Englishmen who thought Trueman should have been chosen earlier in the series. A number of Australians were similarly bemused. 'The reluctance of the England selectors to play him before the fifth Test came as a shock,' wrote Lindwall. 'Trueman bowled much better at the Oval than any of the Australians expected and we were unanimous that, whereas he might have been overrated before, too many people were now under-rating him.' Harvey agrees. 'We were all very surprised England didn't play Freddie in the first four Tests. We had the greatest respect for him in our side. I remember back in 1948 when England dropped Hutton, and it makes you wonder what they do sometimes. They seemed to harm their team rather than improve it, and Freddie, in my view, was badly missed.'

After England gained a first-innings lead of 31, the Ashes were effectively won on the third afternoon. Australia were dismissed for 162, Lock taking five wickets and Laker four. England were left to score just 132 against a team who'd made the fatal mistake of going into the match without a specialist spinner. The home side ended day three on 38 for 1 after losing Hutton to a run-out. Although an English win seemed inevitable, John Arlott reflected a nation's anxiety when he wrote: 'The prospect of winning the Ashes after 19 years has been so distant that we have become like some small boy who has looked forward to a special treat for so long that he fears something will happen to stop it – or is himself sick with excitement so that he cannot enjoy it.' Next morning, Trueman journeyed to the Oval with Hutton and caught sight of a newspaper placard outside the ground. It bore a picture of the urn and the message 'LEN – THEY'RE OURS!'

At seven minutes to three on Wednesday 19 August 1953, with the Middlesex duo of Compton and Edrich at the crease, the dream became reality. Four runs were needed when Compton pulled a ball from Morris towards the square-leg boundary in the shadow of the gas-holder. In the commentary box, Brian Johnston cried, 'Oh, is it . . . is it the Ashes?' Then, as the ball completed its historic course, he enthused, 'Yes, England have won the Ashes.' An ecstatic crowd swarmed the field, ignoring appeals to keep off the square. 'And now the race of all time,' declared Johnston. 'What a scene here. No policeman can stop this.' The crowd converged in front of the pavilion, chanting, 'We want Len.' The England team appeared as salutes were shared in the heady afternoon.

It was an emotional end to an extraordinary series, the first watched by significant numbers on television. In an uncanny precursor of 2005, when Michael Vaughan's England regained the urn after eighteen long years, the 1954 *Wisden* proclaimed: 'No other series of Tests captured such public attention. What with day-by-day front page newspaper articles and radio and television broadcasts there were times when industry almost stood still while the man in the street followed the tense battle between bat and ball.' Unlike 2005, there were no all-night benders or open-top bus parades. Bob Platt recalled: 'I once said to Fred, "Bloody hell, Fred, you must have had one hell of a party after that Ashes win at the Oval in '53."

"Party?" he said. "You must be f***ing joking. I had to be back at camp before midnight otherwise I was absent without leave." '

There was a poignant postscript to Trueman's triumph. When he returned to RAF Hemswell, he discovered that Elizabeth Stimpson, the grandmother from whom he'd taken his middle name and who'd delivered him on that cold and snowy night beside Maltby pit yard, had died of heart failure on the second day of the Test, aged eighty-two. 'The family didn't want to tell Freddie while the match was in progress because we thought it would upset him too much,' said his sister Flo. 'We didn't want it to affect his performance, so we waited until the game was over.'

Three weeks after the greatest cricketing day he had known, Trueman played against the Australians for Combined Services at Kingston – a fixture in aid of service charities. He bowled the opening over before walking to his customary fielding position of short leg. Lieutenant Commander Michael Ainsworth, the Combined Services' captain, took umbrage at this presumptuous behaviour and imperiously dismissed him to deep fine leg. 'Major Parnaby always fields at short leg,' snapped Ainsworth, oblivious to Trueman's insistence that if England regarded him as a short-leg specialist, it was not unreasonable to think he might do a good job for Combined Services.

Trueman trudged towards the boundary and gained morbid satisfaction when Major Parnaby promptly dropped Keith Miller off Leicestershire seam bowler Terry Spencer. But his delight turned to despair as Miller tore into the Combined Services' bowlers – himself included – en route to a career-best 262 not out. De Courcy also struck a double hundred as Australia made 592 for 4 declared. After the game, which Combined Services lost by an innings and 261 runs, tempers flared when Trueman articulated his views on Ainsworth's captaincy.

'Trueman, I'll make sure you never play for Combined Services again,' barked the lieutenant.

Trueman, grinning broadly, chuckled, 'You're dead right, sir.'

Ainsworth – steam practically coming out his ears – shot back, 'What the devil do you mean by that?'

To which Trueman replied, 'I was demobbed two days ago.'

7

Mr Bumper Man

On a dull December morning in 1953 Fred Trueman embarked on his first overseas tour. He left for the West Indies with the world at his feet; when he returned four months later it had crumbled around him. What happened on that trip – on and off the field – had a disastrous effect on Trueman's career. Accused of all manner of indiscretions, he would not tour again for another five years.

His problems began before the players left home. Prior to departure, they were briefed by the Foreign Office on the tense political situation in the Caribbean. Since Indian independence in 1947, there'd been a rise in Home Rule movements throughout the Empire. The West Indians wanted free of their colonial masters, who increasingly feared for their old way of life. The players were told not to inflame tensions with a silly action here or foolish remark there. Trueman's response to the guidance issued by Sir Walter Monckton, a member of Sir Winston Churchill's cabinet, was to protest that if he was expected to behave like a diplomat he should be paid like one. His comments went down like a lead balloon.

Len Hutton told his players at the same briefing not to fraternise on tour with their West Indian counterparts. Trueman knew several West Indians from English league cricket and took umbrage at his captain's frosty command. In later life, Hutton claimed his comments had been misconstrued and that he had, in fact, given no such order. But that was not the impression he gave his players. Godfrey Evans wrote: 'He said to us, in effect, "Well, we've got to do these people, haven't we? We've got to do 'em. You mustn't speak to 'em on or off the field. Keep right away from 'em. Don't take any notice of what they say. Get stuck right into the job and beat 'em at all costs."'

There was further friction between the Yorkshire pair. On the journey to London Airport, Hutton's train stopped at Doncaster, where Trueman joined it. 'It was mum's fiftieth birthday and the family went along to see Freddie off,' said Flo Halifax. 'Dad never liked goodbyes and he just shook his hand and said, "Good luck, lad." Freddie had this new suit on and he looked lovely. Anyway, Len Hutton got off the train and sneered, "My God, Trueman, have you brought the whole of Maltby with you?" He said, "No, sir, just the family." We were flabbergasted. We'd never heard someone speak like that before. Freddie gave us all a kiss and off he went.'

Hutton's was the first MCC team to fly on tour. They travelled on a BOAC Stratocruiser – a plane considered state-of-the-art but with a bar so small the players took turns to go for drinks. There wasn't enough fuel to fly direct, so the plane put down in Ireland. The aircraft developed electrical trouble and diverted to Gander in Newfoundland. Hutton's men arrived in Canada in snow a foot deep and in a temperature of minus sixteen. They stayed six hours before the weather deteriorated. Tom Graveney recalled: 'There was a bad blizzard on the way, so at one o'clock in the morning they woke us up and said if you don't get out now, you won't get out for a fortnight. So we packed all our bags and got back on the plane.'

When they landed in Bermuda, exchanging bone-numbing cold for subtropical heat, there were immediate signs all was not well. Charles Palmer, the England player / manager, got a shock as he tried to finalise arrangements for three practice games. 'We found there was a colour bar in Bermuda, which I hadn't been told about. I met my counterpart at the airport, a Bermudian, and the first thing I wanted to talk about with him was the conditions of play and all that sort of thing. We were standing there with thousands of people milling around, and I said, "Well, let's not talk about it here. Come back to the hotel and we can talk about it in an armchair." And then people started semaphoring: "Not allowed to fraternise . . . Black and white . . . Not at the hotel." We had to arrange a special meeting elsewhere.'

The whites impressed on Palmer and the MCC players how important they considered the forthcoming series. While the press billed it the 'Cricket Championship of the World', with England having just beaten Australia and the West Indies having won 3–1 in England when the countries last met in 1950, the whites saw an England triumph as politically advantageous. Palmer remembered: 'All these countries were saying, "We want our independence." And the white people, who had ruled the roost over there for many years, saw the ground crumbling under their feet. Every day on the tour, we were being invited to social functions, invariably with the white people, and it was difficult to refuse. And all the time they would be saying to us, "For God's sake, beat these people, or our lives won't be worth living." It became a big millstone around our necks. We were almost afraid to talk to a white person. We knew what they were going to say. We wanted to win, but not for them. After a while it ate into our souls.'

Hutton, in fact, had ordered fewer social functions. He'd toured the West Indies in 1948 and found the most tiring thing not the cricket but the interminable round of social engagements. He felt it in his team's best interests if they were kept to a minimum. This caused offence not only to the whites, who expected their invitations to be instantly accepted, but to the West Indian players Hutton told his men to ignore. Frank Worrell described his surprise at meeting England cricketers he thought were friends. 'I was beginning to wonder whether I had been the victim of one of Clyde Walcott's practical jokes, but I soon learned I hadn't. Clyde and Everton Weekes told me that they had been trying, ever since the MCC party arrived a week previously, to do everything in their power to entertain our guests, but they had received the same treatment.'

The warm-up games in Bermuda proved of little value. There was no turf wicket, so the matches were played on concrete matting.

Batsmen found it difficult to time the ball, while faster bowlers were severely hampered. In an effort to avoid jarring his front foot, Trueman delivered from outside the matting strip and developed a stutter in his run-up that lasted some weeks.

In the first match proper, against Combined Parishes in Jamaica, Trueman encountered the legendary George Headley. Known as 'The black Bradman' in the Caribbean where, in turn, Bradman was known as the 'The white Headley', the Jamaican had been brought out of retirement in the Birmingham League to play in the Tests, aged forty-four. The Jamaican public raised more than £1,000 to pay his fare, but the great man's powers were well on the wane. After hooking a Trueman bouncer for six early in the second innings, the first major flashpoint of the tour arose when Headley misjudged a pull from a good-length ball from Trueman that reared up viciously and broke his arm.

While the rest of the England players rushed to the veteran, Trueman casually strolled back to his mark. The crowd were incensed by this shabby behaviour and vented their fury in no uncertain terms. Although Headley's injury was entirely accidental, Trueman's antics were beyond the pale. He was given a police escort when he left the ground and became known throughout the Caribbean as 'Mr Bumper Man', one songwriter immortalising him in calypso to the tune of 'What Shall We Do with a Drunken Sailor?'

What shall we do with that Freddie Trueman?
What shall we do with that Freddie Trueman?
What shall we do with that Freddie Trueman?
Now he's bowling bumpers

Head down and up she rises
Head down and up she rises
Head down and up she rises
He's a-bowling bumpers

> *Four hundred on the scoreboard rises*
> *Four hundred on the scoreboard rises*
> *Watch that head it'll be two sizes*
> *And still he's bowling bumpers*

Headley's broken arm kept him out the first of two games between Jamaica and MCC. In the second match, Trueman had him caught off a bouncer that was akin to pouring petrol on a naked flame. As he passed the bowler on his return to the pavilion, Headley growled, 'The crowd ain't gonna like that, man.' To which Trueman replied, 'No, but it'll go down a storm back in Sheffield.' Headley made an unbeaten 53 in the second innings to save Jamaica from defeat but was dropped twice and laboured four hours over his runs.

Although his form scarcely warranted it, Headley was named in the squad for the first Test at Sabina Park after threats were made to dig up the pitch if he didn't play. An injury to Frank Worrell spared the selectors' blushes but Headley's inclusion was widely condemned. 'For sheer vulgar insularity this latest effusion takes the cake,' thundered one British Guiana paper, while the *Trinidad Guardian* lamented: 'Even charity can find no justification for the inclusion of the aged George Headley.' The *Daily Mail*'s Alex Bannister saw enough during the two colony games to convince him Headley was out of his depth. 'To expose such an illustrious figure to the saddest of all sights on a playing field – the formerly supreme artist striving to hold his own long after he has passed his best – made a depressing spectacle. Here was Headley, once spoken about in the same breath as Bradman and Hammond, trying to put back the years to meet the bold challenge of another generation represented by the confident young Freddie Trueman.'

There was further controversy when Headley walked out to bat on day two of the Test. In a pre-arranged move, Hutton set back the field to allow him a single for old times' sake. Hutton intended it 'as a salute and not out of sympathy', but the unforeseen consequence was that Headley faced the final over before lunch from a fired-up Trueman. The over contained several bouncers and the batsman snapped. 'This ain't cricket any more,' bristled Headley. 'This is war.' According to Clyde Walcott, Hutton's action 'probably caused more resentment than any other single incident on the tour'. But the *Daily Telegraph*'s Jim Swanton called it 'a most agreeable gesture', adding, 'international sport is often a grim, humourless business and it is pleasant to think there is still room for an occasional gesture of sentiment. I cannot remember another instance of a cricketer being given a run in a Test match except for tactical reasons or when near the end proceedings descend to the comical.'

Hutton, however, was damned if he did, damned if he didn't. Either he was patronising the great Headley by gifting him a run, or wilfully exposing him to Trueman's terrors. Headley made 16 before Graveney caught him at short leg off Tony Lock's quicker ball, which Walcott termed 'the most blatant throw I have ever seen'. Later in the match, Lock was called for throwing by umpire Perry Burke, who caused an even greater furore by adjudging local debutant J.K. Holt junior lbw six runs short of a maiden Test hundred. According to Bannister, Holt ducked what he thought was a bouncer and 'palpably misjudged a straight ball from Brian Statham to which he offered no stroke'.

The partisan crowd didn't concur, believing Holt should have received latitude from a home official. Bets had been laid on Holt reaching his hundred in a region where it was common for spectators to gamble on approaching milestones. Burke's decision left many in the crowd out of pocket and triggered a deluge of disorder. As hysteria swept the stands, the umpire's wife was slapped in the face. Later that evening, Burke was accosted by a man with a knife and by another brandishing a pistol. One of his sons was beaten up by a gang of youths on his way home from school. Burke's father, also a Test umpire and employed on the wharves, was threatened by stevedores who ranted: 'We have a good mind to throw you into the water.'

Trueman was also the subject of betting as he struggled for form on a lifeless pitch. Towards the end of West Indies' first innings, the England players were puzzled to hear the crowd start shouting 'We want Trueman' when Alan Moss was bowling. Trueman had not

hitherto been popular with the natives before all became clear. After
he re-entered the fray, loud cheers erupted when the scoreboard
ticked up 100 against his bowling analysis; it had previously been 96
and the crowd wanted him to reach his 'century' before close of play.

Trueman returned 2 for 107 in West Indies' 417, figures that
would have been better but for abject fielding. Three catches were
grassed off his bowling – all offered by wicketkeeper Clifford
McWatt, who gave five chances during an innings of 54 from the no.
8 position that swung the momentum West Indies' way. Swanton,
however, was unimpressed. He called Trueman 'barely more than
fast-medium', adding, 'at times he was wretchedly ragged in length,
and also in direction.'

When England batted, Hutton demanded his players eschew risky
strokes to disastrous effect. The tourists were routed for 170 after
prodding about pitifully for ninety overs. 'On such a pitch a total of
170 represented ghastly failure for which neither excuse nor
explanation could be accepted,' opined Bannister. West Indies' captain
Jeff Stollmeyer chose not to enforce the follow-on, raising England's
hopes of saving the game. Those increased when Willie Watson (116)
and Hutton (56) added 130 for the first wicket, followed by 90 for the
second wicket between Watson and Peter May, but the last eight
wickets tumbled for 39 as England lost by 140 runs.

England changed tack for the second Test in Barbados. Out went
Trueman and Moss, with Jim Laker and Ken Suttle recalled to the
squad. Sussex batsman Suttle had pressed his case with top scores of
96 and 62 during the tour match against Barbados that preceded the
Test, but Hutton left him out of the final XI in a move that stunned
the England squad. Hutton opted instead for manager Palmer, a
thirty-four-year-old with an unremarkable record for Worcestershire
and Leicestershire. Palmer had played only one first-class innings on
the trip and hadn't held a bat for around three weeks. He was
unprepared for the rigours of a Test, but Hutton was no admirer of
Suttle, whose place on tour he felt owed too much to a single century
at Lord's in front of Sir Pelham Warner. Trueman thought Palmer's

selection a nonsense and his own omission nonsensical. He didn't hesitate to say so in voluble terms.

The Barbados Test started on 6 February, Trueman's twenty-third birthday. The anniversary was celebrated at the traditional Saturday 'club night' of MCC touring teams – an occasion that got a little out of hand. Two English players – subsequently proved to be Denis Compton and Godfrey Evans – were guilty of bad language and high spirits in the lift of the Marine Hotel where the England team were staying and two women complained to the hotel management. Next morning, Trueman and Lock were identified as culprits and summoned to clear-the-air talks with Hutton, Palmer and the ladies in question. Jim Swanton was also present, having been asked by Palmer to provide moral support.

'I arrived on the Marine balcony to find captain, manager, Messrs Trueman and Lock, all sitting nervously on the edge of their chairs,' wrote Swanton, 'and two English ladies, the larger of whom, whose rank in the ATS could not possibly have been lower than brigadier, holding forth rather in the manner of Bertie Wooster's Aunt Agatha. The theme, of course, was what was expected of English teams abroad and I found myself applauding the lady's admirable sentiments, expressed, as I recall, in a fine, manly baritone, more in sorrow than in anger, and at the same time feeling intensely sorry for poor Len. [John] Arlott, relating this incident [in his biography of Trueman] . . . says that Fred told the captain "it weren't us". As to this all I remember is that at the time Fred was working on the principle of discretion being the better part of valour. For that matter so were we all.'

Life got no easier for Hutton and Palmer during the Test. Walcott hammered 220 as West Indies scored 383, England again replying in desperate fashion on a pitch *Wisden* described as 'perfect for batting'. After ending day two on 53 for 2, England scored 128 runs in 114 overs to end a turgid third day on 181 for 9. Graveney – one of the finest stroke-makers of any generation – followed Hutton's no-risk strategy to the letter, scoring fifteen runs in two hours before patting back a full toss to off-spinner Sonny Ramadhin. 'Ram was bowling

when I came in,' said Graveney, 'and I hit the first two like a rocket
– one at mid-on, one at mid-off. A yard either side and I would have
had eight runs. Len walked down the wicket and said, "We don't
want any of that."' After crawling to 64, Hutton seemingly forgot
his own tactic when the crowd started shouting 'We want our
money back' and 'We want cricket'. In a rush of blood, he twice
lofted Ramadhin's spin partner Alf Valentine for four before falling
to a catch in the deep as he attempted the stroke a third time.

   Trailing by 202 on first innings, England's bowlers toiled again as
the home side made 292 for 2 declared, Holt finally scoring his
maiden hundred after his near miss in Jamaica. Chasing a notional
495, several England players impressed on Hutton the need to
abandon his cautious policy. 'In the first Test, we seemed to play our
cricket in handcuffs, and the first innings at Barbados was even
worse,' wrote Compton. 'It was paralysed cricket. It was time, I
pointed out, to throw away our chains and to allow the stroke
players to play the game their own way. Len said that he wouldn't
interfere with such a policy, and so a new plan went into operation.
We were to attack, and attack we did.'

   Compton, Hutton and May hit half-centuries as England reached
258 for 3 on the sixth morning, raising hopes of an improbable win.
But when Compton was lbw to Stollmeyer for 93, the last six wickets
fell in a heap and England lost by 181 runs. Much to the
consternation of the Caribbean's white population, they were 2–0
down with three Tests to play.

The tour moved to British Guiana, where Trueman's fortunes took
a turn for the worse. In the colony game at Georgetown before the
third Test, he was accused of verbally abusing an umpire in one of
the biggest controversies of his career. After Graveney and Watson
scored sublime double hundreds, sharing a fourth-wicket stand of
402, England were pressing for an innings win when Hutton asked
Trueman for an all-out effort. From his first ball, Trueman had an
apparently plumb lbw rejected by umpire Cecil Kippins. He was
twice no-balled in the same over, had two further lbw appeals

rejected and a catch put down off the final delivery. When Trueman was no-balled again in his second over, Kippins suddenly left his position at the bowler's end to complain to Hutton, who was fielding at gully. They had a brief conversation before Hutton – 'white-faced and agitated' – changed places with Suttle at mid-on.

After play, all hell broke loose in the England dressing room as Trueman was accused of calling Kippins 'a black bastard'. Trueman vehemently protested his innocence and insisted there had been a misunderstanding. Trueman said if Hutton and Palmer believed him guilty, he should like his ticket for the next boat home. Neither thought him innocent – and Trueman was left to carry the can.

All available evidence pointed to Trueman. The incident took place during an over he was bowling, he'd never been short of a word or two, and, as a young man trying his utmost to get back in the Test side, he was not amused by perceived umpiring blunders. According to Bannister, 'it was only too clear that in the heat of the moment *l'enfant terrible* of English cricket had said something which he should not', while Hutton confirmed Trueman was reported to him by the umpire for using bad language.

But Kippins – now in his late eighties and living in America – admits he wrongly identified Trueman as the culprit. 'It was my fault entirely,' he said. 'It wasn't Freddie, it was Johnny Wardle. I mistook one for the other and it was only later I realised what I'd done. It was only my third first-class game and I managed to get their names mixed up when I complained to Hutton. Freddie didn't call me a black "b". It was Wardle who made an abusive remark. That Wardle, I didn't like him. He was my problem, not Freddie. I completely absolve Freddie of any blame and I'm sorry it never happened at the time.'

Kippins claims he did not correct his error because he'd fallen out with Hutton and wanted nothing more to do with him. 'When I walked over to him to complain I'd been abused, do you know what he said? He said, "Why aren't you giving these batsmen out lbw?" He never addressed the complaint that I made. That broke down all communication as far as I was concerned. I never spoke to Hutton again.'

It seems extraordinary such a case of mistaken identity could have been perpetrated, yet such was Kippins's and fellow official Toby Rollox's performance that Hutton successfully appealed their standing in the Georgetown Test. He described their officiating in British Guiana as 'the worst umpiring I have seen in first-class cricket' and requested either Perry Burke and Tom Ewart of Jamaica or Harold Walcott and Cortez Jordan of Barbados be flown in. The British Guiana Cricket Board of Control refused – ostensibly because of the transportation costs involved but, in reality, because of offence incurred to local pride. Prior to the tour, it had been agreed the colony in which each Test was played would provide its own officials. Hutton was thus forced to accept two new Guianans: E.S. 'Wing' Gillette, who'd umpired the corresponding Test in 1948 and since retired, and 'Badge' Menzies, head groundsman at Georgetown Cricket Club, who agreed to stand on one condition – he was allowed to tend his beloved square. Menzies supervised ground arrangements from seven o'clock in the morning until start of play, officiated the action and then worked on the square until late at night.

Despite all the problems leading up to the game, the Georgetown Test was a triumph for Hutton. He led from the front with a magnificent 169 as a more positive England seized control. Having left out Trueman and chosen three spinners, England totalled 435 after winning the toss. West Indies replied with 251 and 256 before England romped to a nine-wicket win. The match, however, produced yet more controversy. On the fourth day, McWatt and Holt's eighth-wicket partnership lifted West Indies from 139 to 237 to inspire hope of avoiding the follow-on. But when McWatt was run out by May from the leg-side boundary, trying to complete a risky two, the partnership ended at 99 and a passionate crowd grew predictably hostile. 'A momentary lull followed, just as though the crowd had not grasped the significance of the event,' wrote Bannister. 'Then the first of hundreds of bottles, tins and boxes streamed in the direction of umpire "Badge" Menzies, who had given McWatt out, and Peter May, the nearest English fieldsman to the unfortunate umpire. One bottle fell at Peter's feet. He and Menzies prudently scampered out of range.'

Not a ball was bowled for ten minutes. Players and umpires stood in the middle of the field, surveying with horror the mounting mess. Compton foolishly lobbed one bottle back towards the crowd, while Wardle attempted to defuse the situation by taking an imaginary swig from a bottle and staggering drunkenly around. Stanley Jones, president of the British Guiana Cricket Board of Control, left the pavilion to talk to Hutton and advised him to take his team off the field until the riot had been quelled. 'No,' replied Hutton, 'I want another wicket or two tonight.' Compton described it as Hutton's finest hour. 'Len never had a greater moment. He was cool, nerveless, quite unconcerned about the demonstrating crowds which surrounded him in angry thousands. He was superbly defiant. It was, if you like, the saying of the century. It was characteristic Len.'

Amid a tinderbox atmosphere, Laker bowled Ramadhin to give Hutton the wicket he craved before close of play. Menzies – still shaking with fear long after stumps – was given a twenty-four-hour police guard outside his house, while England requested riot police stand by for the rest of the match.

In Trinidad, venue for the next Test, two stands were burned down in an arson attack. Throughout the Caribbean, passions flared like a raging inferno. 'What we couldn't make out was whether this trouble with the bottles was politically motivated or just people having too much rum and betting on whether the batsmen would reach their hundred,' reflected Palmer. 'It was extraordinary what some of those boys would bet on if they'd had a rum or two; they'd bet a fortnight's wages.'

Following the bedlam at Bourda, England played a two-day game in Grenada against Windward Islands. Trueman starred with 7 for 69 and continued his good form in the colony match at Queen's Park in Trinidad before the fourth Test. On a jute matting pitch that was a bowler's graveyard, Trueman was England's most successful performer with match figures of 7 for 122 in a seven-wicket win. But he blotted his copybook again by injuring Trinidad tail-ender Wilf Ferguson in an incident that left a bitter taste.

'Fergie' was a cordial leg-spinner affectionately dubbed 'the ugliest man in cricket'. He had a full-moon face and squat features, which were not noticeably improved when Trueman rearranged them with a vicious bouncer from a deliberate no-ball. Alan Moss said the England players were embarrassed by what happened. '"Fergie" was jumping about like a cat on a hot tin roof and on one occasion he jokingly stuck his tongue out at Fred. Next ball, Fred ran about three strides through his bloody mark and hit him. Fergie fell to the floor and everyone went up to see how he was, apart from Fred, who just walked back to his mark as though nothing had happened. It annoyed everybody and was quite ridiculous.' According to Alex Bannister, Trueman 'rolled up his sleeves even higher as he surveyed the scene, leaving a sad but unmistakable impression that he saw himself as the victorious gladiator'. Not until Charles Palmer, acting on skipper Trevor Bailey's suggestion, went to him did Trueman walk down the pitch to sympathise with the batsman, who was being attended by first-aid men who applied an ice pack to a bump high on his cheek.

In his memoirs, Trueman claimed his felling of Ferguson resulted from the batsman calling him 'a white English bastard' – possibly as a wind-up following Trueman's alleged 'black bastard' remark to Kippins. '"No need for that type of talk," I told him. "Say it again to me, and I'll bloody well do you." A couple of overs later he did say it again – and with some venom. "I did ask you not to say that again," I told him . . . I was so angry I delivered the next ball more or less off my normal run-up and it was a bouncer. The ball reared up and he reeled back. His first port of call when he left the pitch was the hospital with a broken jaw. The trip to the dentist to replace his missing teeth had to wait.' Ferguson recovered but was bowled next ball by a lightning full toss from Trueman.

At close of play, Trueman flouted protocol by running off the field ahead of the batsmen and was received in silence by the Queen's

Park members. Moments later, they pointedly applauded the batsmen and the other ten MCC players. It was another black mark against the Yorkshireman.

If Trueman was the fall guy in British Guiana, where Wardle abused umpire Kippins, he was the undisputed villain on this occasion. He was hardly the first pace bowler to have deliberately injured a batsman, but to show no regard for a tail-ender who'd been hit was grossly unsporting – no matter the provocation. Despite the childish posturing in his memoirs, which suggested a man still trying to live up to his macho image, Trueman expressed remorse behind closed doors. Bannister said he was 'upset, sorry and contrite, and genuinely concerned lest Ferguson, who could not be X-rayed until the Monday, had been seriously hurt'.

As the tour continued in combustible vein, with Trueman cast as hell-raiser in chief, newspaper reports grew increasingly unfavourable. Back in Maltby, Dick Trueman could scarcely believe his eyes as day after day brought adverse publicity. Flo Halifax says her father tried to take action. 'Dad got very upset reading all the bad reports in the paper and one day he said, "I've had enough of this, I'm ringing up Yorkshire County Cricket Club because I want him bringing home." Dad got through to the club secretary and said, "Whatever's happening to my lad out there?" The secretary replied, "Don't worry, Mr Trueman, Freddie will tell you all about it in his own words when he sees you again." Dad calmed down eventually, but he was very distressed.'

Despite his immature antics in the colony game, Trueman was recalled for the fourth Test at Trinidad, but his petulant behaviour soon resurfaced. Following an over that contained three no-balls, three bouncers and eight runs off the bat, Trueman angrily snatched his cap from umpire Ellis Achong. 'Thus a thoroughly bad over had a disagreeable ending,' censured Swanton.

Once again, the match was marred by umpiring controversy. Achong and fellow official Ken Woods were guilty of several blunders against the England team, who felt local officials were frightened to give out their fellow countrymen for fear of reprisal. The most blatant error came from the last ball before lunch on the opening day. Holt chopped the delivery from Denis Compton to slip, where Tom Graveney clutched a waist-high catch. Holt turned to go, then suddenly stopped as though he wasn't sure what had happened. Having thought an appeal quite unnecessary, Compton asked Achong for a decision and was told 'Not out'. The England team were stunned – and Graveney exploded. 'I couldn't believe what was happening,' he remembered. 'The ball hit halfway up the bat and I caught it comfortably away to my right. I threw the ball down and stormed off in a temper, which wasn't like me. I remember saying to Achong, "That's the fourth f***ing time you've cheated us."' Later on, at a cocktail party, a woman told Graveney she thought it disgusting how Trueman had thrown down the ball after Holt was reprieved. It was a classic case of Trueman's reputation preceding him.

Graveney's outburst was the second time he'd been in hot water on the tour. Following the Barbados Test, the players held a party at the Yacht Club in an effort to revive flagging spirits. 'Someone approached me and said, "You'll never be any good until you stop Compton and Evans drinking",' recalled Graveney. 'So I gave them a suitable reply. It turned out this person was staying with the Governor-General, who were like gods in their own worlds at that time. The following morning, Charlie Palmer and Len were up at Government House trying to save me from being sent home.'

By now, public expressions of disappointment had become the norm with Hutton's players. However understandable in the heat of battle, they only gave power to the team's detractors. Roy Harewood, sports editor of British Guiana's *Daily Chronicle*, called MCC 'the worst behaved team that has ever left England's shores – at least for these parts', while the *Trinidad Guardian*'s Dick Murray lamented: 'The shocking behaviour on the field of play by some of their players has left me bitterly disappointed in English cricket.' There were a thousand more comments where those came from as

England were damned by word-of-mouth rumour as well as hard evidence.

The *News Chronicle*'s Crawford White offered a more balanced assessment. 'I have never known any company of cricketers as incensed by gross injustices and flagrant decisions as this England side. I cannot condone demonstrations, scenes or quibbles on the field but when these things go on and on, and mistakes seem to build up and up, one must sympathise as well as condemn.' In his post-tour report to MCC, Hutton described the overall standard of umpiring as 'appalling'. He said none of the West Indian umpires were good enough to officiate a Test in England. Hutton felt the biggest problem was inter-island jealousies that prevented the best officials travelling from island to island. He also questioned if the umpires were strong enough to stand up to partisan crowds.

In his own report to MCC, Palmer echoed his captain's sentiments. 'The umpiring has been the subject of much controversy. I wish to deny any allegations that we have assumed dishonesty. We have said that the standard of umpiring at times has not been good. We do not expect umpires who umpire infrequently to match the general standard attained by English umpires who do the job six days a week professionally and who are most likely old first-class cricketers of considerable experience. Furthermore, we realise that the umpiring out here is much more difficult than in England because an umpire here has long periods in the sun which tends to weaken his concentration, and because in places he often works before partisan, noisy and at times even menacing crowds. By analysis we consider that mistakes have been made more against than for MCC (and I repeat this does not imply dishonesty).'

On Trinidad's matting pitch that had not produced a positive result in twenty-one years' Test cricket, the fourth Test was a dreary draw. West Indies made 681 for 8 declared (Trueman 1 for 131 from 33 overs) before England scored 537 to save the follow-on. Towards the end of England's first innings, West Indies' fast bowler Frank King was operating in tandem with Frank Worrell's gentle medium pace. After Laker ducked and dived an over from King, Trueman patted back a docile over from Worrell before the batsmen held a mid-pitch conference. 'I've had a look at 'em both,' announced Trueman, 'and I reckon I can deal with Worrell if you take King.'

'It was a pretty fair assessment of the situation,' recalled Laker. 'In the next over from King I was helped off with blood pouring from a cut over the eye.'

The game produced 1528 runs for twenty-four wickets, *Wisden* noting: 'The complete subjugation of bowlers took away much competitive interest and the cricket was enjoyed only by those who delight in utter dominance by batsmen.'

'You got out when you were tired,' remembered Graveney.

Trueman kept his place for the final Test in Jamaica, where England had to win to level the series. The pitch was hard and shiny like marble, the groundsman telling Hutton: 'Bat first and you should make 700.'

'Our only hope was to bat, then bowl them out with spinners,' said Bailey. 'And Len lost the toss. I've never seen him more depressed.' But Bailey chose the perfect time to produce a brilliant performance. Bowling into the wind, he took 7 for 34 from 16 overs as West Indies were routed for 139. Trueman chipped in with 2 for 39 during a game in which both he and King were warned for excessive use of the bouncer. Hutton followed up with one of his own great performances, digging in to score a superb double hundred in sweltering heat. 'Whatever he does, he has almost lost the capacity to surprise us,' gushed Swanton. 'Yet from the viewpoint of physical stamina and mental concentration this latest innings is a thing apart, at any rate so far as the post-war years are concerned.'

At tea on day three, Hutton had 205 to his name and England were 392 for 7. As he walked off at the break, shattered and sweat-soaked, Hutton unwittingly strolled past Alexander Bustamante, Jamaica's chief minister, who was among a throng of well-wishers in the pavilion. Moments later, the dressing-room door flew open and a large man grabbed Palmer by the lapels and lifted him off the floor. 'This is the crowning insult,' he told the nonplussed manager. 'Your captain has insulted our prime minister.' Palmer replied: 'Put me down a minute – and we'll talk about it.' The brouhaha was resolved – Hutton and Bustamante sharing a drink at close of play – but there followed more adverse headlines England could have done without. 'Morning, noon and night something was happening,' said Palmer. 'It got to the stage where I didn't know where the next arrow was coming from. All I knew was that it was coming.'

Unsettled by the dressing-room disturbance, Hutton did not add to his total after tea and was caught by McWatt off Walcott. He joked the scoreboard entry should have read 'Hutton b Bustamante 205'. Hutton described the allegation he'd insulted Bustamante as 'so baseless it was incredible it was ever made', adding, 'I cannot believe any touring captain anywhere has been obliged to endure such a blatant discourtesy.'

Trueman took three wickets in West Indies' second innings before England sealed a nine-wicket win. It capped a remarkable comeback from 2–0 down as the 'Cricket Championship of the World' ended all square. Hutton was man of the series with 677 runs at 96 but the tour sapped his strength. He managed only fifteen more Test innings and 306 more Test runs following his double hundred at Kingston and reckoned the tour shortened his career by 'perhaps two years'. Trueman was England's second-highest wicket-taker on the trip with 27 at 33.66. He could be satisfied with his efforts on unhelpful pitches.

The tour had thrown up just about everything: riots, umpiring controversies, chucking rows, intimidatory bowling, unsportsman-like behaviour – not to mention its share of captivating cricket. From a diplomatic perspective, however, it was a disaster. *The Times* called it 'the second most controversial tour in cricket history' after Bodyline, while *Wisden* declared its primary purpose, 'to further friendship between man and man, country and country', had not been fulfilled. For Trueman, even the journey back to England was fraught. 'We came home in a banana boat,' said Graveney, 'and Fred was very ill. He was a bad sailor and his stomach was constantly doing somersaults. He and Locky spent most of the time in their cabins. They were terribly sea-sick.'

When he arrived home in Maltby, physically spent and emotionally drained, Trueman enjoyed a quiet reunion with his parents and siblings. 'He came back loaded with all manner of presents,' said Flo. 'There were pearls, nylon stockings and silk scarves for the girls, and various bits and pieces for the boys. Initially, Dad didn't say anything because we were all fussing over him. Then, late at night, Dad said, "There's only one thing I want to know, son. All this trouble, were you behind it?"

'Freddie looked him straight in the eye and said, "No, Dad, honestly. I was made a scapegoat. I wouldn't dare do anything to upset you."

'Dad sat quiet for a moment and nodded his head. He said, "That's good enough for me, son, that's good enough for me."'

8

All I Did Was F***ing Swear

If only the England hierarchy had been so easily convinced. Shortly after returning from West Indies, Fred Trueman's sense of injustice intensified when he was the only player docked his good conduct bonus. It was not so much the £50 shortfall that stuck in his craw – money that would have topped a £500 tour salary – but the fact he'd been singled out for special treatment. Few players could claim a totally clean slate after a raft of incidents on and off the field. Angered by MCC's decision, Trueman wrote to Lord's requesting an explanation, only to be told the subject was closed. He encountered a similar brick wall when he challenged Len Hutton. Trueman claimed the England captain muttered about circumstances beyond his control and how it all depended on the way individuals interpreted matters. But as proved by a brief entry in the MCC Cricket Committee minutes of 25 May 1954, Hutton was instrumental in imposing the sanction:

> The reward for discipline during the tour should be given to all the professional cricketers of the team with the exception of F.S. Trueman. This was in accordance with the recommendation of the Captain and Manager at the time of their interview with the President and the Treasurer.

The reason for the decision is not recorded and MCC cannot locate documents from the West Indies series. Lord's houses records of just about every tour MCC/England has undertaken but material relating to the so-called second most controversial tour in history and the Bodyline tour is missing. However, Richard Hutton possesses a copy of his father's captain's report. This starts with a general overview of events which has this to say about Trueman and the 'black bastard' episode:

> Trueman was reported to me by the umpire for using obscene language. I think it only fair to say on Trueman's behalf that in the previous over the batsman had certainly been out lbw on two if not three occasions. Unfortunately, Trueman, being high-spirited and outspoken, said something which he very much regretted afterwards, but, as far as I know, this was the only occasion on which he used bad language.

Hutton's contention that Trueman regretted what he said contradicts the player's own version, which is that he was innocent, and also that of the umpire, who admits Johnny Wardle was the culprit. Hutton went on to appraise each player individually, with the longest entry reserved for Trueman:

> Trueman gave me much concern and until a big improvement is made in his general conduct and cricket manners I do not think he is suitable for MCC Tours, particularly a tour such as the one to the West Indies. No captain could wish to have a better trier than Trueman. He is very keen and wanted to do well, and this was probably responsible for some of his aggressive actions on the field. Cricket today does require characters and, in Trueman, cricket has got a character and ultimately I think something can be done with him under capable leadership. There is no vice, envy or jealousy in Trueman and I had some good reports of him on the tour from several reliable people. Unfortunately, during the first match of the tour, he hit George Headley, who had flown out to Jamaica to play against us and received a testimonial of approximately £1,100, subscribed by the public in Jamaica. The incident was looked upon in rather a bad light by the Jamaican spectators. This made him the subject of much publicity and also his aggressive manner on-and-off the field [sic]. One official in Jamaica accused him of throwing the ball and bowling four no-balls out of six which was, I

feel, very unkind to a young cricketer. Mr Palmer and I did all we could to help Trueman and he was most distressed when he made that fatal slip in Georgetown with the umpire.

Hutton's assertion that something could be done with Trueman 'under capable leadership' appeared to say little for his own abilities, but the tone of his report was fair and balanced. Further reference to the Georgetown episode, however, can leave little doubt that Trueman was primarily docked £50 for an incident in which he was actually blameless.

Wardle, who appears not to have spoken up on Trueman's behalf, was the subject of the strongest criticism in Hutton's report. The captain wrote of his Yorkshire team-mate:

Here is a man who was extremely popular on the field during the tour. The crowds liked him and everywhere it was remarked 'How good this chap Wardle is', but from the inside point of view of the team spirit and relationship with the players Wardle showed jealousy, bitterness and envy at times, which was most embarrassing for me and for several other members of the team. Wardle's case should, I feel, be discussed in Committee before selection is made for future overseas tours.

Despite the plethora of controversial incidents, most of Hutton's appraisals were favourable. Tom Graveney, who threw the ball down in a fit of fury at Trinidad and told the umpire 'that's the fourth f***ing time you've cheated us', was described by Hutton as 'an excellent chap to have' and 'very willing to assist in every way both on and off the field'. Denis Compton, who lobbed a bottle back towards the crowd during the Georgetown riot and was guilty of high spirits in the lift of the Marine Hotel in Barbados, was 'a great help in every way'. Godfrey Evans – his partner in crime in the hotel fracas – was also 'a great help', while Tony Lock – blamed for the hotel incident with Trueman – was 'a great trier' whose 'conduct as far as I was concerned, on and off the field, was good'. And yet Trueman was the only one picked out for punishment.

The charge sheet against him was not insubstantial. Regardless of the 'black bastard' episode, Trueman showed no concern on the field after injuring George Headley accidentally or Wilf Ferguson intentionally. He ignored Hutton's instruction not to fraternise with West Indian players. He caused unnecessary offence by refusing to attend a cocktail party in honour of the team after a local dignitary called his bowling action a throw. He angrily snatched his cap from the umpire during the Trinidad Test and was guilty of exaggerated antics and colourful language. On that basis, Trueman probably did deserve to lose his good conduct money, but, equally, so did players such as Graveney, who freely admitted swearing at the umpire in Trinidad – an incident Hutton called 'the most embarrassing on the field'.

In his 1956 autobiography, Hutton pulled no punches in his assessment of Trueman. He described him as his 'problem child' and confessed he was 'constantly wondering about him'. Hutton said Trueman 'almost needed a manager to himself', adding: 'He became very much my "piccaninny" in the tropics and every happening with which he was connected affected me considerably.'

Compton was also critical of Trueman. 'Fred Trueman, by his behaviour on the field, had a substantial share in making difficulties for us right from the start. A bowler, particularly a fast bowler, is no doubt entitled to his exclamations of disappointment when the batsman misses and the ball brushes past the wicket, or is edged and the catch not taken: Miller, for example, could be expressive and Lindwall could look very expressive indeed. But Fiery Fred brought exclamation and expression and demonstration on these occasions to a new and extraordinary level. He would stand poised in the middle of the wicket, hands on hips, a most intimidating expression on his face (it almost frightened me, quite apart from the West Indian batsmen) and used language which was both unusual and colourful, and could be heard at least by the batsman. On occasion the wicketkeeper, if he hadn't held what Fred, alone perhaps, had considered to be a chance, would come within the scope of a vigorous expletive. Fred seemed to like being the centre of attention on these occasions, even to consider that it was quite an amusing joke. I think he was the only one who saw a funny side to his behaviour. His fellows of the MCC side by and large did not, and the West Indians used to be incensed, and showed their feelings in jeers and boos and answering demonstrations. This seemed to egg Trueman on to greater expressiveness and colour in his language, and as the tour went on he got worse and worse rather than better and better. His behaviour had the most unfortunate effect on the game and on the atmosphere in which we played it.'

Compton, however, was in a minority. Most players thought Trueman harshly treated and agreed with his view he'd been made a scapegoat. Brian Statham said stories concerning Trueman's so-called wild behaviour were 'grossly exaggerated', while Peter May felt publicity given to his conduct was 'a bit unfair' and that he was 'too readily given the label of bad boy'. Tom Graveney says Trueman was 'blamed for things he simply didn't do' and that 'there were quite a few scoundrels on that tour – Godfrey, Denis, and all that lot'. Even the West Indians leapt to his defence. Sir Everton Weekes, whom Trueman first greeted with the immortal words, 'So you're one of those bloody three Ws, are you?' insists his behaviour was greatly embellished, while Frank Worrell wrote Trueman was 'not the arch trouble-maker he has been accused of being' and 'there were players on that tour who have more to be ashamed of'.

Trueman, however, was a convenient fall guy. Following such a combustible series, it surely suited MCC – and particularly Hutton and Palmer – to find someone like him to take the rap. Rather than find fault with several of the team, which would have suggested they were badly managed, the captain and manager recommended only one man be penalised. And who better than one whose face didn't fit, whose background and breeding were different from the norm. For Fred Trueman, it must be remembered, didn't just hail from a poor family – but one perceived as a bunch of gypsies. His father was said to always be spitting. His eldest brother was quick with his fists. Trueman came from a family that developed if not quite a siege mentality in the face of condescension then certainly a determination to stand up for itself and not be put down. He was positively encouraged to speak his mind; it mattered not whether he was addressing an authority figure or the milkman.

Indeed, the very key to understanding Trueman, the essence of what made him such a rebellious figure and so different from his peers, is found in that tough and uncompromising upbringing. He was hardly the first cricketer to have hailed from a mining background – Harold Larwood, for instance, was a pit pony boy in Nottinghamshire during the early part of the twentieth century. But Trueman not only grew up in a less subservient age than the mild-mannered Larwood, he was raised in an environment in which his family was perceived not so much as members of a mining community but a social underclass. If he found difficult the transition to the Yorkshire and England teams in the days of amateurs and professionals, gentlemen and players, who could blame him? Few could have handled the leap with aplomb. 'When Fred first came into the England side he was as rough as a bag of nails,' remembered Graveney. 'He hadn't learned the finer points of living, but, as soon as he did, he was good to everyone. The Fred Trueman of those days was a rough diamond who said what he thought and it got him into trouble. He wasn't deliberately nasty – he just behaved in the way he thought fiery fast bowlers should behave.'

While his conduct in the Caribbean is hard to condone, Trueman's biggest crime seems to have been a lack of etiquette. He did not have the social skills of such as the debonair Compton, the decorum expected of a touring cricketer. Palmer recalled the type of incident that was clearly held against the young Yorkshireman. 'I remember in a bar one night, this fellow came up. He said he had a friend in Yorkshire and did Fred know him? And instead of Fred saying, "No, but I'll look out for him," or some such words, he said, "Never 'eard of the bugger." They were little things, but they didn't go down very well in a highly sensitive situation.' Palmer conceded Trueman was 'pulled out of Yorkshire and put in a context which was entirely alien to his upbringing' and 'catapulted into a society of which he had no experience whatsoever'.

Alex Bannister described Trueman as 'a bit of a nuisance because he never stopped talking'. He also recalled an exchange involving Trueman at a dinner party that highlighted how the player inadvertently said the wrong thing.

'Do you work here?' Trueman asked a certain gentleman.

'Yes,' came the answer.

'How long have you been here?' added Trueman.

'About eighteen months.'

'Got a good job?'

'Not bad – I'm the governor-general.'

Another story from that tour has Trueman flirting with a woman at a cocktail party. 'Would you like to come outside?' he allegedly asked. To which she purportedly replied, 'Well, Mr Trueman, as a woman I'm extremely flattered, but as the governor's wife I'm absolutely disgusted.' As with so many anecdotes attached to his name, humour was never far from the surface. Ditto, one suspects, the 'Curse of the Truemans'.

Notwithstanding his lack of propriety, there was general agreement among the England team that Trueman would have benefited from better handling. Compton felt Hutton should have taken a firmer line at the start of the tour, that the captain afforded him too much leeway. 'Len Hutton had told us that here we had rather an unpredictable boy, a fiery character – but we were to leave him to Len, Yorkshireman to Yorkshireman, as Len, apparently, understood Fred and could handle him. I never got the impression that Len had the faintest notion how to handle him.' Compton revealed he tried to discipline Trueman while deputising for Hutton in a colony game. 'Trueman's language on that occasion lacked nothing of its customary vividness, to such an extent that I felt obliged to call him over before the others and to tell him quite plainly that if he didn't behave himself I'd at least try to ensure that he'd be on the next boat for home. It had some effect, and I know that Fred was penitent afterwards.'

Godfrey Evans also considered Hutton soft in his approach. 'He took the view, rightly I think, that Fred was a bowler of class and spirit, and that if the best were to be got out of him then care would have to be taken not to break his spirit. So Len handled him leniently, too leniently in my view. Fred would have been in no way harmed if Len had applied much more discipline: what Fred needed was a firm hand, and he didn't get it from Len, for understandable but for the wrong reasons.'

Wisden was similarly critical of Hutton. 'Earlier and firmer handling of the most recalcitrant member, the fiery Trueman, might have avoided several situations, but, anxious not to dim the spark of Trueman's hostility and aggressiveness, Hutton probably waited too long before calling his lively colt to heel.' Hutton therefore gave Trueman his head for tactical reasons and then penalised him financially for losing his head – a contradiction lost neither on Trueman nor his team-mates.

One of cricket's greatest batsmen, Hutton was a deep and complex individual. Some found him aloof and strangely withdrawn; he inspired more through personal achievement than managerial acumen. Hutton believed the primary duty of a captain was to avoid 'a smell' and disliked any form of confrontation. Trueman, who often sought confrontation and certainly never shirked it, was cut from an altogether different cloth. 'Len was essentially a pre-war Yorkshire cricketer, and pre-war Yorkshire cricketers would not have been like Fred Trueman,' said Trevor Bailey. 'In terms of personality, Len and Fred were chalk and cheese. Fred wasn't a diplomat and was very plain spoken. He was much too flamboyant for someone like Len.' Several Yorkshire players claim Hutton never understood Trueman. 'Len never seemed to take to Fred,' said Bryan Stott. 'He never really seemed to be comfortable with Fred.' According to Ted Lester, 'Len was very difficult – in fact, almost impossible – to get to know. As far as I could tell, he never helped Fred at all.'

Hutton also hailed from an unusual background – in his case, a Moravian community in Fulneck, near Pudsey. The Moravians were the earliest Protestant sect in fifteenth-century Europe and believed in hard graft and Christian discipline. The Fulneck settlement was self-supporting, with tailors, weavers, glovers and joiners working together for the common good. Richard Hutton says his father was heavily influenced by this way of life. 'He wasn't a religious person – I think he was fairly agnostic about it – but the Moravian way of life was embedded in him. One of their characteristics is self-reliance, and he was extremely self-reliant. He was independently minded; I think that was really the foundation of his character.

'By nature, he was a very shy person. I think he found relationships quite difficult because of his natural shyness. He was diffident. He could also be indecisive in that, being such a big thinker, he needed a lot of time for things to pass through his mind and come out the other end. He was thorough. He was also whimsical. He was modest and he was the opposite of Trueman in that respect. My father let his bat and achievements do the talking, whereas Fred was different. I think at times he thought Fred talked too much and should learn to shut his gob from time to time.'

Although Trueman never tired of describing Hutton as the greatest batsman he saw, he never warmed to him personally. Early in his career, he recalled being asked as a favour by Hutton to take part in one of his benefit games in Middlesbrough. They travelled north in Hutton's car and stayed at the ground until late in the evening. On the way home, Trueman was staggered when Hutton swung his car into the forecourt of Leeds railway station instead of taking him back to Maltby. It was 10.40 p.m. and although Trueman managed to catch the last train to Rotherham, he was too late for the last train and bus back to Maltby, so had to walk the remaining eight miles with his kit bag on his shoulder.

Trueman also felt Hutton had a strange sense of humour. During a train journey to Bristol for a match against Gloucestershire, Trueman went to the buffet and asked if anyone wanted anything brought back. 'I'll have twenty Senior Service,' replied Hutton. When Trueman returned, Hutton thanked him but made no attempt to pay the 2s 6d the cigarettes had cost. Trueman felt too embarrassed to ask for the money, so let the matter drop. Some forty years later, Trueman was guest speaker at a sporting dinner in Hutton's honour when, much to his astonishment, Hutton recalled the train journey to Bristol and the thorny matter of the unpaid-for cigarettes. 'No doubt, Fred, you believed I had forgotten this and that you would never be paid the money I owe you,' said Hutton. Then, in full view of the startled audience, he counted out thirteen one-penny pieces and placed them on the table in front of him. 'See, I didn't forget,' laughed Hutton. 'By my reckoning, two shillings and sixpence in current money is twelve-and-a-half pence. There's thirteen pence there, Fred, so you've made a half-pence profit.'

Trueman recalled: 'Len thought this hilarious. Even when he sat down again he was still chuckling to himself, while the audience sat there like Peter Sutcliffe's jury.'

In the West Indies, Trueman felt Hutton had no time for him. Whenever he asked to have a word with his captain, the reply was invariably, 'Some other time.' He resented Hutton's insistence on being called 'skipper' – to Trueman he had always simply been 'Len' – and considered him pernickety. Although Hutton had overseen Test triumphs against India and Australia, he was sensitive to ongoing opposition to the professional captaincy and admitted: 'There was hardly enough time to look after myself, let alone anyone else.' Whenever incidents flared as with the umpire at Georgetown, Trueman believed Hutton did not take time to establish the facts. He thought Hutton's leadership too knee-jerk and said he tried to be more of a diplomat than a captain.

In Hutton's defence, Trueman considered players like Compton begrudged the fact that Hutton was in charge and detected jealousy towards him from senior players. Trueman said there was a north–south divide in the dressing room and that some southerners talked in derogatory terms behind Hutton's back. He claimed to have threatened one or two of the captain's strongest critics, which caused further ill-feeling. Trueman also confided to friends and relatives another significant source of tension between himself and Hutton. He claimed to have caught the captain in a compromising position with a black woman, which made him 'a marked man' in Hutton's eyes. One member of Trueman's family revealed, 'Fred told us he walked on to the veranda outside his hotel room one night and saw Hutton on his own veranda with a black woman. Next morning, Len took Fred to one side and said, "What were you doing on the veranda, Trueman?" To which Fred replied, "More to the point, captain, what were you doing?" Fred said this caused a lot of friction.' Trueman alleged there were various drunken and debauched goings-on in the Caribbean of which he had no part, which only increased his resentment about losing his bonus. Bob Platt said: 'Fred never got over being docked his bonus. He used to say, "Some players on that tour were shagging the blacks and all I did was f***ing swear."'

Trueman saw little of his team-mates off the field. He and Tony Lock – the other greenhorn of the group – were effectively left to their own devices. At the start of the trip, Hutton told Lock to 'look after Trueman' – even though Lock, too, was on his first overseas tour. The youngsters shared rooms and became good friends, finding common ground in their extrovert natures. Jim Laker described the decision to pair them up as bafflingly inept. 'Here were two youngsters of somewhat turbulent character – even though different in manner – on their first trip away from England, and they were allowed to go their own way. What a managerial blunder that was. Each of them should have been paired with a senior member.' Laker also had cause to rue Hutton's man-management. One night, he and his captain were sitting in a bar with Tom Graveney and Brian Statham when Hutton asked Statham if he'd like to go on the trip to Australia the following winter. Statham replied he'd love to go, whereupon Hutton put the same question to Graveney, who answered likewise. Hutton then turned to Laker and said, 'Now then, Jim, what will you have to drink?'

Although Hutton's people skills left much to be desired, he'd have benefited in the West Indies from a stronger manager. By common consent, Charles Palmer was a likeable fellow but not the disciplinarian such a tough tour required. Hutton's preferred candidate was Billy Griffith, who'd performed a managerial role on the previous tour of West Indies in 1947–48, but the Sussex wicketkeeper could not be spared from his duties as MCC assistant secretary. Only when efforts to enlist Yorkshire secretary John Nash fell through did MCC turn to Palmer, who'd no experience of the region and was given no assistant to help him.

Diminutive, bespectacled and three years Hutton's junior, Palmer was not favoured with the appearance of authority. Jim Swanton felt the role of player/manager compromised Palmer and called his appointment 'just about the worst decision ever to come out of Lord's'. However, Hutton felt 'no manager could have tried harder, been more diplomatic, or done his onerous job better', while Alex Bannister proclaimed Palmer 'an oasis of commonsense in every situation'.

Reflecting on the tour in 1989, Bannister said Hutton and Palmer were let down by the Foreign Office. He thought Sir Walter Monckton's pre-tour briefing risibly inadequate – Palmer, for instance, had no idea about the colour bar in Bermuda – and said 'the true extent of the cultural and political changes then taking place in the scattered islands became evident only by bitter experience'. Bannister also thought the on-field shenanigans nothing compared to contemporary cricket. 'The worst of the incidents on the field in 1954 pale into insignificance beside the all too often rebellious behaviour sadly reflecting modern cricket times.' Clyde Walcott, however, took the opposite view. He described the 1953–54 tour as 'stormier than Bodyline' and said if the current system of disciplining players under the International Cricket Council's code of conduct had been in place, 'half of Hutton's players would have been fined or suspended'.

Fuelled by a sense of victimisation, Trueman started the 1954 season in spirited style. He took forty-four wickets in his first ten games, bowling with notable pace and control. But his efforts cut no ice with MCC, whose opposition towards him was further revealed by a letter from Gubby Allen – one of its prominent committee members – to Palmer. The letter was penned after Palmer was summoned to Lord's to address criticism of his management in the West Indies:

Dear Charlie

Just a line to congratulate you on a fine performance yesterday.

You had to take a section of the committee which was, and I know what I am talking about, very hostile to the events of last winter and were looking for any slip up on your part which would help their case. You were so very clear and forthright in your answers that they got absolutely nowhere.

I am convinced that had Trueman not been a member of the team, that had you been given a different brief and more power, and that had Len been persuaded that a bloody battle did not necessarily involve a lack of courtesy, much of the trouble would not have occurred.

Looking to the future now, I would like your opinion. Do you think a manager on a rather higher level is a solution and indeed a worthwhile proposition, especially if Len is to captain?

Yours

Gubby

Trueman was not among the twenty players sounded out by MCC on 6 June for the winter tour to Australia and New Zealand. Nor was he chosen for the first Test of the summer against Pakistan the following week – nor, indeed, for any of the four-match series. Instead, England relied on a pace attack of Statham, Frank Tyson and Peter Loader complemented by the lesser speed of Bailey and Alec Bedser. Although a golden era for English pace bowling, it did not require the sleuthing skills of Sherlock Holmes to deduce that Trueman was persona non grata after the West Indies trip. In addition, he had a highly influential critic in Swanton, whom some felt practically picked the side as *Daily Telegraph* correspondent. While several journalists defended Trueman, arguing his antics had been overblown, the powerful Swanton twisted the knife. In *West Indian Adventure*, published that summer, he wrote: 'His need is control in all its aspects, on the field and off it, and I confess I would not be happy to see his name again in a touring team, irrespective of the number of wickets he may have got, unless I was convinced of a radical change of outlook.' Trueman, who subscribed to the theory that Swanton was a snob, retorted he had 'no time for such people'.

In the popular press, much was made of the battle for a winter tour place between Trueman and Tyson. When Yorkshire visited Northamptonshire in July, the fixture was billed as a shoot-out between them. The contest failed to produce a winner – both men capturing four wickets – but did spawn a celebrated Trueman epigram. On the first day, Tyson bowled Wardle with a lightning ball that splayed the stumps as the batsman retreated. As Wardle walked off, Trueman passed him on his way to the middle and sneered, 'What sort of bloody shot was that?' Shortly afterwards, Trueman was bowled by another Tyson thunderbolt and returned to the dressing room where Wardle taunted, 'And what sort of bloody shot was that?' To which Trueman – never denied the last word – replied, 'Aye, I slipped on that pile of shit you left in the crease.' The last laugh, however, belonged to Tyson. When the squad was announced a few days later, he was in and Trueman was out.

On statistics alone, Trueman's omission was absurd. He'd taken 86 first-class wickets at 15 against Tyson's 52 at 23. He'd captured more wickets than Statham, Loader, Bailey or Bedser, the other pace bowlers chosen to sail, and done his utmost to recover from a troublesome winter. Trueman ended that season with 134 wickets at 15 – thirteen more than Bedser, his nearest England rival. He was the country's seventh highest wicket-taker and, in August, returned what would remain career-best figures of 8 for 28 against Kent at Dover. Only Derbyshire's Cliff Gladwin – 136 at 16 – claimed more wickets by a pace bowler in 1954.

Trueman was at home with his parents in Maltby when the squad was announced. Dick Trueman was so angry he told him that if England wanted him again, he should tell them where to go. In an unguarded moment, Fred said as much to a local journalist, who thankfully didn't print the comment. Most papers came down heavily on his side, this extract from the *News Chronicle* a typical reaction:

FREDDIE TRUEMAN is OUT. The problem boy of the West Indies tour – the dark-haired Yorkshire tornado who would have packed the stadia of Melbourne and Sydney – is evidently too tough to be let loose in Australia. Although he has been bowling better than ever in his career, he is NOT in the MCC 17 to go. Yorkshire will be shocked by the omission. Australia will be bitterly disappointed. Putting the position at its mildest, Trueman has received harsh treatment and, without him, this is not our strongest team.

In the *Yorkshire Post*, J.M. Kilburn diplomatically declared Trueman the 'better bowling proposition for Australia at this moment, but there can be no questioning Tyson's potentiality'. The *Sheffield Star*'s Frank Stainton thought the selectors' decision betrayed social prejudice. He cited 'a school of thought' that considered 'one of the first qualifications for such a tour is the knowledge that the soup is not taken with a dessert spoon, and that a black tie is customary with a dinner jacket'. Stainton claimed 'such questions are of more importance than cricketing prowess when engaged on an MCC tour'.

Reflecting a mood of national disappointment, the Yorkshire public showed what it thought of Trueman's treatment during the county's next match, against Derbyshire at Headingley. When Yorkshire took the field on the first day, Trueman was given a reception that raised the hairs on the back of his neck. Moved by the crowd's solidarity, he responded with three wickets in his first seven balls and six in total as Derbyshire bore the brunt of his displeasure. No less revealing was the reception afforded Hutton when the England captain misfielded off Trueman. He was barracked by the crowd, which clearly blamed him for Trueman's exclusion.

Hutton, who'd only just been passed fit for Australia following the stresses of the Caribbean and retained as captain by a single vote, always maintained he wanted Trueman in his squad. He said 'Trueman had my vote for Australia but the majority were against him' and insisted his claims had 'fair consideration'. However, only a few weeks earlier, Hutton had written in his captain's report from West Indies, 'Until a big improvement is made in his general conduct and cricket manners, I do not think he is suitable for MCC tours.' Hutton said his initial strategy had been to take Trueman Down Under – a plan upset by Bedser's unavailability for West Indies. Consequently, Hutton felt Trueman 'went one tour too early', adding, 'if his maiden tour had been to Australia and not to the touchy West Indian islands, I think it would have been better for him and better for English cricket.'

In the event, Trueman missed out on Australia by a single vote – a close shave that hardly mollified him. He also gained sympathy from within the squad. Vic Wilson, a late addition to the party as cover for knee injury victim Compton, said, 'It was obvious to just about everyone who went in 54–55 that Fred should have gone, just as it was obvious why he didn't go. It all harked back to 53–54. I'm convinced it was Len's decision not to take him. Fortunately for Len, Frank Tyson came off in Australia and we won the Ashes. If he hadn't, and we'd lost the series, I'm sure more people would have said that Fred should have gone.'

Reaction Down Under was similarly incredulous. The Australian cricket writer Ray Robinson opined that 'a speed attack without Trueman is like a horror film without Boris Karloff', while Australia's players were also perplexed. 'Most of us were baffled,' admitted Neil Harvey. 'I know if I had to pick a side and Freddie was available, he'd be the first fast bowler I'd pick.' Instead of packing the stadia of Melbourne and Sydney, where brilliant bowling by Tyson inspired a 3–1 win, Trueman spent the winter as a furniture salesman for a Bradford firm. One national newspaper wanted to send him to Australia to cover the tour but Yorkshire refused on the grounds he might have to criticise fellow players. There were also moves to tempt him back into football. Bill Anderson got in touch to offer a professional contract at Lincoln City, but the threat of injury once more prevailed.

There was at least one happy occasion during a miserable close season. In March 1955, Trueman married Enid Chapman, the twenty-three-year-old daughter of Rodney Chapman, Mayor of Scarborough from 1947 to 1951. They'd met at the 1950 Scarborough Festival during a cocktail party given by her father. Enid, a cashier in her father's auctioneering business, was a beautiful blonde with an outgoing nature. She had a model's high cheekbones and a cheeky smile, plus a model's penchant for clothes and shoes. More than a thousand people gathered outside All Saints' Church in Falsgrave, Scarborough, keen for a glimpse of the happy couple. Some even climbed the roofs of neighbouring buildings in an effort to gain a better vantage point.

The marriage was an unlikely mix of Scarborough high society and working-class South Yorkshire. 'I've never been to a wedding like it,' said Ted Lester. 'It was a clash of cultures to say the least. The Chapmans were well-off, highly respected members of Scarborough society, while the Truemans were from a totally different background. Fred's lot was on one side of the church and Enid's on the other. You wouldn't have believed it possible the Chapmans and Truemans could possibly have mixed.'

Although from different social strata, husband and wife shared the same sense of humour. Enid, too, had a colourful vocabulary – more Maltby Main Colliery than Scarborough Town Hall. 'She could be very Jekyll and Hyde,' remembered Lester. 'One minute she'd be very prim and proper and then, when people's backs were turned, she'd let her hair down with the best of them. I remember a party when Fred got up and started telling rude jokes. Enid kept saying, "Tell 'em that one, Fred," and that sort of thing. Anyway, nearly everyone left. It was very embarrassing; it was dreadful. It was very blue. It was about the only time I'd ever been in a pub with Fred and I never wanted to go again.'

Enid, however, could be genuinely funny. 'I was with her and Fred once in a pub in Scarborough,' recalled John Hampshire. 'It was Sunday lunchtime and Enid was chatting to a load of people on one side of the bar and Fred was expounding with his pipe on the other side. Fred said to someone, "Aye, she's married a bloody genius, ya know (he pronounced it "genie-arse"). Enid overheard and said, "Aye, the trouble with you, Fred, is you're all arse and no genie." The pub erupted.'

Enid needed her sense of humour while the Ashes were taking place. As Tyson swept all before him with 28 wickets at 20, her husband's mood was not improved by reports proclaiming him the fastest bowler to tour Down Under. 'Fred was absolutely downcast that winter,' said Enid. 'He was gutted. He was a pain to live with. All he wanted was to be in Australia and he was absolutely adamant he should have gone.' Enid also blamed Hutton for Trueman's omission. 'That man was ignorant. He knew I was Fred's wife and yet he walked past me one day three times at Headingley. On the third time he did it, I tapped him on the shoulder and told him straight. I said, "Are you blind? Do you need some glasses? That's the third time you've walked past me and I'm Fred's wife." Hutton thought he was a cut above. He thought he was Mr Wonderful, but he wasn't.'

It is a scarcely known – and scarcely credible – fact that no sooner had Tyson returned from Australia than he accompanied the Truemans on their honeymoon. The Blue Cars Company of London had donated a trip to the three outstanding cricketers of 1954, selecting Trueman, Tyson and Worcestershire batsman Peter Richardson. The trip took the form of a coach excursion to Nice and the Côte d'Azur in southern France and included members of the public. 'It should have been a friction-loaded fortnight,' wrote Tyson, 'for I had just returned from a successful Australian tour from which Fred had been omitted. Surprisingly, the holiday proved incident-free and the only spats were between the newly-weds!'

Tyson went on: 'The two weeks we spent on the bus gave me a good opportunity to observe "Fiery" at close quarters. I found him blunt in his opinions and willing to express them in the most colourful terms in any company. His bawdy humour and inexhaustible fund of risqué jokes made him immensely popular with the other holidaymakers. Before we had even crossed the Channel,

"Fiery" had commandeered the courier's microphone and launched upon an endless tirade of funny stories; for 2000 kilometres he scarcely paused to draw breath – and never repeated a story. Fred made no apology for his lack of savoir-faire. Dining one evening in the restaurant of our plush hotel on the Boulevard Victor Hugo in Nice, "Fiery" summoned the wine waiter from the other side of the room with the clarion call of "Hey chuff!" When the startled flunkey arrived he was told to "Bring some wine. Some of that white stuff, not the red. That makes me go to sleep and I don't intend to do much sleeping on my honeymoon!"'

It took a heel injury to Tyson in June 1955 to bring Trueman back into the England fold. He played the second Test against South Africa at Lord's but returned 2 for 112 and was dropped. Over-anxious to impress, Trueman lost his line and was no-balled for dragging. Statham took the plaudits with second-innings figures of 7 for 39, but Trueman at least consoled himself with the thought he'd not been permanently black-balled. There was a further fillip to his England hopes when Hutton retired after persistent back problems, the captaincy passing to Peter May. Hutton appeared only ten times for Yorkshire that summer and announced his departure at the end of the season.

Trueman finished 1955 strongly, claiming the second hat-trick of his career against Nottinghamshire at Scarborough en route to 153 wickets at 16. But it wasn't enough to help Yorkshire to the Championship. For the second year running, Yardley's side finished runners-up to Surrey, who won twenty-three of their twenty-eight games compared with Yorkshire's twenty-one. Yardley also retired that winter as Billy Sutcliffe – son of Herbert – became Yorkshire captain. However, 1956 was a poor summer for Sutcliffe's men and a dire one for Trueman, who made little impression as the team finished seventh. Throughout the year he was bothered by niggles – a strained left side, sciatica, blistered feet. Although recalled for the second and third Ashes Tests at Lord's and Leeds, he couldn't do himself justice. Trueman still managed 5 for 90 during the second innings at Lord's, where he again deputised for the injured Tyson, but he was dropped for the fourth Test at Old Trafford, where Jim Laker returned a world record 19 for 90 as England retained the Ashes.

To add to his depression, Trueman felt poorly treated by chairman of selectors Gubby Allen during the game at Leeds. Before a large crowd, Allen placed a handkerchief on a length in the nets and instructed Trueman to hit it. For once in his life, Trueman kept his mouth shut, did as he was told and let others fight his corner. One of the strongest rebukes came from Bill Bowes, a team-mate of Allen's on the Bodyline tour. Bowes wrote it was unforgivable for Allen to have subjected an England player to such an ordeal, adding that Allen had no talent worth comparing to Trueman's. However, Doug Insole, who played in the game and witnessed the incident, believes Allen acted with the best of intentions. 'Fred was having a bad spell and bowling very wide on the crease. Consequently, he was having to pitch the ball comfortably outside off stump to have any chance of getting a wicket; he certainly wasn't going to get lbws. Gubby had him bowl an over in the nets and pointed out to him – because the ground was so wet – how far he was bowling outside off stump because the marks were clearly visible in the turf. Fred didn't enjoy being told what to do but there was no malice from Gubby in my opinion. I got the impression he was doing it solely to be helpful. Fred, however, was very offended. Afterwards, he was going, "f***ing Gubby Allen this and f***ing Gubby Allen that". But you can't kick spectators out of the ground because net practice is going on.'

In a summer of slow, wet pitches, Trueman managed only 59 wickets in thirty-one games. He was eighth in the Yorkshire averages and nowhere in the national charts. Bob Platt said 1956 was the only time he saw Trueman concerned about his form. 'Fred was genuinely worried about his bowling that year. I think it knocked him sideways a little bit. He'd had one or two injury problems and was being buggered about by England, and I think it got to him. I never saw him like that before or since.' Trueman's self-doubt intensified with the announcement of the winter squad to tour South Africa. Once again he was omitted as the selectors chose a pace quartet of Tyson, Statham, Loader and Bailey. Although his figures that year were hardly compelling, Trueman bowled well against Australia at Lord's and felt – as many press and public felt – he'd done enough to be picked on reputation. His exclusion led to further accusations of prejudice and prompted MCC to take the unprecedented step of insisting there had been no discrimination. Most newspapers, however, were not convinced. The *Daily Sketch*'s Stratton Smith called Trueman's omission a public outrage:

> *This latest smear on Trueman is unbearable. The Yorkshire lad, on my reckoning, is being pilloried by the cricket overlords as a permanent example to those who might be tempted to be themselves on tour. They dare not say he isn't good enough . . . I seem to think the pin-striped brigade at Lord's haven't recognised that Freddie has changed. In the West Indies, he was a young, high-spirited lad fresh out of the services. Now he's a pipe-smoking, reasonable married man – not a boy.*

Insole, the England vice-captain, admits Trueman's omission was double-edged. 'I think the West Indies fall-out was a factor. There was still that feeling he might cause problems. Fred believed he should have gone to South Africa but he'd had a pretty poor season in 1956. He wasn't bowling well at the time and there were others ahead of him in the pecking order.' While Wardle helped England to a 2–2 draw, stealing the show with twenty-six wickets, Trueman contented himself with a short trip to India. He joined a party led by Geoffrey Howard – manager of Hutton's 1954–55 tour – for the Bengal Cricket Association's silver jubilee celebrations. During the trip, Howard's men shared a flight with Pandit Nehru, the Indian premier. Howard sat next to Nehru on the plane, getting up only once during the journey to visit the toilet. 'When I came back, there was Fred Trueman in my seat, giving Nehru a real ear-bashing about the state of his country.'

It was impossible, of course, for MCC to ignore Trueman forever. In 1957, he was finally 'reprieved', playing all five Tests against West Indies and taking twenty-two wickets – four more than anybody else. After claiming four wickets in each of the first two Tests, Trueman produced what the *Daily Telegraph* called 'the finest sustained bowling performance of his career to date' in the third match at Nottingham. On a prime batting pitch in heatwave conditions, he took five wickets in the first innings and four in the second as England were held in a high-scoring draw. During this game, May handed Trueman the ball with the words, 'Come on, Fred, England is expecting.' To which Trueman replied, 'Is she, skipper? Is that why they call her the mother country?' England won the series 3–0 and Trueman's rehabilitation was complete, but the pain of his treatment between 1954 and 1957 would never disappear.

In 1964, the BBC made a film about Trueman's life that included an extraordinary exchange between him and Hutton that sought to cast light on that career-damaging period. Trueman interviewed his captain about the 1953–54 West Indies tour in an attempt to find out what he'd done wrong. Hutton tried to back out at the last minute when Trueman made clear what he was going to ask, but Hutton had already signed a contract to appear. Introducing the clip in a sheepskin coat at a deserted Scarborough cricket ground after vehemently protesting his innocence on all charges, Trueman says: 'That tour planted firmly in my mind that I would never be chosen to play for England again while Len Hutton was captain. And, what's more, I never was. He described me as being his problem child. I don't know what he means, but there's one thing, I'm aiming to find out . . .' The pair are then shown side-by-side in a television studio, their chairs half-turned to face each other like a chat show host and his guest, but the atmosphere is more Spanish Inquisition than cordial conversation as Trueman interrogates his former skipper . . .

Trueman: And the man who can tell us something about it is my old friend and skipper Len Hutton, who is now Sir Leonard. Hello, Len, how are you?

Hutton (*stiffly*): Fine, thank you.

Trueman: Good. Now, Len, this tour of the West Indies, '53–54, was I really as bad as the press and the papers made me out to be? Was I really this firebrand, naughty boy stuff?

Hutton (*shifting uneasily*): Well, so far as I can remember, the only incident I know was with the umpire at Georgetown. Er, apart from that incident, I think, possibly, there was a great deal of press talk and probably it was rather elaborated, many of the incidents, and possibly your run to the wicket, your appeals, which are always a bit, er, noisy and a bit, er, loud, probably tended to give the impression that you were very hostile and, er, a sort of temperamental sort of cricketer.

Trueman: Yeah, but when you appeal, really, I mean, you've got to appeal with confidence. I don't like this half-hearted business and the umpire then gives it out if he hears like a squeak, which happens at times. I like to hear the real confident appeal. Do you agree with me on this, Len?

Hutton: Yes, I do, except when I'm battin' (*sic*). Lindwall used to appeal very hard when I was battin' and, er, I never enjoyed it very much. I always prefer as a batsman a gentle sort of appeal (*smiles*).

Trueman: Yeah, probably so. We differ a bit on opinions there. But anyway, that's nothing to worry about. But there were a lot of things in the West Indies, Len, that I heard myself when I came back that were just not true, they couldn't possibly have happened.

Hutton (*nods*): Hmm, I should imagine they were very much elaborated and, er, you certainly had, I think, in many ways, a rather raw deal in the West Indies.

Trueman: Well, that's very kind of you to say so, Len. I thank you for that very much indeed. But, er, I remember an incident where Tom Graveney caught a ball at slip, the last ball before lunch, at Trinidad, in the Test match. And the umpire, Ellis Achong, said 'not out' off Denis Compton, who was bowling his chinamen and googlies. And with that, Tom Graveney picked the ball up and slammed the ball into the floor and walked off. And only three nights later, at a cocktail party, an official one we had to go to as MCC players, somebody said, at that party, that they thought it was disgusting the show I put up when I caught that ball at slip, and I slammed it into the ground. Now you know as well as I do that this is not true.

(*Hutton nods gravely and mouths a silent 'yes'*)

Trueman: Tom Graveney was the man who caught the ball and threw it on the floor. And Tom – I'll defend Tom in every way because he turned round, while he was there, and said, 'You've got the wrong person, it was me who did that.' And they said, 'You're trying to cover up for him,' or something like that, so these are some of the things that came back.

Hutton: Yes, well, I think it's all very unfortunate, I think it's all past, and I think it's better really to be forgotten.

Trueman: Yes, probably so, but . . .

Hutton (*cuts in*): I think you were unfortunate in being a very promising player at that time, and you looked like being very good which, of course, you have become. And therefore there was a certain amount of jealousy, a certain amount of envy, which, er, of course, as you know does take place in teams, in cricket teams, in football teams and that sort of thing.

Trueman: Yes, I agree.

Hutton: And personally, I think you did very well to overcome that and to settle down and become a mature Test player as you did. But in those early days you had a pretty hard time – not only with the England side, but occasions with Yorkshire.

Trueman: Yes, but I will always think that the press and senior players influenced you a great deal by saying that you couldn't handle me. Well, this was wrong, completely.

Hutton (*grimacing*): Well, er, you know full well that on the field, and that sort of thing, we got on well.

Trueman: I don't think for one minute you were backed up by your senior players as you should have been, 'cos I think they were very, very jealous of you, especially being a Yorkshireman being appointed captain of England, and being a professional as well. And I stuck up for you in a lot of ways, because this was where a lot of trouble came with the players because of some of the things they said about you. I idolised you in those days. You were the greatest thing that I ever saw. And the things they said about you, I stuck up for you. And this brought a tendency of nasty feeling in the place because, I quite agree, I threatened one or two of them if they didn't stop talking about you behind your back that I'd hang 'em one on (*Hutton laughs*), as they say in Yorkshire. And I would have done, too, because I was so upset. And I realised, immediately I was there, that the senior players did not co-operate enough with the youngsters as far as I was concerned.

Hutton: But then people do talk about one's back (*sic*). Lindwall and Miller talked about my back (*sic*), and they called me many names, and I didn't mind it at all because, er, the reason they did it was that they couldn't get me out sometimes.

Trueman: That's right. Well, I quite agree, you were a very difficult man to get out when you decided to get your head down.

(*Hutton appears startled by the remark*)

Trueman: Well, thank you, Len, very much indeed for some of the nice things you've said.

Hutton gulps and looks relieved his ordeal is over. The clip concludes with a beaming Trueman announcing: 'What you've just heard will probably change the opinion of quite a few people I know.'

Trueman's sense of triumph was short-lived. Hutton's admission he'd had 'a raw deal' was of little consolation to a man who never played for England again under his captaincy and who missed twenty-three of England's next twenty-six Tests after the West Indies trip. Effectively blacklisted for three long years, Trueman paid a heavy price for his first tour failings. As he reflected, 'The career of a top-class cricketer is short. I was overlooked when in the prime of my career and over the years have often been given to ponder what might have been. In my opinion, I was treated abysmally by Len in his role as England captain and also by the MCC. I'll never be able to forgive Len or the MCC for that.'

9

The Tempest and the Flood Tide

The captain who understood Fred Trueman best wasn't an international superstar like Len Hutton but a man barely good enough for county cricket. Ronnie Burnet was a controversial choice as Yorkshire skipper in 1958. Six months short of his fortieth birthday, he hadn't even played a first-class match. His only experience was playing for the second team, whom he'd led to the Minor Counties title, and of captaining Baildon in the Bradford League. Burnet was an amateur who worked as director of a chemical firm. Round-faced and rotund, he looked more like a member of the Yorkshire committee than the playing staff. According to Ray Illingworth, Burnet had just three weaknesses – he couldn't bat, couldn't bowl and couldn't field. 'But take away those three shortcomings,' said Illingworth, 'and Ronnie did an absolutely fantastic job for Yorkshire cricket.'

The job Burnet was appointed to do was sort out the strife in the Yorkshire dressing room. It had been a viper's nest of poisonous self-interest since Trueman first knew it in 1949. A cantankerous camp under Norman Yardley had been no less crabby under Billy Sutcliffe, who resigned the captaincy after senior players circulated a petition demanding his removal. Trueman refused to sign it and called Sutcliffe's departure 'a bloody disgrace'. Like Yardley before him, Sutcliffe struggled to handle Johnny Wardle, an insidious influence behind the scenes. Wardle had little respect for Sutcliffe's leadership and desperately wanted the captaincy himself. In an effort to instil harmony, Yorkshire bypassed Wardle and turned instead to the ageing Burnet, whose man-management skills were in spectacular contrast to his cricketing abilities.

Burnet took the first step towards unifying the squad by sacking Wardle in the middle of the season. He'd had one spat too many with his senior professional and took action with support of the Yorkshire committee. At the time of his removal, Wardle had been chosen by England to tour Australia later that year. When this paradox was pointed out to Yorkshire's cricket chairman Brian Sellers, he intoned: 'He may be good enough for England, but not for Yorkshire.' After criticising the county in a series of articles for the *Daily Mail*, Wardle's tour place was revoked and he bowed out of top-flight cricket aged thirty-five. 'But for the volcanic eruption of 1958, his graceful action, square shoulders, fair hair and gravelly voice might have been part of the first-class scene for years to come,' lamented *Wisden*.

Burnet's decisive handling of Wardle came as no surprise to Trueman. He'd detected a strong leader when he played one game under Burnet for the second XI in 1955. Brian Close and Bob Appleyard also took part and Burnet put both men firmly in their place. When Close complained about opening the batting, Burnet told him: 'You'll open – or you'll go home.' When Appleyard kicked up his usual stink about being taken off, Burnet ordered him to take his sweater and do as he was told. 'It was from that moment that I thought Ronnie Burnet would make a good first-team captain,' said Trueman. 'I supported him right from the start, although I knew we would have to do a bit of carrying.'

One of Burnet's first moves after replacing Sutcliffe was to pick Trueman's brains over a friendly drink. This small but significant gesture made Trueman feel valued, something he'd not really known in his Yorkshire career. Trueman was one of a handful of survivors from the Yorkshire team of 1949 and Burnet recognised the sense in getting him on side. But it was no superficial gesture on the captain's part; Burnet knew instinctively how to handle players and get them working for the common good. It was exactly the quality he'd displayed in the second XI, where his young charges gave everything for a player unfit to lace their boots. Now those same youngsters graduated to the first team, eager to perform for a man who treated them with the right blend of fatherly care and schoolmasterly discipline. What Yorkshire lacked in experience they made up for in spirit and togetherness. The viper's nest was replaced by a family atmosphere in which Trueman thrived and Yorkshire flourished.

Burnet's influence over Trueman was no less effective on the field. He encouraged him, cajoled him and was generous in his praise. Burnet offered Trueman tactical assistance and was never too proud to accept it in return. With careful nurturing and sensitive guidance, he steered him towards the peak of his powers. 'Ronnie coming in was the best thing that could have happened to Fred,' said Don Wilson. 'Fred needed someone to believe in him, someone who trusted him. When he played earlier in the fifties, I think Fred thought everyone was playing for themselves. Under Ronnie, the sense of "team" was very strong and everybody wanted each other to do well.'

Bob Platt says Burnet had a positive effect on Trueman's behaviour. 'Fred started cooling down under Ronnie in 1958. He felt wanted and respected under Ronnie. He toed the line more and started to mellow. His verbals became more comical and light-hearted.'

A motivator par excellence, Burnet was a friendly, straightforward type. He drank with the players and classed them as friends while retaining an appropriate air of detachment. 'Ronnie was an affable bloke, but he wouldn't put up with any silly-bugger work,' added Platt. 'All the team had total confidence in him as a leader and a man. Everyone accepted his limitations as a cricketer, but he got plenty of help and advice from Fred and Raymond, with Closey chipping in as well. I certainly don't remember anyone ever saying, "What the f***ing hell's the captain doing?"'

There was immediately a positive sign for the Trueman/Burnet relationship. Trueman took a hat-trick in Burnet's first game against

MCC at Lord's, having Roy Swetman caught by Close, bowling Mick
Allen and sending back Roy Tattersall lbw. It was a sparkling season
for Trueman but a soggy one for Yorkshire, who finished eleventh
in the Championship. Play was impossible on twenty-four days, with
significant rainfall on many others. In between the downpours,
Trueman finished fourth in the national averages with 106 wickets at
13. He played all five Tests against New Zealand, taking 15 wickets
at 17 to help England to a 4–0 win. Trueman's impressive form and
improved conduct made him a shoo-in for the winter tour to
Australia. Selection was all the sweeter for having missed Hutton's
trip of four years earlier.

The sixteen-man party led by Peter May was considered one of
the strongest picked to leave English shores. The batting was
spearheaded by May, Tom Graveney and Colin Cowdrey. The pace
bowling was headed by Trueman, Frank Tyson and Brian Statham,
with Jim Laker and Tony Lock providing the spin. Not even the loss
of Wardle seemed likely to undermine England, who were generally
expected to retain the Ashes. Shortly before the players sailed, a
parcel arrived at Trueman's parents' house. 'It was sent by Keith
Miller and addressed to Freddie,' remembered Flo Halifax. 'Inside
the parcel was a piece of cork. Attached to the cork was the message,
"This is what you'll be bowling on, lad."'

Trueman's hopes of a stress-free trip were quickly dispelled. As
the players boarded SS *Iberia*, the England manager Freddie Brown
humiliated Trueman in front of the squad. 'Any trouble from you,
Trueman, and you're on a slow boat home.' It was not a comment
to cultivate harmony. Brown, in fact, was a preposterous blusterer.
Born in Peru and educated at Cambridge, he usually wore a white
silk neckerchief, which enhanced the impression of a bumptious
windbag. A one-time captain of Northamptonshire and England,
Brown was a bully who preyed on weakness or quirk of character.
Along with Hutton and Denis Compton, he gave Brian Close such a
torrid time on his first tour of Australia in 1950–51 that the teenager
admitted contemplating suicide. Trueman liked Brown as much as
he liked Gubby Allen, whom he loathed. He felt they epitomised the

pompous nature of English cricket in the days of amateurs and professionals, gentlemen and players. Trueman branded Brown 'a snob, bad-mannered, ignorant and a bigot'. He said Brown was rude whenever he spoke to him and treated him with contempt.

After an attack of lumbago forced him out the first Test in Brisbane, Trueman had a further contretemps with Brown. The manager told him that if he didn't get fit he'd have to go home because 'we don't want unfit people on this trip'. Trueman was incensed – not least because Willie Watson had injured his leg on the journey out and had to have an operation, something that did not inspire similar stricture from Brown. Sensing he would need to put his foot down to prevent the tour degenerating into the sort of disaster that was his West Indian experience, Trueman complained to May about Brown's behaviour. He told the captain that unless matters improved he would be going home after the Ashes instead of continuing to New Zealand with the rest of the squad. Concerned at the growing ill-feeling between bowler and manager, May ordered Brown to give Trueman a wide berth and told him to act in a manner more befitting someone with managerial responsibility.

In stark contrast to his relationship with Hutton, Trueman got on famously with May. He found him approachable and always willing to spare time for a chat. Charterhouse-educated and naturally bashful, May was not an obvious ally. But they had profound respect for each other's talent and savoured their duels in county cricket as much as they savoured their common successes. 'If Trueman dismissed May, his whole attitude, and probably his voice, said "Done thi" in tones of infinite satisfaction,' wrote J.M. Kilburn. 'If May drove a beautiful boundary, or stopped a yorker or evaded a bumper, his shy half-smile indicated "One to me, Fred". They relished the battle even more deeply than it was relished by spectators.'

There was little for either to relish at Brisbane. While Trueman rested his back, England crashed to an eight-wicket defeat brought about by abject batting. Although fit for the second Test in Melbourne, Trueman was omitted. Another eight-wicket defeat saw him recalled for the third Test at Sydney, where Miller's forewarning he would be bowling on pitches that resembled cork proved not so frivolous after all. The Sydney surface had none of the life Tyson and Statham exploited four years earlier, Trueman managing only 1 for 46 in a hard-fought draw, but he went down a storm with the Sydney public. Jack Fingleton noted 'many Australians don't care much for authority and they have a secret liking for anybody who cocks a snook at it', thereby ensuring Trueman an instant following on the notorious Hill.

At one stage, Trueman was fielding in front of the Hill in between overs as the temperature nudged 100 degrees. A spectator held up a can of Foster's and shouted, 'Hey, Fred, you look in need of a beer, mate.' Trueman replied he could sink the contents without them touching the sides and asked May if he could take a swig from the can as a friendly gesture. May agreed it would be good PR and when Trueman obliged, the Hill erupted. Trueman returned to the boundary after his next over to find about twenty cans lined up for him in front of the fence.

Australia's cricketers were not so generous. Richie Benaud's men retained the Ashes with a ten-wicket victory in the fourth Test at Adelaide, where Trueman (four wickets), Statham (three) and Tyson (one) appeared together for the only time. Australia completed a 4–0 triumph with a comfortable nine-wicket win at Melbourne but their success was tainted by controversy. The standard of umpiring was heavily criticised, Trueman noting it had 'as much impartiality as a religious zealot', while the actions of pace bowlers Ian Meckiff and Gordon Rorke were roundly condemned. Meckiff, a left-armer from Victoria who topped Australia's averages with 17 wickets at 17, was called for throwing in 1963 and never played again. Rorke, a giant right-armer from New South Wales, had a jerky action and such a pronounced drag he often delivered from eighteen yards. 'It was a miserable tour,' remembered Graveney. 'The problem was we were never a team. Freddie Brown, in particular, did a very bad job. He was rude to Fred and quite a few others and was a very stuck-up individual – at least when he was sober.'

In his post-tour report to MCC, Brown was subtly reproving of Trueman:

The only player who needed any correction was Trueman, but I think it is only fair to him to say that he was always willing to listen and that he took notice of things told to him and proved himself popular with the rest of the team. In my opinion he has learned a great deal from this tour and I have found that if he is told the reason for not doing a certain thing he is easily managed.

May's report criticised several players. Raman Subba Row was 'a disappointment to me'; Ted Dexter made 'stupid mistakes in every department'; Jim Laker had a 'large chip on his shoulder' and was 'too self-centred'; Peter Loader was 'temperamental at times, which is rather tiresome'. It might have been Hutton's 1953–54 report in reverse as May reserved his main praise for Trueman:

There was a great transformation and, to my mind, he was the greatest success of the tour. He was wonderfully loyal in every way and he was always conscious of the press focus, which was trying to upset him. On the field, he was always in the game – batting extremely sensibly, catching well and bowling with every ounce of effort. He became a most popular member of the side, and it was nice to see that the players were laughing with him and not at him. If it was possible, I would recommend Trueman for an extra bonus.

The extra bonus did not materialise but the wheel had turned full circle for Trueman. Helped by Burnet at Yorkshire and May with England, the player supposedly unsuitable for overseas tours had become the 'greatest success' of an overseas tour. After his early problems with Yorkshire and England, he'd matured as a bowler and also as a person. He was twenty-eight years old, one of the game's biggest draws, and was about to enter the years of his pomp.

Trueman returned to a Yorkshire side of which little was expected in 1959. Before the season began, Brian Sellers predicted they would need at least another three years to become Championship contenders, but to Sellers's surprise and the game's in general, Burnet's young team made off with the title, ending Surrey's sequence of seven successive Championships.

Trueman was at the heart of the shock success. He topped the bowling with 92 wickets at 18 and had a decisive hand in seven of the team's fourteen victories; five of Yorkshire's seven defeats occurred while he was on Test duty. Two of those defeats came in successive games at Somerset and Gloucestershire in late August and almost cost Burnet's team the title. In the latter match at Bristol, Yorkshire were bowled out for 35 in their first innings as pace bowler Tony Brown took 7 for 11. 'That night, Ronnie Burnet and myself were sitting in the bar of the team hotel, drowning our sorrows,' remembered Bob Platt. 'It was about ten o'clock and the night porter came round ringing his bell, saying, "Telephone call for Mr Burnet." Ronnie said to me, "You know who that will be, don't you? We've just been bowled out for 35 and made a complete arse of it. It'll be Brian Sellers playing hell wanting me to change the bloody team." Well, the night porter must have come round about four times and on each occasion Ronnie said, "I'm not answering it, Bob. We've come this far with the players we've got – and we're carrying on."'

Burnet's faith was richly rewarded. Needing to win their last match at Sussex to clinch the title, Yorkshire chased 215 in 105 minutes to achieve a five-wicket victory with seven minutes to spare. Bryan Stott (96) and Doug Padgett (79) were the heroes, adding 141 for the third wicket in just over an hour. Trueman chipped in with 11 from the no. 5 position before Illingworth and Bolus saw the side home. His task complete, Burnet resigned the captaincy and handed over to Vic Wilson – Yorkshire's first professional captain of the twentieth century.

Burnet retired with 897 runs at 12.63 but his contribution was worth more than dry statistics. He united a once-divided club and gave new life to its most potent weapon: F.S. Trueman. 'I would have gone through a brick wall for him,' said Trueman. 'He was such a wonderful person that the fact of his not being an outstanding player made us ready to do more for him. If anyone achieved a good performance for Yorkshire or England, Ronnie was always first with the praise and congratulations. He made you feel good inside.'

Reflecting on how he welded the team together, Burnet said, 'If I did anything useful in 1958–59, I like to think that the change in attitude of the older and more established players in the side was decisive. They realised cricket was a game they could actually enjoy, even though it was a deadly serious matter and we were always going out for a win. I am quite sure that this change of attitude rescued the international careers of Close and Trueman, and that Illingworth was completely on the right track, as he was later to prove.'

Testimony that Trueman's international career was revitalised came during the winter of 1959–60. Six years after his Caribbean nightmare, he returned to the West Indies and enjoyed the happiest and most successful of his four overseas tours. England won the five-Test series 1–0, Trueman starring with 21 wickets at 26. It was a notable triumph for the tourists, who were undergoing a transitional period and performed out of their skins in suffocating heat.

This time, Trueman had no problem with the England manager. Walter Robins, a nimble all-rounder who'd played nineteen Tests before the war, was an equally strong character with no-nonsense views. Like Trueman, he had a keen sense of humour and they pulled each other's leg without fear or favour. Trueman responded to Robins's banter, while Robins admired Trueman's skill and stamina.

Trueman also hit it off with West Indian crowds, showing them his lighter, more humorous side. 'Trueman bowled so well and clowned with such success that the past was forgotten,' observed writer and historian C.L.R. James. Trueman even had a laugh with Cecil Kippins, the umpire at the centre of the 'black bastard' row. 'Freddie and I got on very well in '59–60,' said Kippins. 'He was a different character then. What Freddie suffered from before was the captaincy of Hutton. He was our biggest problem in '53–54. Freddie and I had great fun in one game in '59–60. I always wore a hat when I was umpiring and Freddie took it off my head and put it on his own. When he finally took it off again, he started scratching his head as though there'd been bugs in my hair. It had the players and spectators in gales of laughter.'

England's victory came during the second Test in Trinidad – a match marred by crowd trouble. After England made 382, Trueman took four wickets to reduce West Indies to 94 for 7. When local boy Charan Singh was then run out, the 30,000 crowd unleashed its frustration. 'Hardly had umpire Lee Kow's finger gone up than it started,' wrote Alan Ross, the *Observer* cricket correspondent. 'First an ugly, growing roar of protest, then a storm of boos, finally, from far back in the open stand to the right of the pavilion, the bottles. Lobbed like hand grenades the opening volleys bounced separately along the boundary edge. Within seconds these had grown into thick showers, not from this stand, only, but from all round the ground. May called his boundary fielders in, and in no time at all only a tiny island round the pitch was free of bottles.'

Trueman was one of those fielding near the boundary when the riot broke out. As spectators rushed past, one reassured: 'Don't worry, Fred. We ain't gonna touch you, man. We want dem umpires.' Just to be safe, Trueman made his way to the square and grabbed a stump for protection. Statham also grabbed a stump, the pair guarding the team's flanks as the players left the field.

The mayhem, however, continued apace. There had been much drinking and gambling, a controversial umpiring decision and, worse still, West Indies were losing. 'The whole playing area was a confusion of darting figures, of gesticulating mobs, of isolated but brutal fights which the pathetically few police present – there were fifteen of them – could do nothing to break up,' added Ross. 'A fire hose was hauled onto the field and trained on groups of bottle-throwers. The pressure was low and it merely spluttered out in pools at the firemen's feet like an elephant urinating.'

It took forty-five minutes to quell the riot and no further play was possible that day. Trueman, who completed a five-wicket return as

West Indies were dismissed for 112 en route to a 256-run defeat, reflected, 'We play our cricket hard in Yorkshire but we don't throw bottles about. However, that's mainly because we get thruppence a piece back on them.'

Trueman's performances on tour were put into context by the fact five West Indians averaged 40 plus. Garry Sobers led the way with 709 runs at 101.28, Trueman dismissing him four times in eight innings. 'I think that series was Fred's finest hour,' said Ted Dexter. 'On real shirt-front pitches against a fine batting side he bowled as well as I've ever seen an international bowler.' A terrific trip for Trueman was topped when he was made senior professional after Statham returned home following the fourth Test. When informed of his elevation, Trueman told reporters, 'The first thing these buggers will have to do is cut out the bloody swearing.'

Such was his workload in West Indies, Trueman lost more than a stone in weight, but the stresses in no way diminished his effectiveness. In 1960, he enjoyed his most prolific season, taking more first-class wickets – 175 – than anyone in the country, including 132 for Yorkshire as they retained the Championship. For the only times in his career, Trueman took 14 wickets in a match, performing the feat twice in the space of four weeks. He captured 14 for 125 against Northamptonshire at Bramall Lane and 14 for 123 against Surrey on an Oval pitch so placid it made those in the West Indies seem like minefields.

Trueman was equally devastating in that summer's Test series against South Africa. He claimed 25 wickets at 20 as England ran out 3–0 winners. Statham took 27 wickets at 18 as they effectively won the rubber on their own. It was the first time they'd bowled together in all five Tests and established the duo as a top-class partnership.

Trueman and Statham first played together in 1954, opening the bowling against West Indies in Jamaica, but a combination of Trueman's international exile and England's pace bowling strength meant they appeared only seventeen times in harness before the opening Test of the 1960 series. Considering their names were inextricably linked, Trueman and Statham were not paired as often as one might imagine. They combined thirty-five times in Trueman's sixty-seven and Statham's seventy Tests, Trueman also opening the bowling in Test cricket with Alec Bedser and Peter Loader (five times), Frank Tyson, Alan Moss, Len Coldwell and Derek Shackleton (three), Trevor Bailey, David Larter and Fred Rumsey (two), and once with Harold Rhodes, Les Jackson, Jack Flavell and John Price. Trueman, in fact, never had a fixed opening partner throughout his career.

For Yorkshire, he took the new ball 802 times in first-class cricket. Discounting the Roses match at Old Trafford in 1966, when he bowled the only two balls of Lancashire's first innings before the home side declared, he was partnered on the other 801 occasions by Tony Nicholson (188 times), Mel Ryan (126), Bob Appleyard (101), Bob Platt (98), Mike Cowan (70), Richard Hutton (37), David Pickles (29), Alec Coxon (27), Brian Close and Norman Yardley (21), Bill Foord (18), Philip Hodgson (11), Ray Illingworth (10), John Whitehead and John Waring (eight), Brian James and Don Wilson (six); twice by Eric Baraclough, Eric Burgin, Jack van Geloven, Peter Broughton and Peter Stringer; and once by William Holdsworth, Johnny Wardle, Ken Taylor, Keith Gillhouley, Brian Bolus and Chris Old. Trueman's attitude to this avalanche of associates was summed up whenever he heard Platt boasting he used to be his partner at Yorkshire. 'Aye, one of f***ing twenty-eight, Platty.'

Although Trueman therefore had a staggering forty-two opening partners for Yorkshire and England, Statham was by far the most recognisable. Born in Gorton, Manchester, in June 1930, the youngest of four brothers, Statham played his early cricket for Whitworth Street before joining Stockport in the Central Lancashire League. A talented footballer, he represented the same boys' club as Roger Byrne, the Manchester United and England full-back. Byrne was one of eight Busby Babes killed in the Munich air disaster of 6 February 1958 – Trueman's twenty-seventh birthday. Statham was good enough at football to be offered trials by Liverpool, Manchester City, Bury and Stockport County, but his father, a dentist, forbade him to attend. He wanted him to continue his education but when Lancashire offered a trial in 1949, Statham senior relented on condition his son made the grade within three years. Statham junior satisfied the proviso with two years to spare, making his first-class debut on his twentieth birthday. *Wisden* described him as 'a youngster who carried his flannels in a canvas bag, and his boots in a brown paper parcel'.

The young Statham acquired a hat-trick of nicknames: 'Whippet', on account of his whippy, loose-limbed action; 'Greyhound', because of his smooth, effortless approach to the crease; and, most enduring, 'George'. The latter – ostensibly incongruous for a man christened John Brian Statham – originated because some Lancashire players considered the presence of wicketkeeper George Duckworth in the Championship-winning teams of the 1920s a lucky charm and it was felt success would not return until Lancashire had another 'George'. Winston Place, a tall opening batsman, volunteered for the sobriquet after the war and, when he retired, Statham took it on. As it was felt no one could possibly follow Statham, the 'George' tradition eventually lapsed.

'George', often extended to 'Gentleman George', was a character in the less flamboyant sense. He prepared for action with 'a fag, a cough and a cup of coffee' and had a singular habit of talking to his feet – apologising to them after a long, hard day or exhorting them to greater endeavour. Statham was double-jointed and removed his sweater by reaching down his back to the hem before pulling it up back over his shoulders. He could put his right arm behind his head, run it under his chin and tickle his right ear, as well as wrap both legs around his neck to form a kind of scarf.

Confirming the verity that opposites attract, Trueman and Statham were chalk and cheese. As bowlers, Trueman swung the ball away; Statham nipped it back. Trueman's action was classically side-on; Statham's too open-chested for purists. Trueman flourished through flashes of flair; Statham's style was patient and probing. Trueman frequently used the bouncer; Statham had to be persuaded to bowl one. Trueman demanded the wind at his back; Statham was content bowling into its teeth. Trueman screamed, 'I'll pin thee t'bloody sightscreen'; Statham simply stated, 'If they miss, I hit.' Neville Cardus described Trueman as the thunderclap to Statham's lightning, while J.M. Kilburn observed that 'Statham obliterates opposing batting like the inexorable flood tide; Trueman shatters by tempest.'

Their differences in character were no less pronounced. Trueman was a self-confessed 'arrogant bastard' on the field; Statham was quiet and self-effacing. Trueman was demonstrative in word and deed; Statham was a placid, poker-faced assassin. Trueman drank in moderation; Statham filled up lustily from the legs. Trueman actively courted the limelight; Statham avoided it with equal vigour. Their myriad diversities explained their rapport. It is doubtful whether Trueman would have got on as well with someone who also demanded attention and headlines, whether there would have been room for two large egos in the same relationship. Statham, however, was no threat to his appeal – although perhaps more popular at dressing-room level.

Trueman and Statham worked as a team, even gifting singles to turn around batsmen. Because Trueman swung the ball away, he preferred bowling at right-handers. Statham often posed more threat to left-handers, to whom inswing, in contrast, then became out-swing. Statham was considered an unlucky bowler, one who frequently beat right and left-hander alike. 'No fast bowler has been more regularly condemned to achieve his conquests two or three times over,' wrote Kilburn. 'The number of times he has defeated the stroke to see the ball miss the stumps or the edge of the bat is incalculable and incredible. Without the philosophic resignation that is his natural blessing and cultivated reaction he would have committed suicide, or turned batsman, long ago.'

Some felt Trueman benefited from Statham's misfortune and metronomic accuracy. They thought batsmen more likely to go for their shots against Trueman because he was less consistent in line and length. Trueman was essentially an attacking bowler, a man who tried to mix things up. He regularly bowled to aggressive fields and eschewed the protection of a third man, meaning that edges which did not fly to the wicketkeeper or slips invariably found their way to the boundary. According to Sobers, 'there was an element of truth in the "Statham makes it easy for Fred" theory because batsmen tried to chase Fred's deliveries sometimes if no boundaries were coming, and maybe he did pick up one or two extra wickets. A feeling among some batsmen at the time was that if they could keep Statham out they could go for their shots against Trueman.'

The theory, however, had no statistical basis. Not only did Trueman take a vast number of wickets without Statham in county cricket, he had a much better record in Tests when Statham wasn't playing. In thirty-two Tests without Statham, Trueman took 164 wickets at 17.93. In their thirty-five Tests together, he claimed 143 wickets at 25.76 against Statham's 141 at 25.71, proving just how equal their partnership was. Statham, too, had a better average in Trueman's absence. In his thirty-five Tests sans Trueman, he took 111 wickets at 23.73. Only once did Trueman and Statham each take four or more wickets in the same innings, against West Indies at Trent Bridge in 1957. Usually, one would claim a sizeable haul while the other performed a supporting role.

The contrasting challenges posed by the pair meant some favoured facing one or the other. 'I preferred to face Fred because I could never see where or how I was going to score a run off Brian,' wrote Trevor Bailey. 'He never seemed to serve up anything remotely resembling a half-volley; just a non-stop diet of balls pitching just outside the off stump, which were fractionally short and would hit the stumps, interspersed with the occasional yorker. Fred did more with the ball but at least he did occasionally, and often deliberately, send down a half-volley.' However, Bailey added, 'class batsmen like Tom Graveney and Colin Cowdrey preferred facing Brian because the unexpected was less likely to occur, whereas Fred was more volatile and aggressive and always liable to produce that late away-swinger, which only outstanding players touch and I simply missed.'

Neil Harvey also thought Trueman more likely to take his wicket.

'Freddie was the better bowler and more likely to get you out. In fact, he was one of those few blokes who could bowl well no matter where he played – in England, Australia, the West Indies, wherever. Brian, in contrast, didn't bowl as well in Australia as he did in England, and he wasn't as adaptable as Freddie. One of the best things about Freddie was his versatility, such as when he slowed down to bowl off-cutters against us at Leeds in 1961.'

The match in question was one of Trueman's finest. Before his adoring home crowd, he produced a sensational spell to beat Australia almost single-handed. After taking five wickets in the tourists' first innings as they slumped from 187 for 2 to 237 all out, he inspired an even greater disintegration second time round. Bowling off-cutters off a shortened run, he aimed at dust patches on and outside the right-hander's off stump and claimed 5 for 0 in twenty-seven balls to send Australia tumbling from 99 for 2 to 109 for 8, finishing with six wickets in the innings and eleven in the match. Trueman, by then, was a thinking bowler, no longer concerned with out-and-out speed. His stock delivery was the pitched-up away swinger, while he used the bumper to intelligent effect. Trueman also had the skill to bring the ball back, meaning batsmen could not depend on it swinging away or holding its line. As John Arlott observed, 'Statham was accurate; Tyson was fast; Fred was everything.'

The 1961 series was bittersweet for Trueman. His efforts at Headingley earned England their sole victory as Australia retained the Ashes with a 2–1 win, but he was dropped after an average game in the fourth Test at Manchester. Trueman took 1 for 147 at Old Trafford as Richie Benaud – bowling round the wicket into rough outside the right-hander's leg stump – won the match as England collapsed in pursuit of 256 from 150 for 1 to 201 all out. Trueman was dumped despite being England's leading wicket-taker in the series with 20 at 26, the punishment fuelling his belief that MCC never stopped looking for an excuse to drop him.

There was also a frustrating end to his season with Yorkshire.

Targeting their first hat-trick of titles since the 1930s, the county were pipped into second place by Hampshire, who confounded forecasts of a modest season. Trueman took 155 first-class wickets at 19 – down from the high peak of 1960 but still richly impressive. He did not tour Pakistan and India during the winter – or, for that matter, India in 1963–64, in an era when it was common for England to leave their best players at home for sub-continental trips.

Trueman returned for the home series against Pakistan in 1962, claiming 22 wickets at 19 as England won 4–0. He also helped Yorkshire clinch their third Championship in four summers, finishing third in the national averages with 153 wickets at 17. The only blot on his benefit season came on that notorious occasion Vic Wilson sent him home from Taunton for arriving late. It was the nadir of their relationship as Trueman continued his trend of either getting on with his captains like a house on fire or well-nigh wanting to set them on fire.

A farmer from Scampston near Malton in North Yorkshire, Wilson was a powerful left-hand batsman. Good enough to be chosen for the 1954–55 tour of Australia, he was twelfth man in all five Tests and never quite managed an England cap. As team-mates during the 1950s, Trueman and Wilson were never close. According to Bob Platt, they tolerated each other at best. 'Fred and I sometimes picked Vic up at Malton if we were playing at Scarborough and they didn't always speak to one another then. It was never amiable between the pair.' Platt likens their relationship to that of Darren Gough and David Byas, who didn't see eye-to-eye as Yorkshire team-mates in the nineties and noughties. 'Vic and Byas were quite similar. Both were bloody nice blokes, but, for want of a better term, east-coast farmers. They couldn't really see any areas of grey.'

Unlike Burnet, Wilson rarely sought Trueman's input. 'Vic once declared at Cardiff,' said Platt. 'We'd had Glamorgan on the floor for two-and-a-quarter days and he left them something like eighty-eight an hour because Gilbert Parkhouse was lame and he thought Gilbert wouldn't bat. He asked one or two of us what we thought

and we said, "Well, I don't know, Vic, it's a bit of a bloody risk," and
he didn't go to Fred. Anyway, Vic declared and Fred said, "This
f***er's played since 1946 and he's learnt f*** all about the game." Of
course, Gilbert Parkhouse came out with a bloody runner, opened
the batting and won the match. It was a total bloody give-away.'

Notwithstanding his strategic shortcomings, Wilson could point
to a successful record. In his three seasons in charge, Yorkshire won
52 first-class games, drew 42 and lost 17. He had reason to be
profoundly grateful to Trueman, who played 81 of those 111 fixtures
and took 396 wickets at 15. Trueman laboured tirelessly under
Wilson's captaincy, bowling more than 1000 overs in all three
seasons. This extraordinary feat of endeavour provided the
backdrop to one of the most famous Trueman anecdotes. After
Wilson retired in September 1962, Trueman travelled with his
England colleagues to contest the Ashes. On board the SS *Canberra*,
England captain Ted Dexter encountered Gordon Pirie, the long-
distance runner born in Leeds. Dexter asked Pirie to take exercise
sessions with the players and the Olympic star soon had them
running up and down the ship's decks. One man, however, refused
to take part. Having slogged his guts out all summer, Trueman
wanted nothing more than to sit in a deckchair and recharge his
batteries. Pirie, however, would not be deterred. Trueman said their
confab went something like this:

Pirie: I'm going to devise some exercises to strengthen your legs.

Trueman: I'll have you know my legs have just carried me through
    more than 1,000 overs in the county season. What makes you
    think they need strengthening?

Pirie: All the same, I could toughen them up with just a few
    exercises. I would also recommend you stop eating steaks and go
    on a diet of salad and nuts.

Trueman: Er, tell me, Mr Pirie, have you ever run against a chap
    called Vladimir Kuts?

Pirie: Of course.

Trueman: Aye, and if I remember rightly, Kuts was on his lap of honour before you crossed the finish line. (Then, with a menacing look overboard) Incidentally, can you swim?

The story sounds as though it might be taller than the Empire State Building but Pirie confirmed its veracity on *Test Match Special*. Even Pirie, however, must have secretly admired Trueman's stamina. In addition to bowling more than 1000 overs in each season from 1959 to 1962, Trueman bowled more than 700 overs in a summer on eight occasions and, in his entire first-class career, sent down 15,968 six-ball and 494.4 eight-ball overs – a staggering 99,764 deliveries. During that time, he sprinted more than two million yards (around 1200 miles) – not including the walk back to his mark. It is a record to make the modern glut of fitness trainers, dieticians and sundry nonentities choke on their muesli as well as shame contemporary fast bowlers who expend nowhere near the same energy – at least not outside the gym.

To put Trueman's workload into context, Steve Harmison has only twice bowled more than 500 first-class overs in a season, his most taxing campaign coming in 1999 when he sent down 565.5 overs for 64 wickets at 27. Although there are fewer first-class games nowadays, more one-day cricket and less chance for England bowlers to play county matches because of central contracts, the comparison is stark. No pace bowler has bowled more than 700 first-class overs in an English season since Andy Caddick sent down 763.5 for Somerset and England in 1999.

Even more remarkable, Trueman was hardly injured. Apart from one or two back problems on his tours of Australia and a few stresses and strains in his younger years, he was so reliable a captain could have set his watch by him. Trueman played 459 of the 689 first-class games undertaken by Yorkshire between his debut and retirement, notwithstanding international obligations. No bowler of comparable pace has exceeded his career total of 603 first-class matches.

'I don't recall Fred ever being injured,' said Geoffrey Boycott. 'He once fell down while bowling at Sheffield and I thought, shit, he's broken his bloody ankle, but he got straight back up again. It was

bloody phenomenal, really. His fitness record was something else.'
Yorkshire left-armer Mike Cowan remembers Trueman suffering
one injury but even that didn't keep him out of action. 'Fred once
pulled an intercostal muscle and the doctor suggested he wear a
support, so there was England's finest pulling on a bloody girdle. I
said, "Bloody hell, Fred, how long have you had the girdle?" He said,
"Ever since wife found it in back of car."'

Trueman's stamina was founded on prodigious physique. He was
5ft 10in tall and built not unlike a North American bison. At his peak,
Trueman weighed thirteen-and-a-half stone and measured forty-six
inches across the chest. He also possessed an ample posterior, which
cushioned the violent jolt of delivery. Jim Swanton once remarked
on the size of Trueman's stern as he passed him lying on a massage
table. 'A big spike needs a big hammer to drive it home,' declared
Trueman, much to Swanton's distaste. At a dinner in Leeds in 2007
to mark the thirtieth anniversary of his 100th first-class hundred,
Boycott told a startled audience that Trueman, in fact, had a
diminutive spike. 'Fred only had a little tiddler,' laughed Boycott as
he gave an unexpectedly graphic insight into the Yorkshire dressing
room.

In common with most players of his time, Trueman got fit by
bowling – not pumping weights. It wasn't unusual for him to turn up
for a new season carrying a few extra pounds with the deliberate
intention of bowling them off. Trueman and his peers were naturally
fit, having grown up in a much more mobile era. There were no
televisions or computers to provide distraction as children played for
hours outdoors.

Despite the huge strains on him, Trueman never gave less than
100 per cent. There were times his pace understandably dropped but
team-mates insist he tried as hard at the end of a day as he did at the
start. His attitude was the same whether he was playing against
Australia in a vital Test match or a bunch of students with nothing
at stake. 'We once played one of the university sides,' said Cowan.
'They were just a bunch of kids and yet Fred tore in as though his life
depended on it. Fred never liked students anyway – "f***ing jazz

hats", he used to call them – but that didn't explain the effort he showed. On the way home I said, "Bloody hell, Fred, you slipped yourself a bit today, didn't you?" He said, "Aye, I always do when I come here, and do you want to know why? It's because these games count towards the first-class averages, and when it comes to picking the Test side they're not interested in who you've got but how many."'

Don Wilson was another struck by Trueman's fortitude. 'I've never seen a man with as much enthusiasm. I've never seen a chap try so hard. I played county cricket with Fred for many years and never saw him consciously hold back.'

Trueman was helped by the prevailing attitude towards training and practice. There were no regimented net sessions before every game or compulsion to undertake countless exercises. Brian Statham was by no means the only one who warmed up with 'a fag, a cough and a cup of coffee' instead of several push-ups and a run around the outfield. Trueman got ready by twirling his arms a few times and smoking a pipe, not by wearing himself out before the match had started. Modern bowlers, alas, have no such luxury. Were Trueman playing today, he would be obliged to take part in pre-match warm-ups which, in the case of Twenty20 fixtures, appear to last longer than the games themselves.

In Trueman's time, even pre-season training was short and sweet. There'd be a bit of net practice, a spot of jogging, then off to the pub to catch up on gossip. 'The highlight of the year for me was reporting back to Headingley for pre-season training,' said Wilson. 'Not because of the training itself – that was over in a flash and very straightforward. It was because we all used to go up the road afterwards to the Skyrack pub and literally sit there, mouths agog, listening to Fred's stories about what had happened on tour during the winter. He invariably had some great tales to tell.'

Doubtless the Pirie anecdote was high on the list when Trueman returned from Australia in 1963. There were certainly plenty to choose from, with Trueman at the heart of a colourful trip. It was an unusual tour to say the least. The England manager was Bernard Marmaduke Fitzalan-Howard, better known as the 16th Duke of Norfolk. An MCC committee member and ex-MCC president, he was appointed following a chance remark over drinks at Lord's. No sooner had England arrived Down Under than the portly Duke commanded attention. He was close to the Queen and had horse racing connections, and interest focused not so much on the cricket but whether his horses might be seen on Australian tracks.

To add to the sideshow, Dexter's wife, Susan, a fashion model, arrived in Australia for a series of engagements, prompting much speculation about what she'd be wearing. When England batsman David Sheppard undertook to preach in several churches, Trueman was among those concerned that the real purpose of the tour – to win back the Ashes – was being overlooked. He told one reporter the England players were 'not sure whether they were playing under Jockey Club rules, working for Dexter Enterprises or taking part in a missionary hunt'. Another black mark followed when the Duke beckoned him over at a function with the words, 'Trueman – over here'. There followed the usual grumblings about Trueman's parents having taken a long time choosing his Christian name and that the Duke, in future, might care to use it.

Trueman claimed they got on well thereafter and that the Duke even said, 'Just call me "Dukie".' This, however, seems highly unlikely. According to the journalist Ian Wooldridge, His Grace told reporters at the start of the trip, 'I wish this to be an entirely informal tour. You will merely address me as "Sir".' The Duke caused a commotion midway through the series when he made a flying visit back to England to attend to 'private duties'. Pressed on his return, he said he had gone to 'feed the ducks'. The real reason, however, was to help conduct a rehearsal in London for the funeral of Winston Churchill, who, as it turned out, didn't pass away for another two years.

Amid such bizarre goings-on, the cricket seemed almost inconsequential. Trueman needed pain-killing injections to get through the drawn first Test in Brisbane after suffering a displaced bone at the base of his spine. The ailment sparked fanciful reports he had such a serious congenital spinal weakness he might never play again. When journalists put the idea to his father, Dick Trueman described it as 'bloody daft'.

Trueman was fully recovered for the second Test in Melbourne, where he bowled superbly to help England to their only victory of the series. Trueman took 3 for 83 and 5 for 62 – a performance Sheppard described as 'the finest sustained and accurate fast bowling I have ever seen'. One remark from this game has gone down in folklore. When Sheppard dropped a catch off his bowling, Trueman quipped, 'Kid yourself it's Sunday, Rev, and keep your hands together.' Trueman and Sheppard got on well and were bosom buddies throughout the tour. In a letter to MCC secretary Billy Griffith, England vice-captain Colin Cowdrey confided, 'Freddie Trueman and the Reverend make an intriguing pair and they are often to be seen together. At the Lord Mayor's reception, the Archbishop of Perth stopped for a moment to greet David. When he had moved on Fred queried, "Say, Rev, is that your senior pro?"'

Trueman delivered another classic bon mot before the third Test in Sydney. Asked what he thought of 'our bridge', he replied, 'Your bridge? Our bloody bridge, more like. It was built by a Yorkshire firm and you bastards still haven't paid for it.'

Australia drew level at the SCG, where Trueman felt Dexter cost them the game. He'd advised him to go with two spinners on a dry surface but Dexter kept the three-man pace attack that prospered in Melbourne. Sure enough, the pacemen managed only four wickets between them while off-spinner Fred Titmus was England's leading bowler with 7 for 79. As England's support spinners watched helplessly from the sidelines, Australia romped to an eight-wicket win. Trueman felt Dexter compounded his blunder in the next Test at Adelaide by dropping Worcestershire seamer Len Coldwell on the back of his Sydney display and drafting in Ray Illingworth on a pitch Trueman this time thought conducive to pace. Sure enough, Illingworth took 1 for 108, Titmus 2 for 157, and the game was drawn. Benaud's men retained the Ashes in the final Test at Sydney, where the tactics of both teams were widely condemned. *Wisden* branded the drawn decider 'a dull, lifeless game which did immense harm to cricket, particularly in Australia'.

Although Trueman liked Dexter as a person, he had little respect for his tactical ability. He thought Dexter had 'more f***ing theory than Darwin' and little idea how to implement it. Trueman felt England would have won the series but for Dexter's leadership and was not alone in his view of the captain. 'Ted was one captain I never fully understood,' wrote Statham. 'I don't think anyone in the dressing room did, either. He did things at times that were difficult to understand. He made moves, and bowling changes, which were completely out of keeping with the run of the game and which sometimes resulted in the opposition wriggling off the hook.'

Trueman took twenty wickets in the series to lift his career tally to 236, six behind Statham. The Lancastrian had surpassed Bedser's world record of 236 in the fourth Test when he dismissed Barry Shepherd with the aid of a gully catch by Trueman. Statham returned home after the Ashes and did not go to New Zealand, giving Trueman the chance to seize the record. He did so during the third and final Test in Christchurch, inducing Barry Sinclair to hit his own wicket en route to first-innings figures of 7 for 75.

After receiving a congratulatory telegram from every first-class county apart from Yorkshire, Trueman's frustration increased when he arrived back in England. He discovered he'd been docked £50 of his £150 good conduct bonus and was once again denied explanation. MCC said only it had acted on the recommendation of Dexter and the Duke of Norfolk, the latter having playfully rebuked Sir Robert Menzies for undoing 'the hard disciplinary work of six weeks' when the Australian Prime Minister presented Trueman with a pewter tankard in honour of his birthday during a function in Canberra. Illingworth was also docked £50 and given no reason, the punishment rankling with both men.

When interviewed for this book, Dexter claimed he couldn't remember why Trueman lost part of his money. 'Fred was always on about that – you didn't give me my bloody bonus, and so on, but I really can't recall.' However, Dexter's captain's report makes clear his view on Trueman's contribution. Trueman, he wrote, 'is not a team man off the field' and made 'only a 60 per cent contribution to team input'. Dexter qualified his criticism by saying Trueman 'bowled well and with great heart at all times', adding 'occasional discipline [was] sensibly received'. Dexter described Illingworth as 'selfish' and 'difficult to reprimand' and said Illingworth 'made only a 50 per cent contribution to team spirit'.

The Duke's report was even more damning, contradicting Trueman's claim they got on well:

A fine bowler when it suited him. The least easy person in the team to control. Slack in his ways and not prepared to willingly lend any help in off-the-field duties. His general manner off the field, although improved from earlier days, left a good deal to be desired.

Trueman was furious with MCC's sanction. He called it 'a filthy insult' and told journalists he would never again represent England. Unlike his similar outburst in 1954, he didn't care less if his words were reported. Trueman knew the selectors needed him more than he needed them and that he could more or less say what he liked. Popular opinion was also on his side. As news proliferated of the £50 penalty, Trueman was inundated with offers of recompense. The *Yorkshire Post* reported that a number of his admirers had sent £1 gifts to the paper. When told of their generosity, Trueman responded, 'Send them back, and thank them very much.' In Sydney, the *Sun Herald* revealed Australia's Cricket Supporters' Association had opened a fund for the Englishman. 'We want to share our appreciation of the one player who never failed to play bright cricket in the series,' said Association president Bruce Miles. 'We feel it a great pity that a cricketer who did so much for his side and entertained the crowds should be so penalised.'

Trueman's problems did not end there. Records show a bizarre row broke out after the tour concerning the failure of nine England players – himself included – to notify MCC whether they wanted a commemorative ashtray, cufflinks or a tie clip. MCC complained to the counties about the players' procrastination, demanding they take immediate action. Trueman was the last player to indicate the gift he wanted, requesting an ashtray. The mementos were not sent out until the following close season, a delay exacerbated because MCC got Trueman's initials wrong in their order to the silversmith. The governing body took further umbrage when Trueman and co. did not write back with thanks, once more urging the counties to act.

Trueman's failure to acknowledge MCC's gift is the subject of two letters from Yorkshire in the official tour papers at Lord's. The first, from club secretary John Nash, is addressed to Griffith and dated 1 January 1964:

Dear Billy

I am very sorry to receive your letter on 30 December informing me that Trueman has not been courteous enough to write and thank your President and committee for his memento of the Australian Tour.

I am afraid that for the last ten years, I have been trying to instil a few points of etiquette into this young man, but I am afraid my efforts have not been at all successful.

I will let both Sir William Worsley, our President, and Brian Sellers see your letter and perhaps they will both tell Trueman what they think about such conduct.

Sellers followed up with his own letter to Griffith on 6 January:

Dear Billy

I am very sorry to hear from John Nash that FST has not acknowledged the memento that was sent to him. I had no chance to have a word with him before but I certainly will.

I would suggest that in future he is left off the list as it's quite obvious he does not appreciate the mementos.

Having announced his intention to quit international cricket, Trueman backed down before the first Test against West Indies in

1963. Willie Watson, a member of MCC's selection committee, was sent to make sure he withdrew the threat, proving just how worried MCC was. Trueman agreed – in reality, he needed no persuading – and MCC released the following statement:

> *F.S. Trueman has decided to accept the decision of MCC with regard to the bonus for the recent MCC tour of Australia and, so far as he and MCC are concerned, the matter is closed.*

Despite his shabby treatment by MCC, Trueman needed little motivating for the visit of West Indies. The presence in the tourists' ranks of pace bowlers Wes Hall and Charlie Griffith was alone sufficient. Hall was regarded as the world's fastest bowler and Trueman saw himself as much in competition with his pace rivals as the tourists' batsmen. He took 34 wickets at 17 – his best series aggregate but not enough to prevent West Indies winning 2–1.

The tourists' leading wicket-taker was Griffith, who claimed 32 wickets at 16 – twice the number harvested by Hall. Trueman felt England would have won but for Griffith – but he wasn't paying tribute to his adversary's skill. Rather, he was among those who thought Griffith a 'chucker'. In the 1970s, Trueman revealed a conversation he overheard while relaxing in the bath during the second Test at Lord's. It was between Walter Robins, chairman of selectors, and umpires Syd Buller and Eddie Phillipson. 'I heard him [Robins] say that the umpires should under no circumstances call Griffith for throwing. When they objected he explained that there was a lot of worry about racial tension in London and he feared a riot might be sparked off if Griffith was no-balled.'

Trueman went on: 'When I came out of the bathroom Mr Robins was waiting for me. He had heard me moving about. He asked me if I had overheard the conversation so I had to admit that indeed I had. Then he solemnly asked me to give my word never to disclose it. I promised I would keep silent for a time but told him that I thought it should be made public eventually if only to point out the handicap England had been playing under. I must say I was amazed that the chairman of selectors could give such guidance to umpires.'

Trueman was in scintillating form at Lord's. He took 11 for 152 in a thrilling draw as England held out with one wicket remaining. In the third Test at Edgbaston, Trueman captured 12 for 119, his best Test haul, as England won by 217 runs. He finished the game with six wickets in twenty-four balls at a cost of four runs – an edged boundary by Lance Gibbs. 'With his hair escaping in dark and wild curls, and his run a thing of gathering strength, he took control,' wrote John Woodcock in *The Times*. 'He bowled with his brain as much as with his muscle. Beneath a clouded sky he moved the ball with late and vicious swing, off the seam he cut it like a rattlesnake, this way and that.' Trueman managed six wickets in the fourth Test at Headingley and three in the final game at the Oval, both of which West Indies won.

Despite his heavy workload, 1963 was statistically Trueman's best season. Not only did he top the Test averages but the first-class charts too, claiming 129 wickets at 15. His efforts helped Yorkshire – now captained by Brian Close – to their fourth Championship in five years. Trueman also recorded the fourth and final hat-trick of his career – and third against Nottinghamshire – when he dismissed Geoff Millman, Ian Davison and Bomber Wells in the game at Bradford. The feats that gave him most pleasure, however, came with the bat. Trueman scored his maiden first-class century (104) in Close's first Championship match in charge at Northampton. He hit another first-class hundred in the penultimate game of the season (100 not out) for an England XI against a Young England XI at Scarborough.

The innings against Northamptonshire left an indelible impression on a young Geoffrey Boycott. 'It was right at the start of my career and I hadn't scored a first-class century at that stage. I was out cheaply and was obviously in the team as a batsman, yet there was a fast bowler playing like Jack Hobbs. I thought, crikey, I'm not so sure whether I'm going to make it at this level. Fred played out of his skin. I remember he hit a fellow called Scott straight back over the sightscreen for six. I thought, wow. I'd found it tough going, hard work, and yet there was Fred whacking it for six. He made it look easy.'

It was not always thus. Ray Illingworth says the young Trueman could barely distinguish one end of a bat from the other. 'He was the worst batsman I have ever seen when he first started. If you bowled him four straight balls you could absolutely guarantee that three would knock his hob down. He was hopeless, so it's quite amazing how much he developed and what a fine striker of the ball he became.'

With hard work, Trueman developed into a useful tail-ender. He had a good eye and was a muscular hitter, particularly in the arc between long-on and mid-wicket – aka 'cow corner'. At Middlesbrough in 1965, Trueman struck Hampshire's Derek Shackleton – one of the game's most accurate seamers – for twenty-six in an over. Trueman came in at 47 for 7 and announced: 'What the bloody hell's going on, Shack? Are there snakes in the wicket?' He then hit him for two fours and three sixes.

As a batsman, Trueman had a distinct advantage over most of his peers. Few bowlers were bold enough to test him with a bouncer for fear of retribution, meaning he could play forward with uncommon confidence. One man foolish enough to bounce him during a county match was Somerset's Fred Rumsey. The game at Taunton in 1963 was drifting to a draw when Rumsey let him have one off the full run. Only a few overs of the fixture remained and Rumsey, the Somerset no. 11, assumed he wouldn't be needed to bat again. But after the last Yorkshire wicket fell, captain Harold Stephenson mischievously asked Rumsey to open the Somerset second innings. As Rumsey walked to the wicket, Trueman eagerly pawed the ground. But to the great amusement of the Yorkshire players and the greater relief of Rumsey, Close banished Trueman to the outfield and threw the ball to John Hampshire before giving the final over to Doug Padgett. When an enraged Trueman protested, Close said, 'You'll only end up killing him, Fred, and we could do without that kind of publicity.'

Trueman made one more first-class hundred – 101 not out against Middlesex at Scarborough in 1965. Although never an all-rounder, he scored 9231 first-class runs at 15.56, with twenty-six fifties to go with the hat-trick of hundreds. In addition to his batting, Trueman's fielding improved dramatically. The teenager who dropped a chance off Close in their first match at Cambridge held 438 first-class catches, becoming one of the best short legs in the business.

In the early sixties, whether standing at short leg, striking lower-order runs or sending back batsmen with indecent regularity, Trueman was at the top of his form. A career that underwent a rebirth under Ronnie Burnet reached a glorious apex for club and country. Trueman was the game's best pace bowler, its biggest celebrity, and heralded all points east to west. His professional life had never been better, and yet his private life had never been worse . . .

Give Me the Bloody Ball

The 1964 BBC film of Fred Trueman's life was notable not only for his extraordinary grilling of Sir Leonard Hutton. It was also remarkable for a scathing attack on Trueman by his wife that left him hurt and profoundly shaken. In anguished tones, Enid Trueman complained it was impossible to have a normal marriage and bemoaned their lack of quality time. Unscripted television at its most compelling, it was a poignant insight into a crumbling relationship.

The clip begins with Trueman arriving by sports car at his Scarborough home. In a moment of supreme naffness, he gets out the car, taps the roof and declares proudly, 'The old status symbol, this.' Trueman walks towards the front door where Enid and their only child, Karen, are waiting to greet him. All appears sweetness and light as they exchange hugs and kisses on the doorstep. Once inside it is a different story. After telling four-year-old Karen to run along, Fred and Enid sit opposite each other in armchairs. As with the Hutton exchange, the dialogue takes the form of Trueman as interviewer.

Fred (*smiling broadly*): Now, Mrs Trueman, what's it like being married to a professional cricketer?

Enid (*frowning*): Well, it isn't a bed of roses, I can tell you that for one thing.

Fred (*no longer smiling*): Er, do you ever hear from Freddie when he's thousands of miles away on these MCC tours?

Enid: Oh yes, regular. I get a letter nearly every day, every morning, nearly every other morning, and I always get phone calls, several times on a long tour, which are most expensive, and he's usually very incoherent.

Fred: Er, would you have preferred your husband to have been anything else but a professional cricketer?

Enid (*after a long pause*): Yes, I would have liked a nine-to-five husband, but I know in your case – er, in my husband's case – it's impossible because when you have a gift you have to expound this to its full extent and it was the only thing my husband could possibly have done in the circumstances.

Fred: It's obvious, of course, that a young woman, when she marries a man with a chosen profession, that she is going to have to make a lot of sacrifices.

Enid: Yes, it is usually obvious, but in our case it wasn't so obvious (*the camera pans to Fred, who returns a mortified glance*) because you've had – er, my husband's had – such a difficult kind of success.

(*Fred makes to speak*)

Enid (*cuts in*): Now you've interviewed me, Mr Trueman, let me ask you a couple of questions for a change.

(*Fred clears his throat and laughs nervously*)

Enid (*daggers drawn*): You know what it feels like to be a professional fast bowler, to get all the fame. How do you think it feels to be me?

Fred: I must admit, that is rather difficult, is that.

Enid: Well, would you change places with your wife?

Fred (*visibly riled*): In some ways, yes I would. In some ways, I wouldn't.

Enid: When you're married to a famous person, everyone expects it to be absolutely out of this world and marvellous. You have a car to drive, you have a nice house, nice clothes and you go to famous places and meet famous people, but that isn't all, that isn't the end of it. You can also be a very lonely person in the world on your own while your husband's thousands of miles away.

Fred: Yes, I quite agree with you there. It's very lonely and . . .

Enid: And you won't miss me half as much as I miss you because you've all the social contacts, the cocktail parties, the organised dinners. I have none of those things. I just have the telephone and the reporters and the menace.

Fred: Yes, well, I must admit there's many hours when I'm away that I sit down in my room and I probably watch television – especially if we're in Australia – and I sit and think of back home. And the time that I am really lonely, when I really like to be on my own, is probably when we're away for Christmas. And I sit and think, you know, what's Enid and the baby doing now? It's Christmas Day, and this is when I miss it. I miss both you and the baby when . . .

Enid (*interrupts and says angrily*): You miss the home life we don't have.

Fred: No, I miss you and the baby most of all Christmas mornings because it's great fun, sitting there with both of you, and we're all opening our presents and we're laughing and carrying on and thinking about different things. And it's these festive times when it really is lonely.

Enid: And that's the trouble with our life. We've too much fame and fortune and not enough family life.

Fred: I quite . . .

Enid (*cuts in sharply*): Not enough ordinary existence because people won't allow us to be ordinary.

Fred: I quite agree, darling, that once you come into this profession, your ordinary life, or your private life, has completely gone.

Enid: Finished. If you don't play cricket six days a week, then you play on Sunday for charity matches, and if you don't play enough charity matches they write and ask you to do more.

Fred: This is one of the calls, er, one of the unfortunate calls on famous people. They're expected to do these things and . . .

Enid: Ah, but when are they going to expect to stop?

Fred: Well, this again is one of the sacrifices one has to make because I always think to myself how lucky I am – and I thank God that I'm so lucky – to be able to run around on a cricket field and . . .

Enid: You're not lucky at all, you're gifted.

Fred: I'm still lucky this way, that I'm able to run around on a cricket field and I'm able to bowl. I'm able to have this fame. But even then, you must think, these charity matches I play are for little kids who can't walk, little kids that can't speak, they can't see, they can't hear. And the only thing they get out of life is probably watching these famous sportsmen of all walks of life on television.

Enid: I don't begrudge these people any of these things, I just want a little more home life for my little kid.

Fred (*with Churchillian grandeur*): Well, I can assure you, my darling, that this won't go on forever. Age beats everything – and one day it's bound to beat me.

The item ends incongruously as Enid, suddenly smiling, states, 'Well, as long as it doesn't do it this season with the Australians, then we won't worry about it too much.' The camera pans back to Fred, who runs his hand across his face and says, 'Phew, I feel as though I've been hit for six. After being shot down in flames like that, it's reminded me, I'm going shooting this afternoon . . .'

The programme, broadcast in May 1964, was the talk of the cricketing circuit for weeks. If Fred and Enid argued like that on national television, one can only imagine what happened when the cameras weren't there. Within weeks he'd moved out, vowing never to return. He booked into a hotel before staying with friends.

Although the first few years of their marriage were happy, the relationship worsened at the start of the sixties. The strain of long periods apart – in those days, cricket tours lasted six months or more – took a heavy toll. Some marriages survived; others didn't. With Fred and Enid, there was the additional pressure of the 'Curse of the Truemans' and his vast celebrity, which deprived them of valuable time together. A classic example came after Trueman's twelve-wicket haul against West Indies at Edgbaston in 1963. When Enid arrived at the team hotel, hoping they could go for a meal to celebrate, she couldn't get near him. A swarm of reporters and well-wishers swamped him. 'One day you won't have your bloody friends hanging on your back,' she shouted and, with that, turned on her heels.

For all the love they shared, Fred and Enid were contrasting characters. Enid had a taste for high life and parties, for dancing, socialising and having fun. Fred, for all his gregarious exterior and love of the limelight, was a self-confessed loner away from the game. Whereas Enid wanted to paint the town red, Fred had no appetite for skipping around dance floors. Very often he wanted nothing more than to put his feet up after a long day's play, watch television and smoke his pipe. Enid – young, attractive and naturally outgoing – was the antithesis of the stay-at-home wife. She wanted to experience every sway of the swinging sixties. 'Mum and Dad were different,' said daughter Karen. 'Mum wanted to do this, Dad wanted to do that. Mum was young, she was beautiful, she wanted to go out and have a good time, and she was prevented from doing that by Dad's career. She was too young to be held back.'

Living in Scarborough also posed problems. Rail connections were unreliable and it took Trueman a good two hours to drive to Yorkshire's home grounds such as Leeds and Sheffield. If Yorkshire were playing at Headingley, he'd leave Scarborough early in the morning and arrive home not much before bedtime. Enid, who had no desire to leave the area where she grew up, became naturally frustrated at their lack of a life.

Doug Insole recalls how Trueman struggled with his geographical isolation. 'When I was an England selector, Sunday was a rest day for the Test players and they could go home if they wanted – provided they were back by a certain time. The selectors took it in turns to have Sundays on duty and it was my turn one particular game when the team were staying at a hotel in Nottingham. When I got there in the afternoon, Fred was the only one around and I said, "Didn't you fancy going home, then, Fred?" He said, "Oh, living at bloody Scarborough, it's a hell of a long way, what with all the weekend traffic and what have you. I'm just too knackered to go home. It doesn't do me any favours with the missus, but I simply can't do it, Doug, lad." It was rather melancholy really. He'd been staying pretty much by himself all weekend, and I got the impression it wasn't the first time.'

Even when Trueman was at home, there were constant demands on his free time – invitations to speak at dinners, requests to play in charity games, enquiries from reporters, and so on. Over time, the arguments with Enid grew increasingly hostile and absurdly trivial. In her frustration, she might complain about the way Trueman set the table for dinner as minor rows mushroomed into major ones. Sometimes the rows got so bad that Trueman stormed out the house and slept in his car (he claimed to have spent the night in a Leeds car park before taking 5 for 0 against Australia at Headingley in 1961). For Trueman, the years of his cricketing pomp were an escape from 'the torture and the pain', a chance to get away from the never-ending quarrels.

Having intended to leave Enid once and for all, Trueman made one last attempt to make the marriage work. He returned to Scarborough a few months later to see Karen and was shocked to discover that Enid was pregnant. He moved back in, and in March 1965 Enid gave birth to twins, Rebecca and Rodney. Fred and Enid weren't so much papering over minor cracks, however, as major chasms. Trueman resigned himself to the fact it was never going to work and walked out for good a few weeks later. He and Enid lived apart before finally divorcing in 1972.

Reflecting on their marriage, Enid believes there was fault on both sides. 'I suppose it was six of one and half-a-dozen of the other. I think I should perhaps have been more sympathetic to Fred's situation. I was fiery at that time, he was fiery, and it was a case of yin and yang. Cricket always came first with Fred, and I sometimes got annoyed about it when I was young. I remember beating him over the head with tulips one year when he came home on our wedding anniversary about four hours late. I wrapped the tulips around his head. He said he'd been having a drink with the boys.

'Unfortunately, things went wrong between us and there were difficult periods. In sixteen years of marriage, I think we had about two Christmases together. Of course, Fred was such a huge celebrity that it was very difficult to have a normal marriage. I was a cricket widow, but despite all the problems, I loved him very much.'

Although his personal problems boiled over in 1964, it was the year Trueman broke cricket's equivalent of the four-minute mile. In August, he became the first man to 300 Test wickets – a milestone previously thought unreachable.

Trueman went into that summer's Ashes series with 284 Test wickets to his name. As befitted a man who knew every record in *Wisden*, he was entirely conscious of the looming landmark. The series began on a soggy note. The first Test at Trent Bridge was drawn after half the game was lost to the weather. Trueman had three victims in the first innings but went wicketless in the second, *Wisden* noting that despite employing five slips he 'preferred to test O'Neill with a series of short-pitched, harmless bouncers'. Half the second Test at Lord's was also washed out, Trueman taking six wickets in another draw to lift his total to 293.

There would have been no greater fairytale had he taken his 300th wicket in the third Test at Headingley. Instead, he had one of the worst games of his career and was largely responsible for the loss of the Ashes in the only match that produced a result. With Australia 178 for 7 in reply to England's first-innings 268, and with spinners Fred Titmus and Norman Gifford bowling well, Ted Dexter took the new ball. He thought Trueman and Jack Flavell more likely to finish off the tail – a move that backfired disastrously. Believing Peter Burge, Australia's no. 4, susceptible to the bouncer, Trueman plied him with a succession of short balls. The upshot was that Burge – 38 when the new ball was taken – walked off with 160 to his name by the time Trueman finally had him caught on the hook. Trueman's tactic was brainless – not least because Dexter refused him protection on the leg-side boundary for much of the innings. Burge simply picked off what *Wisden* termed 'a generous supply of medium-pace long hops' and Australia rallied to 389, ultimately winning by seven wickets.

Trueman was dropped for the fourth Test at Old Trafford – three

short of 300 and despite England having to win to stay in the series.
Had another pace bowler succeeded at Manchester, Trueman could
have found himself permanently jettisoned. Well into his thirty-
fourth year, he'd shown by his abject display at Headingley he could
no longer summon the pace of yore. In his mind's eye, Trueman
could still pin the likes of Burge t'bloody sightscreen but advancing
years had taken their toll.

The Old Trafford pitch was a batsman's paradise and neither quick
bowlers John Price and Fred Rumsey nor medium-pacer Tom
Cartwright got much joy – although Cartwright had remarkable first-
innings figures of 2 for 118 from 77 overs. Australia captain Bobby
Simpson made a triple century and England's Ken Barrington a
double as 600 played 600 in a tedious draw. Overall, Trueman was
left to reflect it was perhaps not a bad game to miss. He was recalled
for the final Test at the Oval, which Colin Cowdrey admitted several
England players thought would be his last.

After rain washed out the opening day, England posted a paltry
182. Propelled by Bill Lawry's 94, Australia ended day two on 245
for 5, well placed to gain a match-winning lead. Trueman had
bowled poorly and there seemed a real chance he wouldn't get his
300th wicket after all. According to Cowdrey, Trueman took the field
on the third day with none of his customary swagger. 'He was
understandably and visibly tense. He could not find his rhythm. He
knew that he was bowling badly. To add to his depression, Australia
were rapidly running out of batsmen to bowl at. The more anxious
he became, the worse he got, until, in the end, Ted Dexter had to
take him off. The words must have sounded like a life sentence to
Trueman. His jaw sank down on his chest as he walked from short
leg at one end to short leg at the other, cursing his luck and visibly
ageing.'

Just before lunch, Australia were 343 for 6 and Trueman had
bowled twenty-six wicketless overs for eighty runs. Dexter was
looking around for someone to bowl – and looking everywhere but
in Trueman's direction. Peter Parfitt, the Middlesex left-hander and
occasional off-spinner, recalled: 'There was only one over to go

The young Fred, right, with mother, Ethel, and eldest brother, Arthur. *Family Collection*

Scotch Springs, circled, where Trueman was born beside Maltby Main pit yard. *Courtesy of Maltby News*

Above: The brotherhood: Arthur and Fred. *Family Collection*

Below: Trueman's sister, Stella, who died of cancer in her early twenties. *Family Collection*

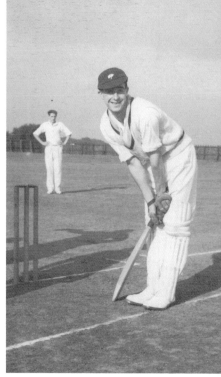

Above left: Trueman practises ahead of his first-class debut at Cambridge University. *Family Collection*

Above right: The stance that brought over 9000 first-class runs. *Family Collection*

Below: The classic, side-on action. Yorkshire versus Essex, 1951. *Family Collection*

The men who shaped Trueman's cricketing destiny. Arthur Mitchell *(top left)*, Cyril Turner *(top right)*, George Hirst *(bottom right)*, Maurice Leyland *(bottom left)*, Bill Bowes *(centre)*.

Bill Bowes presents Trueman with a testimonial from Maltby Urban District Council in recognition of his performances against India in 1952. *Daily Mail/Rex Features*

Ethel Trueman, right, at Maltby sports day.
Family Collection

Dick and Ethel Trueman outside
10 Tennyson Road, Maltby.
Family Collection

Trueman with Station Adjutant Flight Lieutenant L.S. Robinson at RAF Hemswell.

Daily Mail/Rex Features

Below left: Fred and Enid on their wedding day, March 1955.

Ross Parry Syndication/Yorkshire Post

Below: Playing for Lincoln City reserves, November 1952.

Family Collection

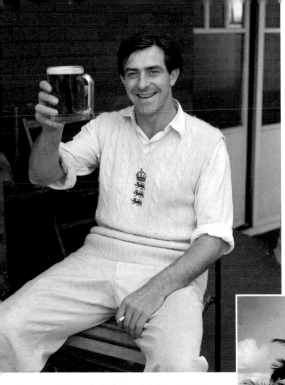

A pint and a cigarette after another match-winning performance, but the beer-drinking image was purely a myth, while Trueman preferred his smoke from a pipe.

Press Association Images

Below: An informal photograph of the MCC squad in the Caribbean, 1953-54. *Back row (l-r):* Dick Spooner, Willie Watson, Johnny Wardle, Charles Palmer (player/manager), Denis Compton, Ken Suttle, Godfrey Evans, Peter May. *Front row (l-r):* Fred Trueman, Tony Lock, Tom Graveney, Alan Moss, Len Hutton (captain), Brian Statham, Jim Laker, Trevor Bailey.

Above: A rare moment of relaxation during the stormy 1953-54 West Indies tour. Trueman in trunks at Montego Bay (Len Hutton is second from right).

The old firm:
Trueman and
Statham.

*Ross Parry Syndication/
Yorkshire Post*

Trueman working
as a furniture
salesman after
being left out of
the 1954-55 tour
of Australia.

Daily Mail/Rex Features

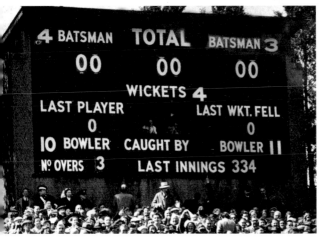

The scoreboard tells the story of Trueman's destruction of India on his Test debut at Headingley.

Bob Thomas/Popperfoto/ Getty Images

Yorkshire County Cricket Club, 1957. *Back row (l-r):* George Alcock (masseur), Johnny Wardle, Bob Platt, Mike Cowan, Ken Taylor, Cyril Turner (scorer). *Middle row (l-r):* Arthur Mitchell (coach), Ronnie Burnet, Brian Close, Doug Padgett, Fred Trueman, Jimmy Binks, Bob Appleyard, Maurice Leyland (coach). *Front row (l-r):* Peter Barrett (assistant secretary), Frank Lowson, Ray Illingworth, Willie Watson, Billy Sutcliffe (captain), Vic Wilson, John Nash (secretary). *Popperfoto/Getty Images*

Trueman goes past Pankaj Roy's outside edge en route to career-best Test figures of 8 for 31 against India at Old Trafford in 1952.

Central Press/Hulton Archive/ Getty Images

Trueman pounces at short leg to dismiss Keith Miller off the bowling of Jim Laker during England's Ashes-clinching victory at the Oval in 1953. *Daily Mail/Rex Features*

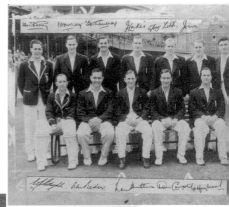

The England team pose before the 1953 Oval Test. *Back row (l-r):* Trevor Bailey, Peter May, Tom Graveney, Jim Laker, Tony Lock, Johnny Wardle (twelfth man), Fred Trueman. *Front row (l-r):* Bill Edrich, Alec Bedser, Len Hutton (captain), Denis Compton, Godfrey Evans. *Daily Mail/Rex Features*

Trueman embraces Colin Cowdrey who has taken the catch at the Oval in 1964 to give him his 300th Test wicket.

Allsport/Hulton Archive/Getty Images

The moment when the record
300th Test wicket was taken,
as Trueman has Australia's Neil
Hawke caught by Cowdrey.
Central Press/Hulton Archive/Getty Images

Trueman bursts on
stage at Club Fiesta in
Stockton-on-Tees during
his ill-fated stint as
a stand-up comedian.
*Central Press/Hulton Archive/
Getty Images*

With members of the *Dad's Army* cast. *(L-r):* Ian Lavender, Clive Dunn, Arthur Lowe, Arnold Ridley (partially hidden), Bill Pertwee, Fred Trueman, John Laurie. *Evening Standard/Getty Images*

Competitive to the end. Trueman bowling in later life. *Family Collection*

Fred and Veronica
on their wedding
day, February 1973.
Family Collection

'Nah then'.
Presenting pub
game show *Indoor
League* on Yorkshire
Television.
ITV/Rex Features

Above: Trueman arriving for the meeting that would confirm Geoffrey Boycott's sacking from Yorkshire in 1983. The move sparked a revolution that saw the committee overthrown and Trueman lose his seat.

Ross Parry Syndication/Yorkshire Post

Below: The *Test Match Special* team pose during the 1993 Trent Bridge Ashes Test. *Back row (l-r):* Peter Baxter, Neville Oliver, Jonathan Agnew, Bill Frindall, David Lloyd. *Front row (l-r):* Fred Trueman, Brian Johnston, Trevor Bailey.

David Munden/Popperfoto/Getty Images

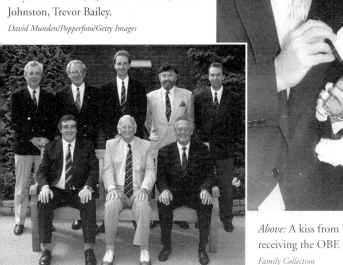

Above: A kiss from Veronica after receiving the OBE in 1989.

Family Collection

Trueman talks to the Duchess of Kent, daughter of former Yorkshire President Sir William Worsley. *Family Collection*

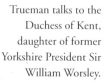

The strain shows on Rebecca's face during the blessing of her marriage to Damon Welch, son of film star Raquel, at Bolton Abbey in the Yorkshire Dales. The couple are flanked by their famous in-laws. *Family Collection*

'That bastard Boycott'. Trueman in action on the after-dinner circuit. *Family Collection*

Fred and Veronica at Mary's Tomb during a visit to the Holy Land in 1997. *Family Collection*

Below: Rebecca is all smiles at her wedding to Welborn Ferrene in 1998. *Family Collection*

Bottom left: Skipton-based brewers, Copper Dragon, created this ale dedicated to Fred Trueman to coincide with the unveiling of his statue.
Yorkshire Picture Library

Below: 'Gotcha!' Veronica at the statue to her late husband at Skipton's Canal Basin.
Family Collection

The England team applaud England's greatest fast bowler after news of Trueman's death casts a dark shadow over the one-day international against Sri Lanka at Headingley on 1 July 2006.
Andrew Yates/AFP/Getty Images

Trueman's coffin is driven to Bolton Abbey for his funeral on 6 July 2006.
Christopher Furlong/Getty Images

Flo Halifax and Dennis Trueman at a tribute dinner to their brother at Leeds's Queens Hotel in 2010.
Family Collection

before lunch and Edward Dexter said, "Come on, Parf, have a bowl."
I said, "It's pointless putting me on, Edward. We've got Fred here, he
desperately wants the 300 wickets and he's not going to be knackered
bowling one over." Anyway, Fred overheard and said, "Give me the
bloody ball. I'll f***ing bowl." '

Trueman practically snatched the ball from Dexter's grasp and
marked out his run at the pavilion end. His first three deliveries were
wildly inaccurate, reflecting his and the crowd's growing agitation.
The fourth was on target but kept out comfortably. Then, out of the
sultry summer's day, divine redemption . . .

Trueman's fifth ball bowled Ian Redpath and his sixth was edged
by Graham McKenzie to Cowdrey at slip. He had saved himself and
was on a hat-trick for the record 300. In the sort of party-pooping
moment only cricket can provide, there was no time for the hat-trick
delivery as the teams trooped off for lunch, leaving Trueman, the
large Oval crowd and a vast television and radio audience in
unbearable suspense.

Throughout the forty-minute interval, Trueman was in a state of
constant anxiety. 'He ate and drank nothing, merely sat down, stood
up, prowled around and then sat down before going through the
whole meaningless routine again,' recalled Cowdrey. 'He was rarely
a man to show his nerves but that day he could not conceal his
agitation. He wanted that 300th wicket more than anything in the
world.'

After Cartwright bowled the first over after lunch, Trueman ran
in for the hat-trick ball. He had planned to bowl the perfect, pitched-
up away swinger designed to clip the top of off stump but the
delivery was a ghastly anticlimax, passing well wide of off stump
without inducing the batsman, Neil Hawke, to play a stroke.
Trueman ploughed on without reward for another half-hour before
the new ball became available. Then, at 2.40 p.m. on Saturday 15
August 1964, came the immortal moment. In the commentary box,
John Arlott described it:

'Trueman with a bit of a scowl at the batsman. Doesn't even look friendly

towards his fieldsmen at the moment. In his thirty-first over, has two wickets – wants a third. Trueman in again. Bowls to Hawke, and Hawke goes forward, and he's caught. (Deafening applause) *There's the 300.* (Arlott pauses as the applause continues) *There was no nicer touch than Trueman congratulating Hawke.* (Applause) *Caught by Cowdrey.* (Applause) *Neil Hawke can never have come into the pavilion to a greater ovation in his life, but they weren't looking at him. Fred Trueman's 300th Test wicket – the first man in the history of cricket to achieve the figure, when Hawke played a half-hearted stroke outside the off stump to a ball that perhaps left him a little, took the outside edge and Cowdrey swooped on it, two hands. It was high in the air. Up went Trueman, up went the crowd. Stood to him, cheered him, and, as Hawke walked away, Trueman congratulated him. And the score – Australia 367 for nine.'*

Amid the euphoria, Arlott's eyes had slightly deceived him. The catch was taken not high to Cowdrey's right but down by the fielder's right knee. 'It was straightforward, but sharp, coming firmly at a good height just to my right, and I took it comfortably,' remembered Cowdrey. 'But, easy or not, it was several minutes before my heart resumed its normal pace. It would have been on my conscience for the rest of my days had I dropped that catch.' As the ball lodged in Cowdrey's hands, Trueman threw his arms skyward and feigned to keel over. His team-mates rushed to pat him on the back as he stood, relieved, in the centre of the pitch. Trueman humbly acknowledged the crowd, where his father was among the cheering throng. He rounded off the innings by having Grahame Corling caught at slip before the match petered out in a watery draw.

As he walked off the field, Trueman asked umpire Jack Crapp for the historic ball. There was no love lost between the pair, who never got on when Crapp played for Gloucestershire. According to *Guardian* writer Frank Keating, a friend of Crapp, the umpire first declined to hand the ball over and then almost certainly gave Trueman the wrong ball.

Writing after Trueman's death in 2006, Keating revealed: 'Just before he died a quarter of a century ago, Jack confided: "Always too full of himself was Fred, and in our playing days I'd not overcared for his 'bullying' attitude, especially his bowling nasty bouncers at some of the young county batsmen on the circuit. Anyway, once he'd got his famous 300th that day at the Oval, Trueman tried to grab the ball off me, saying he wanted it engraved for posterity. He began swearing at me, but I stuck to the letter of the law and said he'd first have to ask permission during the change of innings from the Surrey secretary Arthur McIntyre. He goes off in a huff to do this, and meanwhile, still annoyed in our umps' room, I just toss the ball into a large box in which there were already a dozen or so spare balls, all worn about the same. Then Fred barges in rudely demanding his souvenir, saying Mr McIntyre's given permission – so I simply go back to the box, dip in, and throw him the first ball that comes to hand, don't I? So I suppose there's a one-in-12 chance that Fred engraved the right ball."'

Keating said he dared not disclose the secret in Trueman's lifetime, knowing the bowler had had the treasured ball mounted. In his dotage, Trueman was even pictured kissing it in fond remembrance.

Right ball or not, Trueman was in a mood to celebrate after creating history. Following a quick drink with the Australians, with Hawke thrilled to have been the historic victim as 'it was the only way anyone will ever remember me', Trueman went to the *Black and White Minstrel Show* at London's Victoria Palace. The show, first broadcast on television in the late 1950s, featured singalong dance routines involving stereotypical blacked-up characters. It attracted more than eight million customers during a ten-year run, while a touring version played to more than six million people in holiday resorts. Intended as good, clean family fun, incorporating a blend of traditional American minstrel songs and music hall numbers, the show became a stage pariah as Britain became increasingly multi-racial. It was considered offensive and effectively banned, the last shows playing in 1987.

Trueman was a close friend of Leslie Crowther, the show's presenter, whom he'd met during the 1957 Scarborough Festival.

Crowther had been appearing in *The Fol-de-Rols*, a long-running variety show at Scarborough's Floral Hall, and Trueman and several Yorkshire players had gone along to watch. Afterwards, Trueman invited Crowther – a keen cricket fan – back to the team hotel for a drink. They struck up a friendship – Trueman was even godfather to Crowther's son, Nicholas – and got together whenever the Black and Whites came to Scarborough.

Trueman's trip to Victoria Palace on the night of his 300th was not allowed to pass unnoticed by Crowther. As the comedian told *The Cricketer*: 'We were delighted and flattered, and I was able to say at the end of the performance, "Ladies and gentlemen, in the wings stands a great man who has just achieved a record in cricket that has never been done before." I didn't even have to mention his name; they knew it alright. The whole house stood up, and to that standing ovation Fred came on in tears.'

Afterwards, Trueman returned to the team hotel in something of a daze. Tom Cartwright recalled: 'It was quite late, and Fred came in. He'd been feted quite a bit all day, and he sat down for about ten minutes. I suppose he was looking for somebody who was still up, and he just sat there quietly, as if he was trying to take it all in. It was an emotional few minutes. It was obvious that it meant an awful lot to him.'

Predictably, it did not seem to mean anywhere near as much to Yorkshire County Cricket Club. Once again, Trueman received a congratulatory telegram from every county but his own. Not until the following spring did Yorkshire mark his historic achievement. He was presented with a silver tea service at the annual pre-season lunch – only he wasn't. As Yorkshire president Sir William Worsley handed him the gift, he noticed it hadn't been inscribed. He told Trueman he would arrange for an appropriate message to be added, leaving an embarrassed Trueman to return to his seat empty-handed – much to his team-mates' amusement. A few months later, Trueman happened to be in the club office when a committee member casually pointed to the tea service standing in a corner. It had been there several weeks, gathering dust, shoved to one side, awaiting not renewed presentation – simply Trueman's collection.

In the aftermath of his 300th wicket, Trueman was asked whether he thought anyone would beat his record. 'I don't know,' he laughed, 'but if they do, they'll be tired.' His words echoed those of Yorkshire and England all-rounder George Hirst, asked the same question after scoring 2000 runs and taking 200 wickets in 1906. What once seemed impossible has today become commonplace. At the time of writing, twenty-four bowlers had reached the 300 mark, five of whom had gone on to 400, two to 500, one to 600, one to 700 and one – Sri Lanka's Muttiah Muralitharan – to 800. Trueman's final tally of 307 wickets stood as a record for twelve years before being beaten by West Indian Lance Gibbs. Somewhat uncharitably, Trueman noted Gibbs 'crawled' past his record and that the off-spinner 'bought' his wickets whereas Trueman 'took' his. Just as no one can take away from Neil Armstrong the distinction of being the first man on the moon, however, so Trueman's name will forever be associated with that day at the Oval when he became the first bowler to climb cricket's Everest.

Although no longer the force of his heyday, Trueman was still England's leading wicket-taker in 1964 with 17 at 23.47, but it wasn't enough to earn him a place on the winter tour to South Africa. Once again he was shattered and stung. According to Parfitt, there was a strong rumour that Mike Smith – who'd taken over the captaincy from Dexter – didn't think he could handle Trueman. Cartwright also detected an undercurrent. 'He desperately wanted to go, but I think there might have been a feeling in some quarters that, with a five-month tour, if he wasn't playing in the Tests, he might have created some distraction.' England opted for pace bowlers John Price and David Brown, with support from Cartwright and Trueman's Yorkshire team-mate, Tony Nicholson. When Nicholson withdrew through injury, England turned not to Trueman but to Sussex's Ian Thomson.

In reality, both Trueman and England had a case. Trueman could point to a new world record, twelve years' international service and

a return in 1964 of 100 first-class wickets at 21, which helped
Yorkshire finish fifth in the Championship. England could argue that
Trueman had cost the Ashes with his profligate display at
Headingley, that his pace was in decline and that Cartwright that
season had taken 134 wickets at 15, Nicholson 76 at 15, Thomson
116 at 16 and Brown 86 at 19. Only Price, with 76 at 28, had an
inferior average to Trueman. According to J.M. Kilburn, Trueman
'could not evade the touch of time's finger' and 'was no longer
guaranteed to dominate early batsmen or bring tail-enders to
summary dispatch'. However, Kilburn added, 'Though Trueman
was clearly not the fast bowler England and Yorkshire wanted in
1964, his advocates could reasonably ask who was better.'

One man adamant Trueman should have gone is Geoffrey
Boycott. 'It was my first tour and Fred was better than some who
went, definitely. To my mind, he should have played a lot more
for England and the only reason he didn't was because some people
thought he was a handful. But a bad boy? I would say Fred was
different, that's all. I mean, what did he do, rob a bank, hit old
ladies over the head? He said a few words, but so what? He was
playing professional sport and fast bowling is all about aggression.
That's what you want. That's the sort of character you want in
your team. I don't know what England wanted. I'm sad Fred didn't
play another twenty-five Tests or something and take more
wickets.'

Instead of plying his trade in apartheid South Africa, Trueman
toured Jamaica with Rothmans Cavaliers. The Cavaliers were an ad
hoc side that usually comprised Test players whose countries were
not touring, or who were not required for their Test team. They
played an important role in the evolution of one-day cricket,
contesting forty-over games against county sides on Sunday
afternoons in a forerunner of the John Player League. While the
Cavaliers were in action in the Caribbean, England's bowling
department in South Africa was decimated by injury. Price strained
a stomach muscle, Brown damaged his heel and Cartwright broke a
bone in his foot. The situation was so dire that Somerset's Ken

Palmer – out coaching in Johannesburg – was drafted in for the final Test at Port Elizabeth.

When news of Palmer's selection reached West Indies, it was more than Trueman's dignity could bear. 'Look at this,' he fumed, brandishing his newspaper in a state of high dudgeon. 'Look who's opening the bowling for England in the Test in South Africa – Ian Thomson and Kenny bleeding Palmer. And here am I bowling for bloody cigarette coupons.'

Just as Trueman never forgave Len Hutton for leaving him at home in 1954–55, so he never excused Mike Smith for not taking him to South Africa. Richard Hutton recalled: 'Many years later Fred got an invite to Mike Smith's seventieth birthday party, which Warwickshire were putting on. He replied to the invitation with the words, "He left me at home in 1964–65 – and I'm stopping at home now."'

Trueman played two more Tests before the final curtain fell. In 1965, New Zealand and South Africa visited for three Tests apiece, Trueman appearing in the first two games against the Kiwis. He took six wickets at 39 but the touch of time's finger had now become a squeeze. In what proved his last Test appearance, at Lord's, Trueman was described in the *Guardian* as one of the England attack's 'honest plodders . . . who, in his time, has scared the pants off every batsman from Woolloongabba to Old Trafford. But not any longer . . . By last night the experts were saying that not even he could cope with another Test.' The paper added that if Trueman had been 'a careful man', he would have retired after his 300th Test wicket. 'That would have been the moment to quit . . . The great men of cricket, however, have a habit of going out in anti-climax. When Bradman played his last Test innings he didn't survive an over and he didn't get a run.'

As he was fond of telling anyone who'd listen, Trueman finished with 307 Test wickets at 21.57. Rather than bask in the splendour of those statistics, he blamed those who'd denied him chances to improve them. 'I will always have a chip on my shoulder that I should have played a lot more times for England,' he wrote. 'I estimate I was robbed of at least thirty-five Tests. I should have been the first man to play a hundred times for England. Instead, my record was not as good as it could have been.'

Although 1965 saw an anticlimactic end to his international career, Trueman finished fifth in the national averages with 127 wickets at 14. But his relationship with Yorkshire further deteriorated. In June, he was reprimanded after agreeing to write a book and produce newspaper articles without the club's consent. He was warned another breach of contract could result in dismissal. A few weeks later, another storm erupted when he was accused of 'not trying' by Yorkshire chairman Brian Sellers during the Roses game at Bramall Lane and suspended for one match. After his dismissal from Taunton in 1962, it was the greatest humiliation of his county career. Sellers reckoned Trueman should have made a better attempt to run out Harry Pilling from his position at mid on, but Trueman – who'd just bowled flat out for an hour – protested he was still in the process of putting on his sweater when Tony Nicholson ran in to bowl. Sellers rubbished the excuse and told Trueman that one more offence and he'd be finished by the club. He called him 'a bastard' in front of his team-mates.

Trueman recalled: 'Sitting there in the dressing room was my eldest brother Arthur, a big, proud man. The chairman was the luckiest man in the whole of Yorkshire that day because Arthur is a hard man and very strong from working in the pit and proud of his younger brother, and it would not have surprised me if he had struck him there and then. I managed to smooth things over. If he had said that a few years before I would probably have thumped him myself, but by then I was the senior professional and had to try to set an example.'

However, Richard Hutton says Trueman was scared stiff of Sellers. 'In spite of all his bluster, there were some people Fred could be very timid towards – and Brian Sellers was one of them. For all he would say, "That bugger, I shall tell him next time I see him," I think Fred was quite fearful of Brian Sellers. One day, Fred was moaning about Sellers and, just at that moment, Sellers walked into the dressing room. Fred looked up and said meekly, "Hello, boss."'

Six foot tall and strongly built, Sellers ruled Yorkshire with an iron fist. A modest batsman and brilliant close fielder, he'd led Yorkshire to six titles in the 1930s and was the county's cricket chairman for many years, also serving as a Test selector. 'Brian Sellers was a strict disciplinarian but he could be very funny,' added Hutton. 'We had a bowler called Mel Ryan who was known throughout the county game as being extremely well-hung. One day, we beat Leicestershire at Park Avenue and Mel got six wickets. Sellers came into the dressing room and said, "Well done, boys. Well done, everybody. Well done, Mel. Is it thee cock that's done it?"'

The season ended happily for Trueman and Yorkshire. Although the side finished a disappointing fourth in the Championship, they won the Gillette Cup with a 175-run triumph over arch-rivals Surrey. Trueman took important wickets throughout the tournament – including the first three to reduce Surrey to 27 for 3 in the Lord's final, a match remembered for Boycott's scintillating 146. Chasing 318, Surrey were blown away by Trueman and Ray Illingworth (5 for 29).

An interested spectator was the American film star Gregory Peck, who visited the dressing rooms and talked with the players. 'Fred decided it would be a good idea to take Gregory Peck for a walk around the ground,' remembered Don Wilson. 'Normally, Fred never liked doing that sort of thing because he'd invariably be mobbed. I tagged along and on the way round, we bumped into my mother and father, who never normally came to watch me play. Fred said to my mother, "Mary, I'd like to introduce you to Gregory Peck." My mother looked up at him and said, "And which county do you play for, Mr Peck?" Next thing I know, Gregory Peck is picking my mother off the ground in absolute wonderment, while Fred is lying on the floor howling with laughter.'

After the match, Trueman again found himself on stage at the *Black and White Minstrel Show* at Victoria Palace. This time he had with him the Gillette Cup trophy and his Yorkshire team-mates, who wandered on to a standing ovation. Over the years, the Yorkshire players developed a strong bond with the show's stars, Wilson and Philip Sharpe even spending a week working for the Black and Whites as dressers. The pair also put together a routine based on the show, which the Yorkshire players sometimes performed after games. 'We were like one of the old Glee Clubs where groups of men from a factory got together and formed a choir,' recalled Wilson. 'Sharpey was a wonderful pianist and could write music. But he was very finicky. He had this damn tuning fork and he used to go round telling us where we were getting it wrong. A lot of the grounds we played at used to have marquees around the boundary, like they do at festivals, and after the game someone would invite the boys in for a drink. And they'd always ask us to sing. Most of the lads joined in at one time or other. Fred loved religious songs and, if he was with us, it had to be the twenty-third Psalm.'

Such happy diversions created a special bond between the Yorkshire players of the 1960s, underpinning their on-field success. That isn't to say there weren't arguments – Trueman admitted there were 'rows galore' – but they were the product of an open dressing room under Brian Close. 'Closey had a very healthy attitude that if you said something that was worth listening to, he'd take it on board,' said Boycott. 'Even youngsters like me were encouraged to join the debate; we weren't told to shut up because we were junior. Yes, there were arguments along the way, but people get them out of proportion sometimes. It was a strong dressing room – not a bitchy one – and everything said was for the good of the team.'

No one was allowed to get ideas above his station – not even Trueman. 'If we'd had a poor morning, people might tell Fred he'd bowled like a f***ing drip,' added Boycott. 'That would soon get him going. He'd invariably reply that he was bowling at the wrong f***ing end. There was a lot of back-and-forth stuff – "You should have taken that catch", "There's no way I could have got it", that type of thing, but behind it all was a determination to win.'

Trueman thrived in this challenging environment. He enjoyed the banter and good-natured ribbing. Although the biggest star in the Yorkshire side, he was one of the boys and respected by all. In a dressing room packed with colourful characters, he was the liveliest and larger than life. 'Fred had the most enormous presence in the dressing room,' said Richard Hutton. 'If he wasn't telling jokes he was smoking like a furnace, and he had clothing and fan mail all over the shop. In fact, I have a classic vision of him in the Yorkshire dressing room. I can see him now standing at the window in his Yorkshire cap, jockstrap, cricket socks and heavily toe-capped cricket boots. He'd have a pipe in his mouth and a pair of binoculars to his eyes. He'd be looking around the crowd to see what he could find. He'd say something like, "Bloody hell, sunshine, come and look at this." He'd have spotted an attractive woman in the stands.'

Due to his workload, Trueman often dozed in the dressing room. 'He'd frequently nod off during the lunch break,' said Boycott. 'He'd perhaps have a ham sandwich first and a pot of tea, and the tea would always be laced with sugar, and then he'd tell us all to f*** off while he had a little kip.' John Hampshire, who drove Trueman to away games, recalled: 'Sometimes he fell asleep as soon as we left the ground. If he didn't, he'd be regaling me with tales of his various adventures.'

Trueman spent more time in the opposition dressing room than he did in Yorkshire's. It was an important part of his psychological warfare. A 'Fred session' became an accepted part of games involving the county – as customary as the pre-match toss. 'He'd walk in, look around and casually announce the number of wickets he was going to take,' said Illingworth. 'If a young lad was playing, he'd say something like, "I don't know you, sunshine. Can you hook? You'll be getting plenty of chance out there." Sometimes he drew an imaginary cross on the batsman's forehead. I think it used to intimidate some players, but folk got used to it after a while. The more experienced pros would say to the youngsters, "Look, Fred will be in this morning. He'll try to wind you up with this, that and the other." But it was always very funny. In fact, he spent so much time with the opposition we used to throw his kit bag in after him.'

Doug Insole says opposing teams liked these light-hearted visits. 'I think a lot of players looked forward to them, but the most amazing thing was grown men would actually hold their hands up when Fred said, "Right, which of you buggers hasn't played against me before?" All of a sudden, about four blokes would shoot their hands up and say, "I haven't, Fred." And he'd say, "Well, that's four in the bag for me already, then."'

One of Trueman's favourite targets was Somerset batsman Peter Wight. 'Now Peter was a bloody good player,' said Close. 'He came from the West Indies and got hundreds against a lot of good bowlers – Brian Statham, Peter Loader, he hit them all over the place. But Fred always got the better of him somehow, and whenever we played Somerset he would wander into their dressing room, look around and see Peter sitting in the corner. Fred would say, "Are you playing today, Peter?" and Peter – who had this squawky little voice – would say, "Yes, Fred, I'm playing." Fred would say, "Good, that's two wickets I've got before I've got changed."'

Bob Platt recalled: 'The only time he got cross with me was when I got Peter Wight out at Hull. He said, "What the f***ing hell are you doing? I haven't even bowled at him yet.' Ironically, Wight's solitary success against Yorkshire came on the occasion Trueman was sent home from Taunton. With his nemesis absent, Wight struck 215; in his other thirty first-class innings against the county, he averaged 14.85.

Bravado came as naturally to Trueman as bowling fast. If he wasn't telling opponents what he was going to do, he was telling team-mates what he'd done to opponents. Successes were embellished with elaborate detail as to how this ball had pitched leg and hit off, or vice versa. Barren spells were invariably the product of batsmen's outrageous fortune or the failing eyesight of incompetent umpires. 'I remember one of my first Tests,' said Boycott. 'We were talking in the dressing room beforehand about the Australian batting line-up – Simpson, Lawry, O'Neill, Booth, Burge – five terrific batsmen. Anyway, every time a new name came up Fred would say, "Oh aye,

I'll just slip him a couple of outswingers and a nip-backer and he'll be f***ing gone." Or "That bugger doesn't like the bouncer, so I'll give him one of those and then slip in an outswinger and he'll nick the f***er to slip." I thought, bloody hell, sounds all right, this. Sounds like we should have them out in next to no time. Anyway, when they batted, they never looked like getting out – and Fred never looked like taking a wicket.'

Jimmy Binks, who made 412 consecutive Championship appearances for Yorkshire from his debut in 1955 to his retirement in 1969, remembers a game against Kent at Middlesbrough. 'Colin Cowdrey was in the Kent side and some of us in the dressing room were saying, "Gee, this guy's a really good batsman."

'Fred said, "Rubbish, I'll fill his mouth with leather."

'I said, "What are you going to do, Fred, hit him with your handbag?" He chased me out the dressing room.'

Trueman's apparent ability to make every ball talk became a standing joke on the county circuit. In his eyes, each delivery did something special, as though propelled by Merlin the magician. Richard Hutton once asked Trueman whether he'd ever bowled a straight ball. 'Aye, it were a full toss,' came the lightning reply. 'It went straight through Peter Marner like a stream of piss and knocked out middle stump.' Hutton achieved the only known instance of rendering Trueman speechless. 'Fred, would you call yourself a modest man?' he enquired as the Yorkshire players collapsed in stitches.

Trueman's bluster was ripe for ribbing. Illingworth recalls his reaction to a failed lbw appeal during a game at Bradford. 'Fred was in a right old state, saying, "How the bloody hell could that have missed? I mean, it was a dead straight ball that pitched off-and-middle and did nowt." I said, "Hang on, Fred, you've never bowled a straight ball in your life." The rest of the lads burst out laughing.'

Mike Cowan once teased Trueman after a match against Somerset. 'I'd managed to pick up a few wickets and Fred said to me in the dressing room, "Well bowled, sunshine."

'I said, "Cheers, Fred."

'He said, "What happened?"

'I said, "Well, with the first one, I swung it in late and it took leg stick. The second one pitched leg, moved away and took off."

'Of course, the lads twigged what I was doing and started laughing, but Fred didn't catch on until about the fifth wicket. Eventually, he said, "You bastard." He picked up a boot and let fly and I just managed to get out the way before the boot thudded into the plaster behind me. When I looked round, you could see the heel and stud marks in the plaster. That could have been my bloody face.'

Cowan, however, gave as good as he got. 'Fred had a habit of rubbing Vaseline inside his thighs because his jock-strap used to shake. There used to be a big jar of it on the massage table before we went out to play, and he used to dive his fingers in. So I got a spatula, took the top off the Vaseline and put in some Fiery Jack cream. Fred put his fingers in as usual and rubbed it into his thighs. It was a bloody hot day and he started to complain of this burning sensation between his legs. A couple of the lads knew what I'd done, but we didn't tell Fred because he'd have chinned me. Oh, we pissed ourselves.'

By 1966, Trueman had growing cause to exaggerate his powers, but he still wanted to bowl as often as possible. This caused tension between him and Close. Whereas previous captains used Trueman as shock bowler and stock bowler rolled into one, Close adopted a different tactic. He felt it best to use him in short, sharp bursts, thereby increasing his wicket-taking power. This led to a spectacular bust up at the Scarborough Festival in 1964, with Trueman needing four wickets to reach 100 for the season. When Close took him off after an opening spell of 1 for 18, Trueman was furious. He stomped off to deep fine leg, slagging off the captain to anyone in earshot. MCC had reached 132 for 7 when Close said, 'Come on, then, Fred, finish it off.'

'Bollocks,' came the reply. 'You can stick your f***ing ball. I'm not bowling.'

'Fair enough,' said Close, deadpan. 'Take your sweater off again, Illy.' Trueman got the other three wickets in the second innings.

Throughout their careers, Trueman and Close had a love-hate relationship. Close wrote that Trueman 'wasn't exactly my cup of tea' when they made their debuts in 1949, but they got on better as the years progressed. Each respected the other's skill. Close thought Trueman the best English fast bowler of his generation, while Trueman felt Close had more natural talent than Garry Sobers. Unlike previous captains, Close had not the slightest qualm about standing up to Trueman. Whereas the likes of Norman Yardley and, to a lesser extent, Vic Wilson gave him his head, Close kept Trueman firmly in check.

Six foot tall and utterly fearless, Close was English cricket's Rocky Marciano. He barely flinched when beaten black-and-blue by Wes Hall and Charlie Griffith in 1963 – nor when recalled, aged forty-five, to face their fearsome successors Michael Holding and Andy Roberts. Such was Close's bravery when fielding at short leg, the comedian Eric Morecambe quipped: 'In future, I shall always be able to tell when the cricket season begins – all I have to do is listen to the sound of Brian Close being hit by a cricket ball.'

Trueman was wary of Close's physique. Although he'd still argue with his captain, still tell him to 'bugger off' when necessary, he knew full well that Close was boss. 'Fred never pushed Closey too far because he knew Closey could have thumped him if necessary,' said Bryan Stott. 'Fred knew he couldn't play fast and loose with Brian.' Bob Platt remembers the pair clashing at Oxford. 'They had a row about something in the showers. Next thing I know, Closey's turned on Fred and Fred's sprinted bollock-naked through the dressing room up to the dining room.'

Close admits they had differences of opinion but says Trueman was relatively easy to handle. 'Fred missed a lot of Tests he should have played because people couldn't handle him, but I always found him fairly straightforward. You had to stand up to Fred, and, if you did, he took his place. If he'd been properly led at the start of his career, he'd have played a lot more for England. We argued about tactics and things like that, but it was only because we wanted to win.'

Trueman's tactical advice was not always welcomed. Close preferred the suggestions of Illingworth, who acted as buffer between captain and team. 'Knowing Brian so well, I could say what I wanted to him,' said Illingworth. 'The lads would come to me if there was a problem. He would accept suggestions from me, as his mate, but he was less receptive to Fred or others. I could give Brian a kick up the backside.' Close was utterly obsessed with the game and constantly dreamt up ways to improve. If an idea came to him, he'd ring a player regardless of time of day or night. Once, struck by a sudden flash of inspiration as to why Tony Nicholson was having problems with his action, Close rang him at two o'clock in the morning. 'Skipper, do you know what time it is?' enquired a bleary-eyed Nicholson. Close turned to his wife and said, 'Vivienne, Tony wants to know what time it is – clock's on your side.'

Under Close, Yorkshire won a hat-trick of Championships from 1966. Although Trueman was on the way down, he still managed 101 wickets at 17 that year, 57 at 22 in 1967 and 46 at 22 in 1968. Yorkshire's success was a genuine team effort under a captain who put the game first, his side second and himself last. Runs flowed from such as Boycott, Doug Padgett, Hampshire, Sharpe and Ken Taylor; Binks was one of the all-time great wicketkeepers; Close, Illingworth and Hutton provided wonderful all-round contributions; Trueman, Nicholson and Don Wilson were key performers with the ball, while the fielding – epitomised by Sharpe's stunning work at slip – was superlative. In all, from 1959, Yorkshire won seven Championships and two Gillette Cups in the space of ten years.

Trueman could still produce flashes of the old fire, such as when he skulled Trevor Bailey at Leyton and apologised with the classic, 'Sorry, Trev, there are plenty more I'd rather have hit than thee,' but the bouncers carried more pathos than poison. This was brought home in May 1968, when Trueman was made twelfth man against Warwickshire at Middlesbrough. Trueman was incandescent – not least because he claimed to have heard of Close's decision from Warwickshire captain Alan Smith. 'After all the service I've given to this county, to be treated like this is diabolical,' he told the *Daily Mail*.

Chris Old, the man chosen to replace Trueman, recalled: 'Fred was really upset but he was tremendously encouraging. He said, "Don't worry, lad, it's nothing to do with you. Just go out there and do your best." I didn't know what to say, to be honest.'

There was a final flourish before the fire burned out. Due to Close's unavailability through injury and Test duties, Trueman led Yorkshire seven times during the 1968 season. This included a game against the Australians at Bramall Lane when Yorkshire beat the tourists for the first time since 1902, giving Trueman what he termed his 'ultimate pleasure'. After Trueman won the toss, Yorkshire scored 355 for 9 declared. Australia subsided to 148 in reply (captain Bill Lawry 58) as Trueman contributed three wickets, three catches and a run-out. When Australia followed on, Hutton claimed the key wicket of Lawry with a superb yorker, opening the door for Trueman (three wickets) and Illingworth (four) to dismiss Australia for 138 as Yorkshire completed an innings win. 'That was undoubtedly one of Fred's greatest moments,' said Hutton. 'In many ways, it set the seal on his career. To lead Yorkshire to glory against the old enemy – it didn't really get much better than that.'

Twenty-five years later, Hutton was not a little surprised to find Trueman taking credit for the all-important dismissal of Lawry. 'The *Daily Telegraph* was looking back on a series of sporting events and, on this particular day, was concentrating on our victory against the Australians. Fred was quoted at length in the piece and one of his remarks was, "I knew that as soon as I got Bill Lawry out we were through 'em." My eyes almost dropped on the newspaper. I couldn't believe it. So I wrote to the sports editor with a correction. I thought that's absolutely bloody typical of Fred because, if there's any credit to be grabbed, he'll grab it.'

Following Yorkshire's victory, Jack Fingleton wrote that Trueman would have made a fine Test captain. 'He led Yorkshire in this game from the front, taking wickets, taking catches, and captaining the side with rare generalship. Here, I also thought, was one who could have led England with distinction. He knows the moves, he is a canny thinker, but, then, in all countries, bowlers are strongly believed not to possess the wherewithal to lead their national team. It is an odd belief.'

Trueman led Yorkshire in twenty-eight first-class games – all between 1965 and 1968 when Close was indisposed. Yorkshire won sixteen, drew eight and lost four of those matches, which brought Trueman 92 wickets at 18. 'I'm not sure Fred would have made a good permanent captain,' said Hutton. 'His captaincy was based on charisma and magnetism in that he got everybody firing behind him. I don't know whether that could have been a long-lasting thing. I certainly don't think he was tactically gifted – it was all charisma, with his chest puffed out and that sort of thing.' Don Wilson concurs. 'Fred would have made a poor permanent captain. He needed someone like Closey to say, "Hey, bugger off, Fred." He needed strong men behind him. That's how you got the best out of him.'

Former Yorkshire and England off-spinner Geoff Cope, however, profoundly disagrees. 'Fred would have been a brilliant permanent captain. Not only did he lead by example, he had that ability to make you feel good about yourself. I once played a second-team game at Jesmond and had to travel down afterwards to join the first team at Bath, where Fred was acting skipper. I got there at something like two in the morning and Fred was asleep at reception, waiting for me. He – the great Fred Trueman – had been waiting to make sure that I – a young player with no track record – had arrived all right. The night porter woke him and Fred told me to stay in bed an extra half-hour in the morning to make sure I got as much rest as possible. Then, next morning, he came straight over and said, "How do you feel? Are you tired? Are you fit to play? I know you're running on adrenaline, but be honest with me." He gave the impression he was right there with you, which is exactly what you want from a leader.'

Trueman coveted the Yorkshire captaincy. He relished standing in and the extra responsibility. What's more, Close knew it and felt insecure. He sensed that Trueman was breathing down his neck. 'I remember one morning at Bradford in 1968,' said Hutton. 'Brian was out injured and Fred was acting captain. Brian came into the dressing room and said, "I would like to remind you all that I'm still the Yorkshire captain." It seemed a pointed thing for Closey to say.'

Close's insecurities were hardly eased by an incident that almost shattered his relationship with Trueman. One of Yorkshire's most devoted supporters was Betty O'Neill, who ran a business in Cornwall. Every year she sent five pounds to wherever the team were playing their first game so the players could enjoy a drink on her. In 1968, her money arrived at Harrogate just after Yorkshire had left town. It was redirected to Taunton, only to get waylaid. The cash finally turned up at Close's home six weeks later on the day before he was due at a Yorkshire committee meeting.

When Close turned up for the meeting, Brian Sellers immediately mentioned Mrs O'Neill's cheque and accused him of 'mis-appropriating funds intended for the team'. Close reached into his pocket, pulled out the cheque and angrily threw it on the table. 'Is this the money you're talking about?' he snapped. 'It arrived at my house this morning, as you can see by the postmark.'

Close suspected Trueman had dropped him in it because he'd been in close contact with the committee as acting captain. When he voiced this view, it was hastily shot down. 'One of the committee, Ronnie Burnet, very quickly said, "It hasn't come from Fred,"' wrote Close. 'He said it just a bit too quickly. I was sure I was right. And the meeting finished in no time at all after that . . . I went up to the dressing room, caught Fred's eye and threw Mrs O'Neill's note and cheque on to the table, telling him, "Fred, there's that cheque I've spent." No comment.

'At close of play, I went for a drink with the lads and sure enough, my two most senior players, Ray Illingworth and Jimmy Binks, echoed my thoughts: "The stirring must have come from Fred."

'I saw Fred and told him, "If you want my job so badly, you can have it."'

Close believes there was a simple reason for Trueman's actions. 'He was over the top as one of the great fast bowlers of all time but he did not want to go out of cricket. He could try his hand at medium-paced seaming but the only way he was going to be able to

command a regular place for any length of time was as captain.'
Trueman, however, was temperamentally unsuited to medium pace.
Although he could reduce his speed when necessary, such as when
he destroyed Australia at Leeds in 1961, he was, as John Arlott noted,
'not merely a fast bowler in achievement, he was a fast bowler in the
mind and in the heart'.

With Chris Old hammering ever louder on the door, Trueman
sensed the way the wind was blowing. He'd been turned down for
a second benefit and, in November 1968, announced his retirement
from first-class cricket, thereby ending the stormiest of careers with
the softest of whimpers. Unlike Brian Statham, who'd revealed in
August that 1968 would be his last season, Trueman slipped away
quietly, much to his fans' disappointment.

In truth, there'd been a heavy hint in what proved to be his final
county match. As the Yorkshire players left the field at Scarborough
on Friday 13 September 1968, having failed by one wicket to beat
MCC, the brass band struck up the Harry Parr-Davies number 'Wish
Me Luck as You Wave Me Goodbye'. 'When Fred walked into the
dressing room, there were tears streaming down his face,' said Don
Wilson. 'It was obvious he'd reached the end of the road.'

Rather than face emotional outpourings on every ground, which
is exactly what happened to Statham, Trueman waited for the season
to settle before driving to the home of Yorkshire president Sir
William Worsley to tender his resignation. Worsley was shocked.
He told Trueman he could go on bowling at lesser pace and revealed
the club was to hold a meeting the following week at which
Trueman would probably be offered the captaincy, proving how
right Close was to have felt insecure. Although Trueman wanted the
job more than anything, he'd simultaneously given details of his
retirement to the *Sunday People* and it was too late to stop the presses.
'By a couple of hours I missed being captain of Yorkshire,' he
reflected. 'I'll regret it for the rest of my life.'

There was just one task to complete. Trueman turned his car in
the direction of Maltby and went to see his father. When he arrived
at Tennyson Road, Dick Trueman was sitting in the same chair

where, twenty years earlier, he'd waited for his son to return home with his Yorkshire cap. 'I could see he was deeply moved again,' said Trueman. 'He thought for a bit, then looked at me and said, "Well, I've been very fortunate. I was there to see you start playing cricket and I've lived to see you finish. I can die happy now. And I'll never watch Yorkshire play again.' He never did. Less than two years later, Dick Trueman passed away at the age of seventy-six.

In recognition of his sterling service, Yorkshire gave Trueman a Charles II silver cruet set as a farewell present. Unbelievably, they asked him to pay £120 towards the £220 cost. When he arrived home, Trueman found they hadn't even bothered to inscribe the gift. It was an apposite end to his Yorkshire career.

Ah'll Si'thee

Fred Trueman faced up to life without cricket with none of the certainty that typified his bowling. There was no new career path lined up and waiting, no obvious diversion to fill up his time. His marriage to Enid was effectively over, with residual anger and hurt on both sides. A world once built on solid foundations was suddenly set on shifting sand.

It was around this time that a chance encounter began to assume profound significance. Some three years earlier, at a charity football match, Trueman had met an attractive redhead. She'd been talking to friends while leaning on his car, unaware to whom the vehicle belonged. After Trueman rebuked her in gentle fashion, they started chatting and hit it off. The woman was Veronica Wilson, who co-ran The Swan at Addingham, near Skipton. She'd gone to the game in Keighley, North Yorkshire, to lend her support and help raise funds. Malcolm Davies, a mutual friend, took Trueman back to her pub for a drink. He stayed an hour before heading home, thinking no more of a woman two years his junior.

In 1968, they met for a second time. Trueman had been staying with his solicitor, Jack Mewies, who lived not far from Veronica's pub. Trueman started calling in regularly and a friendship developed between him and Veronica, whose own marriage was on the brink of collapse. They offered each other a shoulder to cry on before friendship evolved into full-blown romance.

By 1970, their bond had strengthened to the point they wanted to live together. They bought a detached bungalow in Flasby, near Skipton, and set about creating a brighter future. Situated in a peaceful corner of the Yorkshire Dales, the stone-built property had everything they wanted: space, comfort, and above all privacy. It backed on to a wood and had extensive gardens, which looked on to the patchwork of the Pennine Hills. All that remained was to sort their divorces. With Mewies's help, Trueman's went through as quietly as possible in November 1972. Veronica's was finalised two months later. They married at Skipton Register Office on 28 February 1973.

Although blissfully happy, Fred and Veronica agonised over the effect their divorces would have on their children. Fred had Karen, Rebecca and Rodney to consider, while Veronica had two children – Sheenagh (born in 1958) and Patrick (1960) – from her marriage to motor mechanic Keith Wilson. Enid was awarded custody of her children, who stayed with her in Scarborough. Veronica was granted custody of Sheenagh and Patrick, who went to live in Flasby. But Trueman found separation from his own children difficult and disturbing. 'I was beside myself worrying about the effect the split would have on them,' he confessed. 'I wondered what they would think of me when they grew up. I wanted them to love and respect me throughout their lives, but tortured myself wondering how this could be possible given the circumstances.'

The circumstances were more traumatic than Trueman ever revealed. Just as his own life was undergoing a period of rebirth, so Enid's was rapidly falling apart. After their estrangement in 1965, Enid began drinking heavily. 'Mum always liked a drink,' said Rodney. 'That has to be said in balance. It was always likely to be a problem if things went wrong in her life. It would be very unfair to Dad or Veronica to say that his leaving caused Mum's drink problems. That tendency to drink was always there.'

Enid's world descended into chaos. She couldn't afford to keep the house she and Fred owned, so she and the children moved in with her mother, who owned a sizeable property nearby. Enid's mother was elderly and needed looking after – something Enid was unable to do because she was hardly capable of looking after herself. 'Mum got to the stage where she couldn't cope with everyday life,' added Rodney. 'She reached the point where she was out of control.'

Fred's answer was to send Rebecca and Rodney to boarding school in Scarborough. 'I don't think Dad really knew what to do,' said Rodney. 'He was a very loving father but he didn't have the emotional capacity for that sort of problem. I was very close to my nana and didn't want to leave her, so living with Dad wasn't an option. In any case, the house at Flasby was full up with Dad, Veronica, Sheenagh and Patrick. Dad was very concerned about my twin sister and me and sent us to boarding school to get us away from that environment, with my big sister Karen having left home by then. But that actually made the situation worse for Mum. The day-to-day challenges of looking after children disappeared, so she had long periods on her own when the temptation to drink was even stronger.'

In 1974, Enid appeared before Scarborough magistrates accused of drink-driving. A policeman told how he'd seen a car at the rear of the town's Derwent Hotel jerk forward about ten yards, then stall. Enid gave a positive breath test of 174 milligrams of alcohol in 100 millilitres of blood. She said she hadn't intended to drive on the road – merely to reverse and park in the hotel's rear entrance. Although over the limit, Enid escaped a ban. The *Yorkshire Post* reported: 'Mr Martin Summers, defending, submitted details of a 1968 High Court case as grounds why she should not be banned. Mrs Trueman's case was almost identical with the six-year-old precedent, claimed Mr Summers, and the magistrates decided in the "very special circumstances" not to ban her.' The paper said Enid – fined £70 and her driving licence endorsed – clutched a tiny jade pig throughout the proceedings, a good luck charm that had belonged to her grandfather.

Rodney says his mother sought help from support groups but nothing seemed to work. It was only when Karen provided her with her first grandchild in 1985 that she finally got better. 'Mum is such a kind, lovely person,' he explained, 'but when a problem like that takes hold, it transforms you. Looking back, if she could change everything, she'd do it in a heartbeat, but what was particularly sad was that Mum, as far as I'm concerned, was a one-man woman. She had a few boyfriends after the divorce but none of them ever lived up to Dad. He was her whole world, really; he was her hero. It must have been incredibly hard for her to be at home with three kids with Dad always away during summer and winter. That was really the root of their problem. I honestly think if they'd just been an ordinary couple who'd been able to live ordinary lives, they'd never have split up.'

Trueman visited his children on a monthly basis. They also took holidays with him at Flasby – especially at Easter. 'For me, the most surreal thing as a child was the massively different worlds we stepped into,' said Rodney. 'One minute we'd be in a world of chaos with a dysfunctional mother; the next, Dad would arrive in a Rolls Royce and we'd be swept off to this lovely house in the Dales. People think because your father's famous and you live in nice houses or go to nice schools that you live a dream life. Well, actually, if you delve into the lives of very famous people, it's probably more chaotic and difficult for the children than anyone can imagine.'

Veronica put huge efforts into making the children's visits happy. She recognised how important they were not only to the children, but to Trueman as well. Trueman's concerns about what his children would think of him when they grew up proved utterly unfounded. Karen, Rebecca and Rodney speak in glowing terms of a father they say showered them with affection, did not have favourites and was as proud of them as they were of him. They also appreciate Veronica's influence. 'Veronica was right for Dad,' said Karen. 'She sorted him, she organised him, she mothered him. She totally looked after him really, and Dad needed that.'

Born and bred in Bradford, Veronica was the daughter of a furniture salesman. She'd gone into selling herself before deciding she wanted to run a business with her friend, Pat Bromley. The ladies settled on pub management and pestered brewery after brewery until Hammond's finally offered them The Swan, half-hoping they wouldn't accept. But Veronica and Pat were determined to succeed in a male-led industry. Trueman's former team-mates say Veronica's strength of character, allied to her organisational skills, rescued Trueman at a time when the twin pillars of his life – cricket and marriage – had collapsed. 'I honestly think that without Veronica, Fred would have been a goner,' said Don Wilson. 'His life was going nowhere at the end of the sixties – his career had finished and his marriage had broken up – and Veronica came along at just the right time. They say that behind every great man is a great woman and, for Fred, Veronica was that woman. She put his life back on track when he needed it most.'

Richard Hutton agrees. 'Without Veronica, Fred might have been dead. She completely organised him and saved his life. Without someone to look after him and help him along, Fred would have been useless. God knows what might have happened if he hadn't met Veronica.'

Prior to settling down with Veronica, Trueman had been drifting. He'd been involved in several failed business enterprises – a sports goods shop, a garage, a frozen food firm – and lost around £8500 of the £9331 he earned from his 1962 Yorkshire benefit, nearly all his savings. He had no business skill and knew only cricket. Without Veronica's guiding hand, he might have stumbled from one disaster to the next.

There was a glaring example in 1969 of the directionless form his life was taking. Trueman had a brief and embarrassing stint as a stand-up comedian, having accepted the job as a casual bet. He'd been watching a comic in a north-east night club and boasting to its owners he could do better. When they called his bluff, he agreed to a four-week stint at Club Fiesta in Stockton-on-Tees. The club was owned by local entrepreneurs Jim and Keith Lipthorpe and attracted a variety of famous stars. Singers Roy Orbison and Shirley Bassey performed there, as did magician Tommy Cooper and comedian Freddie Starr. The Lipthorpe brothers hired attractive hostesses known as the Fiesta Fawns to serve customers who paid £7 to watch top stars and £3 for entertainment by lesser or local acts. Wearing outfits inspired by the Playboy bunnies, the Fawns brought a touch of glamour to the industrial north-east.

The Lipthorpes paid Trueman £500 a week – 'I'd been slogging my guts out on a cricket field for much less' – and devised for him a novel stage entrance. They projected a film of Trueman running up to bowl on a large paper screen as though the audience itself was the batsman. At the point of delivery, Trueman came bursting through the screen with his hands in the air – a performance that invariably made the crowd jump but which friends considered a prostitution of the artistry he'd shown on the cricket field.

As one of the most colourful characters the game has known, Trueman had an array of jokes and stories – many of which he'd devised himself. In the cosseted confines of an all-male dressing room, where conversation was not unknown to dwell on carnal matters, such stories were invariably well-received and added to the camaraderie of a travelling cricket team. In front of a mixed and by no means downmarket audience in a north-east club, they were liable to attract disapproving looks. On his first night, Trueman stormed on stage with an 'L' plate around his neck and proudly announced: 'I'll tell you jokes that'll make the women think they've had their hair done by the Electricity Board.'

Over the course of a forty-five-minute routine, he proved he wasn't joking. One former Yorkshire team-mate who watched him in action said: 'He basically trotted out a stream of lewd jokes and foul language. Some people found it funny, but there were plenty who didn't. To be honest, I think he slightly got the wrong impression of how he should be. Fred seemed to think that sort of humour was the only way to make people laugh, but you don't have to swear all the time to be funny and entertaining.'

It wasn't just jokes about the mother-in-law and what the actress really said to the bishop that formed the core of Trueman's repertoire. His act was sprinkled with racist overtones as he declared:

'You always know when you're flying into Bombay. You can smell it from five thousand feet.'

'There's a snake in India that can kill a man in nine seconds. After five hours in Bombay, you go looking for it.'

'Whenever I'm at a cricket match in India they say, "We don't get the crowds we used to, Fred." I say, "I know, they're all in Leicester and Bradford."'

'Anyone who goes to India should get a VC as big as a frying pan. I don't care if your stomach is made of concrete, their food will find a way through it.'

'After two weeks on the sub-continent, you walk around with the cheeks of your arse so tight together you couldn't get a tram ticket up there.'

Trueman, however, was no racist at heart. Many of his closest friends in cricket were coloured – men such as Garry Sobers, Everton Weekes and Farokh Engineer. Trueman's attitude was a generational thing. He'd been raised in an era where it was acceptable to use such words as 'darkies' and 'wogs' and his attitude and his stage act reflected that fact. 'Fred might have called West Indians "bottles of stout" or "snowy", but affectionately, if you know what I mean,' said Bob Platt. 'It was never meant derogatory. Some of Fred's best mates in cricket were Indian or West Indian. I certainly wouldn't have called him a racist.'

In later life, Trueman had a saying: 'I'm not racist, but I am as far as Imran Khan is concerned.' Although it's a bit like saying you're slightly pregnant, the comment was a clumsy expression of Trueman's dislike for the Pakistan all-rounder rather than a vulgar declaration of white supremacy. 'Fred's attitude reflected his generation,' said Don Wilson, 'and there was always an element of humour in his words. I remember he once walked into the Lancashire dressing room and said, "All you want is a green player, ya know." They said, "Why's that, Fred?" He said, "'Cos then you'd have a bloody snooker set."'

Trueman, however, didn't move with the times. He continued calling West Indians 'bottles of stout' and 'snowy' because, deep down, he didn't find it offensive and couldn't understand anyone who thought it was. Sidney Fielden, a detective sergeant in the South Yorkshire police who served with Trueman on the Yorkshire cricket committee, remembers an incident that summed up his outlook. 'Sidney Hainsworth, the district committee member for Hull, wanted permission for Yorkshire to play a West Indian XI at Hull in the 1980s. There was considerable opposition to this from the cricket committee, of which Fred was a member, and there was a long discussion about the pros and cons. Fred started going on about how he'd bowled against the West Indians in the Caribbean when spectators were falling out of palm trees like "bloody chocolate drops", as he put it. I remember saying, "Fred, if you were to say something like that out of the committee room, in the street, you might get arrested."'

Trueman's stint at Stockton did little for his public image. Don Mosey described it as 'one of the major disasters of his life' and said friends were 'relieved and grateful' when it ended. But Trueman was a natural entertainer and public speaker. When Veronica helped him to sort out his life, he enjoyed a long and lucrative career on the after-dinner circuit. As a shrewd businesswoman, Veronica realised the financial potential of such engagements. 'Fred had no commercial experience. He had no business sense. He had only fame and no idea how to harness it. He had an agent who charged £30 a time for public appearances by Fred but not many bookings were coming in. I wrote to him to say it might be a good idea to end the contract and I took over myself.'

Letters that had previously gone unanswered received prompt replies as Veronica effectively became his agent. Encouraged by the response, she upped his fee to £50, £75, then £100. Trueman felt more at home on the after-dinner circuit and at Rotary Clubs and sportsmen's dinners. The audiences invariably contained cricket lovers with whom he had an instant rapport.

He could still be blue and gratuitously offensive, sometimes struggling to pitch his act. 'Most times, Fred got it spot on and read the audience 100 per cent,' said Peter Parfitt. 'Occasionally, however, he got it wrong and that's when you'd hear comments like, "I listened to that Fred Trueman the other day and I never want to go and hear him again. He was this, that and the other and he was effing and blinding and what have you." Of course, when you speak at a rugby dinner, when you speak at a football dinner, there is plenty of effing and blinding that goes on. But sometimes he misread it. On other occasions I've heard people say, "I listened to that Fred Trueman the other day and he was talking about cricket and it was one of the most wonderful three-quarters of an hour I've spent in my life."'

Most people didn't want the blue material. They respected Trueman for what he was and what he'd achieved. They wanted the cricketing stories he was able to provide – many of which featured himself. If it was blue stuff people wanted, there were plenty of professional alternatives. For many, Trueman was at his best when telling cricketing anecdotes or recounting tales of Brian Close's motoring escapades and sundry collisions with inanimate objects. Blessed with great verbal timing and a tremendous memory, he rarely used a note or crib card. 'I've seen Fred do forty-five minutes in a theatre, take a fifteen-minute break and then do another forty-five minutes without a note to help him,' said Veronica. 'He was a memory man and incredibly fluent. He also had a way of picking up something topical and bringing it into the evening's entertainment. Colin Cowdrey once told me that if Fred had had the chance to go to university, he'd have walked it because he had such a good memory.'

In a life of paradoxes, few were more profound than the fact Trueman hated bad language in certain circumstances. A man of whom former MCC president J.J. Warr proclaimed, 'cricket and the Anglo-Saxon tongue have been enriched by his presence', particularly detested anyone swearing in front of his children. 'If we went to Headingley and somebody swore near us, Dad would get very upset,' said Rodney. 'He would say, "Excuse me, I've got my son here. Please don't use language like that in front of my son." In fact, I can honestly say I never heard my dad swear. If a car pulled out in front of him when he was driving, he would use the word "photographing" rather than the f-word. He was passionate about stuff like that. In many ways, Dad was very old-fashioned. He would always hold doors open for women and that sort of thing. His manners were impeccable.'

Sidney Fielden recalls being asked to have a word with Trueman by former Yorkshire chairman Brian Walsh, who was concerned about Trueman's language ahead of a dinner to honour Sir Leonard Hutton. 'We were planning the 364 dinner in 1988 to honour the fiftieth anniversary of Len's record score of 364 against Australia at the Oval. I was responsible for getting the speakers and managed to line up Denis Compton and Ray Lindwall. Brian Walsh rang me and asked whether I'd managed to get the last speaker. I said I'd got Fred and he said, "Fred Trueman? But what about his language?"

'I said, "He won't use bad language. It's a dinner for Len Hutton and he wouldn't dream of using bad language on an occasion like that."

'Walsh said, "Yes, but have you marked his card?"

'I said, "I wouldn't dream of marking his card." I didn't say a word to Fred, who made the best speech of the night and didn't swear once.'

After settling down with Veronica, Trueman's fortunes turned around. Yorkshire Television signed him to host *Sometimes You Win*, a celebrity chat show with a sporting theme. Trueman interviewed such stars as singer Tom Jones and comedian Jimmy Tarbuck. He asked them to predict the draws in Saturday's football matches, thereby providing tips for pools punters. Impressed with his performance, YTV hired Trueman to present *One Man Business* and *Yorkshire Speaks*, where he talked to everyday people about their life and work.

But the YTV show that really propelled him back into the spotlight was *Indoor League*, which he presented from 1972 to 1978. The programme – broadcast across the full ITV network – featured pub games such as skittles and shove ha'penny and offered ordinary people the chance to appear on television. One of its creators was Sid Waddell, who went on to become the voice of darts. Waddell invented Trueman's weekly opening line, 'Nah then', and his classic parting shot, 'Ah'll si'thee'. When Trueman complained he didn't talk like that, he was told: 'You do now.' Waddell remembered: 'We gave him a pint glass and a pipe and wrote Fred-speak for him – a kind of Yorkshire gobbledegook. "We've got potters and slotters, twiddlers and nudgers", that sort of thing. Fred was great to work with and naturally funny. He was the perfect presenter for that type of show.'

The programme, filmed at Leeds Irish Centre, was effectively the birthplace of televised darts. It threw up a cornucopia of characters that helped draw a regular audience of eight million. There was Mark Sinclair-Scott, an arm-wrestler known as 'The Narcissus of the Knotted Knuckles' (Trueman dubbed him 'The Nancy Boy with the Knotted Knuckles' – although not to his face). There was Des Stabb, an appositely named darts player from Plymouth. Jean Smith played darts in a Para's beret and was certified blind, while Phillip Bootham – aka King Ben – boasted he could ride a unicycle after downing ten pints. In 2003, *Indoor League* topped an *Observer* poll of the ten funniest sports programmes ever invented, while *The Times* said it had 'all the recherché values of *It's A Knockout* and the heady atmosphere of floodlit rugby league'.

Some of the Fred-speak was more entertaining than the action. Introducing one programme dressed in a woolly cardigan with suede panels, Trueman declared: 'Nah then. Just slipped out for a minute from the biggest bonanza of sporting skill I've ever clapped eyes on. We've got sixty-odd of the best players I've ever seen in my life. None of your Charltons and your Geoffrey Boycotts, mind yer. This bunch of lads are kings at those sports you get up 'n' down the land in every pub. There's one fella who's shown up from Scunthorpe in a ten-gallon Stetson hat, and he's floating coins around in the best game of shove ha'penny I've ever happened across. And there's two of the cockiest blokes – students playing table football as though they were Giles and Bremner. So let's get cracking. The first prize in each game's a hundred quid – that's for shove ha'penny, bar billiards, skittles, table football and darts. And remember, all you lot south of Trent, this is real darts on a Yorkshire board – no trebles, no fluky shots, just a hell of a lot of skill.'

During another show, Trueman delivered one of the wackiest links in broadcasting history. With earnest voice and deadpan delivery, he announced: 'Now to the final of what's probably the oldest pub game in England. I hear Henry VIII used to knock the old shove ha'pennys about a bit – that's when he weren't bashing missus. Well, I don't know how Barry Stones or Alan Brown of Durham treat their missuses, but they certainly can nudge a crafty ha'penny. We pick up our shove ha'penny final with Brown leading by sixteen chalks to eight . . .'

It was good clean fun – apart from one occasion when a fight broke out at the table football. One triumphant competitor went to punch the air in delight but succeeded only in punching a spectator. A passage of confused violence followed, exacerbated when a fight from a wedding upstairs at the Irish Centre spilled down into the main room. As punches flew, Waddell had to smuggle Terry Yorath, the Leeds United footballer and guest referee, out the nearest door.

In addition to fronting YTV shows, Trueman made guest appearances on various programmes. In 1970 he featured in *Dad's Army*, the sitcom set in World War Two. Trueman took part in an episode entitled *The Test* in which the Walmington-on-Sea Home Guard led by Captain Mainwaring was challenged to a cricket match by Air Warden Hodges. Trueman played Ernie Egan, a world-class fast bowler recruited by the Warden. After the Warden's men batted first, Mainwaring opened the platoon's reply with Sergeant Wilson. Hodges handed the new ball to Egan, whose first ball was a bouncer that sent Mainwaring diving for cover as surely as a doodlebug. The effort of the delivery caused Egan to strain his shoulder and he had to go off – an ironic twist given Trueman was hardly ever injured.

Mainwaring's men claimed a dramatic victory when last man Private Godfrey improbably struck Hodges for six over square-leg.

Bill Pertwee, who played the irascible Warden, became a good friend of Trueman. He remembers that during filming the cast and crew were invited to a wine promotion by Colman's Mustard. 'We were promised food as well as wine and we set off in a coach. Unfortunately, all the food had been eaten by the time we arrived and so we wined on empty stomachs with the obvious result. Arthur Lowe (Captain Mainwaring) started a singsong with Fred and then they both told several jokes – many of them a little ribald but very, very funny. This continued on the return journey and Fred suggested that we look for a fish and chip shop. We found one in a village and Arthur walked in and ordered "Forty cod and chips please." The startled proprietor said, "I can't do forty." Arthur commanded, "Do the best you can, man." And he did. We eventually returned to our hotel where we were expected to learn our scripts and prepare for the following day's filming. But Fred and Arthur's jokes continued into the early hours.'

Trueman also appeared on comedy game show *Blankety Blank*, the magazine programme *That's Life!*, had a brief stint as team captain on *A Question of Sport* and even had a one-word part in Yorkshire soap opera *Emmerdale Farm*. Trueman was flagged down in the middle of Leeds by gamekeeper Seth Armstrong, who asked whether he knew Yorkshire at all. Trueman replied, 'Slightly,' and gave Armstrong a lift. Trueman joked he was offered a part on rival soap *Crossroads* but didn't get it because he kept remembering his lines.

In 1979, Trueman was honoured on *This Is Your Life*, the biographical show in which the host surprises a special guest. When Eamonn Andrews startled Trueman with the famous red book, Andrews was even more startled by the reply, 'Hey up, Eamonn, lad, you can't tell my life in half-an-hour, ya know.'

Many former cricketers turned out in tribute, including Neil Hawke, Keith Miller, Brian Close and Don Wilson. Leslie Crowther also took part, as did former Lincoln City manager Bill Anderson.

There were recorded tributes from Tommy Stubbs, the Maltby schoolteacher who'd encouraged Trueman in his younger years, and former Prime Minister Harold Wilson. The pièce de résistance was a bizarre family sketch involving Trueman's brothers Arthur, John and Dennis. Filmed at Tennyson Road, Maltby, it showed them lying in the same bed they'd shared as children. The bed was deliberately made to collapse with the brothers still in it, imitating what used to happen for real.

Trueman found the sketch hilarious but for most of the programme looked close to tears. As footage was played of his greatest moments, he bit into the stem of his pipe to stop himself crying. 'Fred was a deeply emotional man,' said Veronica. 'He'd burst into tears at the first line of "God Save the Queen". Sometimes he used to say, "Oh no, I'm going to get emotional," and I used to say, "Fred, there's no need to be afraid of it." He hated showing his emotions in public.'

As well as appearing on television, Trueman tried sports writing for the *Sunday People*. He'd been a columnist for the paper since 1957 and began covering football and rugby league. Trueman derived particular satisfaction from watching rugby but writing was not his strongest suit. One of his first journalistic assignments was a match between Wakefield Trinity and Featherstone Rovers. Trueman made only three lines of notes and neglected to convey the final score. When another sports reporter rang to check the result, Trueman replied, 'They f***ed 'em right.' None the wiser, the reporter enquired as to 'Who f***ed whom?' After much harrumphing and ruffling of notes, it was ascertained Wakefield had f***ed Featherstone 26–14.

Trueman's football writing was similarly hit-and-miss. Following a game at Barnsley, he filed a piece detailing the names of the eleven scouts in attendance – including the magnificently irrelevant detail of one of the scouts' middle names. The only thing missing was the identity of the player the scouts had gone to watch. Although Trueman enjoyed writing, he had little taste for 'personality journalism'. He had neither relish nor aptitude for ferreting out quotes.

He also tried cricket writing but was largely unsuccessful. Trueman's reports were considered too technical for *People* readers, who wanted something spicier than staid descriptions of how to bowl the outswinger. He continued instead with a ghost-written column among the best on the circuit. Derek Hodgson, who collaborated with Trueman during the 1980s, says he had a natural eye for a story. 'I've ghosted an awful lot of people in my time from Matt Busby onwards, but Fred was as good as any of them. He had innate news sense; he scented a story. Sometimes he'd say, "I've got something for you today, lad. You'll like this one." And, sure enough, he'd have some line or other. Very often, it didn't end up in the Trueman column but made a story elsewhere in the paper. Often, it was a story about what the England selectors had decided to do.'

One such story involved Geoffrey Boycott's decision in 1977 to end a self-imposed three-year exile from Test cricket. Trueman discovered that Boycott, having bowed out due to poor form, workload and the fact Mike Denness had been appointed as captain, had contacted the selectors, saying he wanted to return. The Trueman-bylined story, 'Boycott Wants To Come Back', was a major scoop followed up at home and abroad, but Trueman was more enraged by the prospect of Boycott's reappearance than elated at trumping his journalistic rivals. 'Any man who says he doesn't want to play for his country should never be asked again,' he thundered.

Having retired from cricket in 1968, Trueman surprised many by ending his own self-imposed 'exile' four years later. Derbyshire asked him to play in the John Player Sunday League and he took part in six games, taking seven wickets at 22 before a knee injury curtailed his involvement. One of the matches was against Yorkshire at Bradford, Trueman returning 2 for 20 from eight overs – including the wickets of John Hampshire lbw and Philip Sharpe caught behind – in a seven-wicket defeat. As if to prove old habits die hard, he spent more time in the opposition dressing room than he did in Derbyshire's.

Bob Taylor, the former Derbyshire and England wicketkeeper, believes Trueman found his comeback challenging. 'I remember Fred's debut against Surrey at Derby. He was visibly nervous before we went out. He hadn't played for a long time and you could tell by his mannerisms he was very apprehensive. Fred was still accurate and difficult to get away, but I think he soon realised it was pretty hard going.' Taylor retains an indelible image of Trueman's debut. 'The Surrey openers were Micky Stewart and John Edrich. After Fred bowled the first over, he went to field at third man and Micky edged the ball between second slip and gully. I have this picture in my mind of Fred running round and pretty much grovelling on all fours trying to stop the ball going over the boundary. It was quite sad, really, to see the great F.S. Trueman – one of my all-time heroes – grovelling on the ground because he was obviously no longer as fit as he used to be.'

Although professional cricket was now beyond him, Trueman continued to dabble at lesser levels. His love of the game and competitive instinct kept him playing well into his fifties. Trueman represented The Forty Club, a nomadic side that featured a number of former first-class players. Founded in 1936, the club played mainly against private schools. One of his club-mates was Eric Burgin, his former Yorkshire colleague and Sheffield United coach. Burgin says Trueman was as driven to succeed as ever he was during his professional career.

'I remember a match against the Midland District at Trent Bridge. They had some good players in their team like the former Notts batsman Reg Simpson. When we got to the ground, Fred was suffering from a sore back and didn't think he'd be able to bowl. He thought he'd only be able to bat and field. Johnny Wardle was also in our side and he decided to play a trick on Fred. He told him one of our opponents, Norman Horner, the former Warwickshire batsman, was very sorry Fred was injured because he always enjoyed facing his bowling. Fred doled out one or two adjectives in reply and

Norman Horner walked out to open the batting. With no thought whatsoever for his bad back, Fred said, "I'll have a go, skipper." He steamed in and bowled as quick and short as I've ever seen. Horner turned to us in the slips and said, "What the hell's going on?", unaware that Wardle had set it all up. Fred got Horner out after an over or two and then took his sweater. He could still turn it on if he wanted.'

The Forty Club toured the world, playing various club sides. Burgin recalls a trip to Malta. 'A group of us were sat on our hotel balcony one day, taking in the sun, and there were some Germans below us. We were making a bit of noise and the Germans complained to the hotel management. This chap from the hotel came over and said, "Would you mind keeping the noise down, please, there's some Germans below." So Fred leant over the balcony and said, "Oi, what's up with you lot? We've beaten you twice, ya know, and if you want to have another go, we'll beat you again." We didn't have any more trouble from those Germans.'

Trueman's cricketing career did not end there. He played several games for MCC against public schools – occasions that brought out the best in him as he sought to show the 'f***ing jazz hats' a thing or two. He represented Saints Cricket Club (founded by ex-Army officer and Yorkshire committee member Desmond Bailey), which featured ex-professionals who played against schools in northern England. In late 1980, Trueman even set up his own team – the Courage Old England XI, enlisting the help of former Test and county stars such as Denis Compton, Tom Graveney and Basil D'Oliveira to play one-day games for charities and benefits.

Trueman took great delight in finding the old outswinger working again and was quick to point it out to his colleagues, but the red-letter days grew increasingly rare. In later years he took some fearful poundings – a match between a Yorkshire Legends XI and the Yorkshire County Cricket Club Academy, featuring a young Michael Vaughan, a prime example. The former England captain recalls the Academy players were under strict orders not to take advantage of

Trueman's age – only for one man, Steve Bethel, to ignore the command. 'Bethel responded to this by continually smacking Trueman clean out of the ground,' said Vaughan, 'earning himself a major bollocking for failing to show enough respect.'

Trueman also turned out for British Airways Eccentrics XI in places as far flung as Thailand, Mexico and Singapore, for Craven Gentlemen in the Yorkshire Dales and for village club Cracoe in the Dales Evening League. His involvement with Cracoe ended abruptly after he took 5 for 0 on debut against Linton. The opposition successfully complained to the League it was unfair for teams to have to face a former Yorkshire and England bowler – and Trueman was banned.

Trueman initially offered to join Cracoe at the start of the seventies after he and Veronica moved to the area. He wanted to immerse himself in Dales life and become part of the community. When the club secretary went excitedly to the committee to announce the great F.S. Trueman had offered to play, there were grumblings among the committee members. 'Would you thank Mr Trueman for his generous offer,' came the reply, 'but tell him it's batsmen we're after – not bowlers.'

12

That Bloody Boycott's More Slippery than a Bloody Snake

How Yorkshire could have done with batsmen and bowlers following Fred Trueman's exit in 1968. Ray Illingworth also departed at the end of that season, denied the security of a longer contract, while Ken Taylor left to coach in South Africa. When Jimmy Binks retired in 1969 and Brian Close was sacked the following year, half the 1968 side had quit or been axed. There followed the most poisonous period in the county's history – one that revolved around Geoffrey Boycott.

Appointed captain by a casting vote only, Boycott took charge after Close was removed. Having led Yorkshire to four Championships and two Gillette Cups in seven years, Close might have assumed his job was safe. But he'd angered the committee with a perceived reluctance to blood young players and his outspoken opposition to one-day cricket. Given ten minutes to decide whether to resign or be sacked, Close resigned and then changed his mind, forcing Yorkshire to do their own dirty work.

Following the example of Illingworth, who linked up with Leicestershire, Close threw in his lot with a rival county. The likes of Ian Botham, Viv Richards and Joel Garner joined him at Somerset, while Illingworth inspired a golden era at Grace Road, where Leicestershire won five trophies in as many years. Yorkshire, in contrast, struggled in the absence of so many players, becoming a shadow of their former selves. To make matters worse, senior men such as Richard Hutton, Don Wilson and Philip Sharpe actively disliked Boycott, considering him a selfish and inappropriate leader.

Dressing-room discontent grew during Boycott's first season in charge in 1971. Yorkshire finished thirteenth in the Championship, despite Boycott becoming the first Englishman to average over 100 in a county summer. For everyone who feted his achievement, others felt it indicative of the player's self-absorption. The dichotomy between Boycott's individual milestone and Yorkshire's collective mediocrity drew stinging rebuke from Trueman, who had this to say at the annual dinner of Harrogate Cricket Club: 'It will never cease to amaze me that a man can average for the first time in history 100 in every innings he played, yet what did we get? Somewhere near the bottom in the batting points league. I think it is disgusting.'

Never bosom buddies as team-mates, Trueman and Boycott fell out spectacularly during the seventies and eighties. Although they respected each other's talent (just as Boycott considered Trueman a wonderful bowler, so Trueman subscribed to the time-honoured view that Boycott was the man you would want to bat for your life), that was about as far as it went. When asked his opinion of Boycott, Trueman would say, 'As a batsman, yes; as a man, no.' Trueman subscribed to the popular belief that Boycott was more concerned with himself than the team.

By mid-1973, as Yorkshire still floundered, Trueman's opposition to Boycott increased. He began to blast him in his newspaper column with a ferocity with which he blasted out batsmen. 'To be honest, I think he has had long enough in charge to prove whether he can do the job or not,' thundered Trueman. 'The time has now come to find another man capable of doing the job.'

Boycott also became the butt of Trueman's after-dinner jokes. Even stories of Close's motoring mishaps were relegated to secondary status as Trueman tore into the Yorkshire captain. Although the majority of gags were harmless enough, they failed to mask a hostile undertone:

'Boycott attended a wedding once. As the happy couple left the church, the vicar said, "May God go with you," so Boycott buggered off with them for two weeks.'

'I hear Boycott's bought a house by the sea. Perhaps he thinks he can walk on water.'

'Boycott's always been terrified of fast bowling – particularly the Australian fast bowlers Dennis Lillee and Jeff Thomson. One day, Boycott pulled this bird and took her back to his hotel room. "What's your name, luv?" he asked. "Lillian Thomson," she replied. And with that, Boycott shit himself and jumped out the window.'

'What have Geoffrey Boycott and Cinderella got in common? They were both past masters at leaving the ball.'

'It must be nice to go through life knowing you'll never die of a stroke.'

Boycott, however, did not see the funny side. He considered Trueman a malign influence, a backbiter with the naïve notion Yorkshire should still be winning trophies, even though great players such as Trueman had left the club. As Yorkshire limped through the seventies, with only a second-placed finish to Illingworth's Leicestershire in 1975 to lift the gloom, Trueman and Boycott became further opposed.

Their antipathy plumbed new depths when Yorkshire sacked Boycott as captain in 1978. In his newspaper column, Trueman called for Boycott to quit Yorkshire altogether, saying he'd done enough damage. Echoing Oliver Cromwell's entreaty to the Rump Parliament in 1653, the column was headlined 'IN THE NAME OF GOD (AND YORKSHIRE) GO!' With Cromwellian fervour, Trueman fumed: 'When Boycott was appointed seven years ago, I forecast turbulent times ahead for the greatest county club in the world. But my advice fell on cloth ears . . . Boycott is always talking about loyalty, but the only loyalty he seems to know is to himself

. . . Boycott has caused enough trouble. The least he can do is go now . . . Boycott's reign as captain was depressing. The side won nothing.'

Boycott, however, was not for budging. He opted to continue under the captaincy of John Hampshire and then Chris Old, along with the management of Ray Illingworth, who returned to Yorkshire in 1979. Trueman also returned that year as Craven representative on the county committee, serving in addition on the cricket committee. Although the opinions he expressed in his newspaper writings moderated accordingly, his opposition to Boycott simmered in the background, boiling over in 1981 when fresh problems emerged in the form of Boycott's relationship with Illingworth.

Unhappy that Illingworth had left him out of several fixtures at the Scarborough Festival, Boycott responded angrily during a television interview in a York bookshop, saying he would be seeking a 'showdown' with the manager. When Illingworth arrived at Scarborough next day for a match against Northamptonshire, he suspended Boycott for the rest of the season – a decision taken after consultation with Trueman, Old and the Yorkshire committee. As news spread of Boycott's suspension, his supporters drew up a petition calling for Illingworth's head. They then rose to give Boycott a standing ovation as he left North Marine Road like a naughty schoolboy banished from the classroom.

Two weeks after that PR disaster, the Yorkshire committee – in a staggeringly inept move even by the cockeyed standards of Yorkshire cricket – made public the results of an internal poll conducted by Old, which revealed the majority of players no longer wanted Boycott. The findings of the poll – organised in response to newspaper claims Boycott had the players' full support – were unambiguous. To the first question, 'Do you want Geoff Boycott as captain?', there were fifteen votes against, with three abstentions. To the second, 'Do you wish to have him [Boycott] in the side next season?', only two people voted in favour, with ten opposed and four abstaining. Finally, when asked, 'Do you want Raymond Illingworth to continue as manager?', thirteen voted yes, while three abstained.

Amid the ensuing furore, Yorkshire established a sub-committee to conduct an in-depth inquiry into every aspect of the club's management. Headed by retired accountant Peter Dobson, the sub-committee reported its conclusions shortly before the start of the 1982 season. Although there were criticisms of Illingworth's management and Old's captaincy, the real missiles were directed at Boycott. 'Morale can only be rebuilt and true unity of purpose re-established within the team when Mr Boycott is no longer in the team. It is therefore the reluctant recommendation of the majority of the sub-committee that Mr Boycott's services should be dispensed with as soon as possible.'

Rather than sack Boycott and upset his army of followers, particularly when their own stock was so low, the Yorkshire committee decided to set-up a three-man 'peace-keeping' sub-committee of Trueman, Ronnie Burnet and Billy Sutcliffe. Designed 'to help the manager in the day-to-day running of the side', it was to act as a buffer between Illingworth and Boycott and increase Illingworth's ability to push through cricketing decisions. The irony of Trueman being appointed to a peace-keeping body at least raised a chuckle during an otherwise cheerless period for Yorkshire cricket.

The peace-makers had little to do until August 1983, whereupon their decision to reprimand Boycott for slow scoring during a game against Gloucestershire at Cheltenham inadvertently triggered a revolution that led to the Yorkshire committee being overthrown – the nadir of Trueman's fifty years in cricket. When the Yorkshire side arrived at Cheltenham, Boycott immediately caused uproar by telling a young autograph hunter to 'f*** off' as he took the field for a team photo-call. Once the photo was taken, Boycott told another group of youngsters to 'f*** off' when they, too, approached him for his signature. Several Gloucestershire members overheard and Illingworth apologised. 'I am very sorry,' he told them. 'I can't defend him. He was wrong and has been told about it.'

When the match began, Boycott invited further censure by taking 347 balls to score 140 runs in bright sunshine on a plumb batting pitch. With trademark torpor, he laboured 262 deliveries over his hundred and managed only eight runs during the last half-hour when Yorkshire were chasing a fourth batting bonus point. What particularly infuriated Illingworth was Boycott's apparent disregard for a message sent out to him through twelfth man Nick Taylor demanding Boycott get a move on. According to Illingworth, Taylor and Jim Love, the non-striker, Boycott responded to Illingworth's instruction by telling Taylor, 'Go and talk to the other man. I'll continue batting my own way.'

Illingworth referred the matter to Trueman, Burnet and Sutcliffe, who issued the following statement:

> We have had a long discussion with Boycott and listened to his version of events and at his request obtained evidence from other people. We are satisfied in this instance his batting was not in the best interests of the side and he has been told again that he must at all times play the sort of innings the side needs, irrespective of his own personal ambitions.

Boycott's supporters were livid. Led by Sidney Fielden, they demanded a special meeting of the Yorkshire committee. Before that could take place, Trueman and the committee voted unanimously not to offer Boycott a contract for the following season, a decision upheld by the general committee. Yorkshire chairman Michael Crawford cited as reasons for Boycott's dismissal the need to encourage younger players without the current atmosphere of 'dissension and discord which creates a lack of confidence', the public bickering after the Cheltenham episode, the need to put the interests of Yorkshire before one individual, and the threat of established players leaving the club.

Undeterred, Boycott's supporters launched a campaign to reinstate him. The Members 84 Group was formed and the necessary signatures obtained to force the club to stage a special meeting. It meant the decision to sack Boycott was put to the will of the Yorkshire public. Amid near-evangelical scenes at Harrogate's Royal Hall on 21 January 1984, the public nailed its colours to the mast as all three pro-Boycott resolutions were carried. First, that Boycott be offered a contract for 1984 (4115 for, 3109 against); second, a vote of no confidence in the cricket committee (3609 for, 3578 against); and, finally, a vote of no confidence in the general committee (3997 for, 3209 against).

Although the votes were not technically binding, Trueman and his colleagues felt no option but to resign. In every seat across the county, elections took place for a new committee as the majority of the old guard – Trueman included – fought against the pro-Boycott candidates. The Members 84 Group, with Fielden to the fore, canvassed far and wide – knocking on doors, writing letters, telephoning on spec and making it their business to talk to every individual who might influence the result.

In contrast, Trueman, along with ex-players such as Burnet, Sutcliffe and Bob Platt, relied more on reputation than lobbying to win the day. While the *Members 84 Group* was busy drumming up support in all weathers, Trueman's canvassing effectively consisted of a brief letter to Craven members which declared the club 'greater and more important than any individual player' and cited two reasons why Yorkshire were right to sack Boycott. First, his age, 'which is limiting the progress of younger players who become unsettled and leave for other counties', and the fact Yorkshire finished bottom of the Championship in 1983 for the first time in their history, despite Boycott scoring 1941 runs at 55.45. But Trueman's protests fell on deaf ears. A combination of widespread dissatisfaction with the old committee, complacent electioneering on their part and tireless campaigning from the Members 84 Group resulted in a landslide victory for Boycott and his supporters.

Trueman was annihilated – beaten is too soft a word – as he polled just 65 votes in the Craven district against the 128 of Peter Fretwell, a printer from Keighley. Burnet, Sutcliffe and Platt were also ousted as seventeen of the twenty-one Boycott candidates prevailed. The crowning indignity for the old guard came when Boycott – standing in his own district of Wakefield – beat Dr John Turner by 203 votes to 147, leading to the unique occurrence of a current professional serving on the general committee.

This dual role sparked yet more controversy, yet more condemnation from Trueman's revitalised pen in the *Sunday People* and
ultimately alienated many who'd fought so hard to oust Trueman
and co. – most notably Fielden, who was moved to declare: 'Geoff
Boycott is a very great cricketer . . . I wish I had never met him.' Like
many who'd sided with Boycott, Fielden felt it simply wasn't right for
a player to have a foot in both dressing room and committee room.
How could confidentiality and trust exist under such circumstances,
he protested? And what about sensitive matters such as players'
wages and contracts? Having trusted Fielden 'like a brother', Boycott
branded him a 'Judas' and stubbornly clung to the dual role for the
rest of a Yorkshire career that ended in 1986, thereby concluding the
stormiest period in any county's history.

For Trueman, the wounds of 1984 never healed. The greatest living
name in Yorkshire cricket – greater even than Boycott – was snubbed
by Yorkshire's members in favour of someone with no connection to
the first-class game. To think those members had turned against him
upset him more than anything else in his cricketing life. Not even
myriad mistreatments by the Yorkshire and England hierarchies
came close to matching the pain he felt at being rejected by the
county's followers. In echoes of his father's gesture in burning his
pit clothes after returning from his final shift at Maltby Main Colliery,
Trueman threw out his old Yorkshire kit – items of priceless
sentimental value – with barely a thought or tear. Shirts and
sweaters, caps and flannels – all ended on the rubbish heap.

Although Yorkshire's members had not voted against him as such,
merely for Boycott's reinstatement as a player, Trueman took their
decision personally and blamed only one man – Boycott. 'Fred was
shattered when he lost his committee seat,' said Veronica. 'Yorkshire
cricket had been his life. To think the Yorkshire supporters didn't
want him; I don't think he ever got over that. He'd given his all for
them over the years and that was the thanks he got. Some of them
even sent him hate mail. There were drawings of private parts, that
sort of thing, and I used to burn any letters I thought would upset

him. Fred suspected the vote might have been fixed, but he didn't have any proof. Either way, the events of that period had a profound effect.'

When Boycott heard Trueman received hate mail, he tried to put the record straight. 'I wrote to him to say, "Look, I'm really sorry about that, but it's not of my making." I mean, I didn't tell anybody to write nasty letters or say nasty things about him, but it all became very bitter, very personal, and I didn't want that. Fred didn't reply to the letter.' Boycott claims he had nothing against Trueman and was genuinely sorry he lost his seat. 'I was sad and disappointed for him because he was my boyhood hero; I thought a lot about him. But when Fred was voted off the Yorkshire committee he became very bitter, very hostile. It was as if I personally had done him some injustice, some harm, but I hadn't done anything. The situation at Yorkshire was about me, yes, but I hadn't done anything to Fred personally. I never would. But he took it as a personal thing against me.'

Boycott believes Trueman's animosity stemmed from the fact he couldn't accept Yorkshire were no longer a force. 'People like Fred felt Yorkshire should always be strong and should always be winning the Championship, but Yorkshire had no divine right. Even when all the great players had left, Fred felt Yorkshire still had a divine right to keep winning the Championship, and, if they didn't, someone must be to blame – i.e., me. What people like Fred couldn't grasp, what they didn't want to accept, was that the players who took the places of Trueman, Close, Illingworth, etc., simply weren't as good. We just didn't have that quality of player. There was also a big influx of overseas players in county cricket and we weren't allowed to have those at the time. It was like playing with two hands behind your back.'

Boycott's bid to distance himself from the hate mail cut no ice with its resentful recipient. Rather than defuse their differences, Trueman deepened them, stepping up his war against Boycott in print. Having called for Boycott's head as captain and player, Trueman strove to get his hands on as much anti-Boycott material as possible. So determined was he to discredit Boycott he pursued titbits from Fielden, who'd helped bring about his downfall by championing Boycott. 'Following the 1984 election, Fred was very anxious to find stories about Boycott he could use in the *People*,' said Fielden. 'He was always looking for gossip and information. Of course, I wasn't prepared to disclose any confidential stuff about Boycott, even if I'd known it, which I didn't. Although I'd fallen out with Geoffrey over the dual role, which I thought completely unacceptable, it wouldn't have been fair or responsible to give Fred the ammunition to attack Boycott in print.'

Trueman ploughed on anyway. In one post-election piece he seethed: 'Boycott must go because he's one-paced, a run accumulator unable to step up the scoring rate. The kids at the other end are having to throw away their wickets to get some runs on the board.' In another he cited incidents involving Boycott that concerned 'rudeness to a waitress, bad language to a girl photographer and uncouth behaviour in a sponsors' marquee'. In a further attack he branded Boycott's supporters 'sewer rats' – a slur that resulted in an unsuccessful attempt by the Members 84 Group to have Trueman stripped of his honorary life membership. Trueman's relentless criticism of Boycott even resulted in a solicitor's letter, which led to a cooling – if not a cessation – of tabloid thunder.

In his 1987 autobiography, Boycott wrote Trueman 'waged a systematic and virtually unbroken campaign of character assassination against me'. Trueman, who felt he was acting on behalf of many ex-Yorkshire players and Yorkshire cricket in general, was not inclined to dispute the claim. Although angered Boycott's supporters tried to deprive him of his honorary life membership, Trueman, in reality, didn't give a fig. In his eyes, the election defeat was the latest in a long line of cruel cuts and the final straw. Now the man who'd been left to languish at home in Maltby when he fell injured at the start of his Yorkshire career, who'd been suspended for one game for not trying, who'd been turned down for a second benefit, who'd not been sent a telegram of congratulation by Yorkshire after becoming the first man in history to take 300 Test wickets, and who'd endured sundry other indignities, decided enough was enough. He took his ball home and never came back.

It is one of the saddest aspects of the Trueman story – and one of the most depressingly avoidable – that he and Yorkshire effectively severed all ties after that committee split. The ill-feeling between them was never healed due to a combination of Trueman's intransigence and the inertia of successive Yorkshire administrators, some of whom gave the impression of never having heard of Fred Trueman – let alone what he stood for. Two days after Trueman passed away, one prominent Yorkshire board member sent a text message to a radio reporter as Yorkshire neared victory in a Twenty20 game at Durham, which said simply – and quite preposterously given Trueman's contempt for crash-bang-wallop – 'This one's for Fred.' Somehow, it crystallised how Trueman and Yorkshire – although synonymous – were never really on the same wavelength.

Trueman made no attempt to build bridges with the club post-1984. Bob Appleyard invited him to Headingley when he was about to become Yorkshire president in 2006 only to receive the glare that terrified a thousand batsmen. 'I asked Fred whether he'd come to some of the Yorkshire games as my guest, but he wouldn't,' said Appleyard. 'He carried that grudge right to the end.'

Trueman, in fact, felt unwanted at Headingley after retiring as a player. 'We were always made welcome at places like Lancashire and Nottinghamshire, but never at Yorkshire,' said Veronica. 'We once went to Headingley for a Test match and Fred was going on somewhere afterwards to speak, so we took two cars. Fred gave me his pass and said he'd follow me through, so I went in, showed the pass and was let through. Then they stopped Fred and wouldn't let him in. He got in eventually, but the fact they even tried to stop him amazed me. Another time they stopped him, he simply got out his car and allowed all the traffic to build up behind him. This policeman came up and said, "What's going on?" and told the gateman to let him through. That's Yorkshire County Cricket Club. That's what you're dealing with.'

Yorkshire also passed up chances to bury the hatchet with Trueman. In 1998, Fielden nominated him for the presidency only for the committee to block the move. Even Boycott tried to get Trueman made president after joining the Yorkshire board in 2006. Only four years after Trueman's death did the club recognise his contribution to Yorkshire cricket. In 2010, the lower part of Headingley's old Winter Shed – now a small section of the Carnegie Pavilion – was named 'The Trueman Enclosure', but even that smacked of tokenism, the official opening taking place on the penultimate day of the season as if shoved into the schedule as an after-thought.

Fittingly, the ceremony was a shambles. Only a handful of spectators were present in the enclosure's outdoor seats on a day when squally rain blew on a biting wind. As people took their places at the front of the seating area beside the boundary, Boycott – representing the club along with fellow board member Robin Smith – remarked loudly: 'Can't we get on with it? I'm freezing my balls off.' When Smith commenced proceedings without the benefit of a microphone, the whirring of groundsman Andy Fogarty's tractor drowned out his words. It almost goes without saying no one bothered to inform Tony Loffill, the public address announcer, the ceremony was taking place, the majority of spectators looking on from other parts of the ground in total ignorance.

At least 'The Trueman Enclosure' represented a marked improvement on what Trueman thought Yorkshire might do in his honour. Richard Hutton recalled: 'Fred was talking about this one day in the dressing room before coming to the conclusion that "if they name anything after me, sunshine, they'll probably call it The Trueman Shithouse".'

Given they were cricket's answer to Cain and Abel, it is remarkable Trueman and Boycott ever made up, but in early 2003, a few months after Boycott got throat cancer, the unthinkable happened – and the cricket world was stunned. Blithely dismissing twenty years of acrimonious differences in an eye-blink, Trueman telephoned Boycott to offer his support.

His concern for his one-time bête noire surprised friends, family and former team-mates alike. 'No one was more surprised than me,' said Rodney Trueman. 'I could have fallen over when Dad told me. One day he said, "I'm going to see Geoff."

'I said, "Geoff who?"

'He said, "Geoff Boycott."

'I said, "Dad, you've spent all my childhood hating Geoff Boycott and now you're going to see him?"

'He said, "Well, he's got cancer now – that's different."

'And that one sentence told me more about my dad than anything else could. That's the man I loved, the man I respected. We're all flawed human beings, and Dad didn't always know how to show his affections, or manage his very complex nature, but, deep down, he had a heart of gold.'

Although Trueman's gesture was widely praised, he didn't technically make the first move. On the instigation of Rachael Swinglehurst, Boycott's then partner and current wife, Boycott sent Trueman a card on his seventieth birthday in 2001. 'Rachael's a brilliant people person and she said to me, "Why don't you send Fred a card for his birthday?" ' recalled Boycott.

'She said, "You still talk about him, you still obviously like him, and it's a big thing, his seventieth birthday."

'I said, "He'll probably throw it away or spit on it or something," but I sent the card and I'm pleased that I did. It wasn't about getting back together, or anything like that; it was just about me wishing him a happy seventieth birthday and putting on the card some sentiments that I genuinely believed – that he was a truly fantastic, wonderful bowler.'

If that card scraped a light covering of frost off an ice-hardened relationship, Trueman took a pickaxe to the ice when Boycott was diagnosed. 'Fred was absolutely brilliant,' said Boycott, who subsequently made a courageous recovery. 'He used to ring every Sunday about 1 p.m., and although I wasn't able to speak to him at first because I'd had this tube inserted and was struggling to talk, Rachael would speak to him and pass on his messages of goodwill. Fred was incredibly supportive and it meant a hell of a lot. I know he didn't have to pick up the phone.'

And yet the question remains: how genuine was the reconciliation? Could all those years of bitterness simply have been banished? 'It was 100 per cent genuine on Fred's part,' said Bob Platt. 'He had nothing to gain from a reconciliation and went ahead with it despite the fact he knew people such as myself and a number of former Yorkshire players didn't want anything to do with Boycott, even though we felt sorry for him when he fell ill. For years, Fred used to say, "That bloody Boycott's more slippery than a bloody snake in a bath tub of baby oil," and that's what most of us thought – still think. But, deep down, Fred was an old softie.'

That is not to say the patched-up relationship was all roses and chocolates. 'When Fred first made contact with Boycott it was all "Geoffrey this and Geoffrey that",' continued Platt, 'but there were times towards the end of Fred's life when he started calling him "Boycott" again and I thought, "Hello, Fred, I've known you long enough. You mustn't be happy with him again for some reason." You could usually tell what Fred thought depending on whether he called him "Geoffrey" or "Boycott", but the bottom line is whatever Fred thought about Boycott deep down, he was prepared to put the past to one side and let bygones be bygones. In that respect, he was a better man than I and a better man than a good many people in the game who don't like Boycott and never will.'

As well as ending their feud, Trueman made up with Boycott's supporters. He became increasingly friendly with Fielden and BBC *Look North* presenter Harry Gration, whose foot was firmly in Boycott's camp at the height of the troubles. 'When Geoff was under a lot of pressure at Yorkshire and the whole committee was against him, I supported him,' remembered Gration. 'I was sports editor of Radio Leeds at the time and Fred was absolutely livid that my sympathies were with Geoff. All through the seventies and eighties, I got the cold shoulder from him because of that.

But, by the end of his life, I was very proud to count Fred as a friend.'

The true import of Trueman's reconciliation with Boycott can only be understood in light of the 1984 revolution that rocked Yorkshire cricket. It was the darkest period of Trueman's life, a period that tore at his dignity and pride. It was a time of anger and antagonism, humiliation and hate mail, a time that split the club from top to bottom. And, most tragically of all, it was a time when Trueman's personal life came crashing off the rails in a way he regretted for the rest of his days . . .

In the spring of 1984, when the Yorkshire troubles were at their peak, Trueman embarked on a five-year affair with Diane Watkin, a thirty-eight-year-old from Beckenham in Kent. He'd met her on a Leeds–London train while he was on his way to Lord's and she was en route to the Savoy Hotel, where she worked in a boutique. Perhaps the kindest thing to say is that Trueman – traumatised by events at Yorkshire – was emotionally vulnerable at this turbulent time. But that in no way condoned conduct that vindicated at a stroke those who held the view he was a womaniser as opposed to someone who, for want of a better term, *made a mistake*. In Trueman's case, it was a pretty big mistake – one that led to sordid headlines in a Sunday red-top.

In time-honoured fashion, Watkin sold her story to the *News of the World* in return for lurid details of their romps in London. The catalyst was her claim she was pregnant with Trueman's child – a claim he vigorously denied and which was never proved – and that he subsequently didn't want to know her. Naturally, the revelations had a devastating effect on Veronica, who steadfastly stood by him in his hour of shame. The story was published on New Year's Eve 1989 while the Truemans were holidaying at their villa in Spain. They owned a property on the Costa del Sol, where they spent up to twelve weeks each winter. Emphasising the extraordinary celebrity of a fifty-eight-year-old who'd been twenty years retired from first-class cricket, the *News of the World* devoted three pages to its 'shock exclusive'. The main splash – dubbed a 'world exclusive' – was headlined: 'FRED TRUEMAN IS DAD OF MY BABY! JILTED DIANE TELLS OF FIVE-YEAR AFFAIR'.

The worst revelation was Watkin's claim that when she told Trueman she was pregnant, he replied, 'Get rid of it. At your age it could turn out to be a Mongol.' Watkin said Trueman even offered to pay for an abortion. 'I was in love with Freddie and he said he loved me. But now I'm expecting his child, he doesn't want to know.'

Watkin described their first meeting as 'like something out of *Brief Encounter*' and said Trueman came on to her when they stepped off the carriage. 'I gave him my phone number but really thought little more about it. It was about a week later that the phone rang. Fred asked me out to dinner and we went to a Chinese restaurant in Soho. Over the years we ate a lot of Chinese food – Fred just loves it and he's very good with chopsticks and showed me how to use them.'

According to Watkin, they didn't get romantically involved until four months after the first meeting. 'That night we both had a bit to drink and Fred took me to this sweet little flat near Lord's. It has just a small bedroom with a double bed, a lounge with two sofas and a TV, a kitchen and tiny bathroom. Fred brought a bottle of Old Grouse scotch with him and we were both a little tiddly. We just fell into each other's arms.'

Watkin laid bare Trueman's love-making technique. 'As a lover Fred was very caring and considerate – not at all the Wham! Bam! Thank you ma'am! Normally we'd make love once or maybe twice in a night. Fred was actually very quiet – content to sit in front of the TV and puff his pipe before coming to bed. Quite often we didn't talk too much – we were just happy being together. When he'd have a bath, he'd leave the door open and sometimes I'd scrub his back. He was so huge in that tiny bath I used to tell him he reminded me of a walrus! He really knew how to please me, all the secret places where a woman loves to be caressed. He could look at me with that direct, challenging stare – and I felt my legs go weak. I know he comes over as solid and down to earth, but I saw another side to him – tender and passionate at the same time. When I was in his arms the world stopped turning and I could think of nothing but that great muscular body pressed to mine.'

Watkin had the brass neck to call herself Trueman's 'other wife' and said of the night she told him she was pregnant: 'He took a Bible from the drawer beside the bed, went down on his knees in front of me with tears streaming down his face and said: "I swear I'll never leave you." We spent one more night together. Then Fred went home – and the phone stopped ringing.'

Instead it was Trueman's phone that started ringing – up to twenty times an hour. Usually Veronica answered, only to be greeted by stony silence. She contacted the police, who in turn alerted British Telecom. But when the calls kept coming, she found Trueman had stopped the BT trail behind her back. 'I called BT to check on their progress and they told me they'd stopped the trail on Mr Trueman's instigation. By this time, of course, I'd sussed out what was going on and I said, "Look, this has got nothing to do with Mr Trueman. This is to do with me. I'm Mrs Trueman. I reported it in the first place and the police are acting on my account." A few days later, the local policeman, a friend of ours, bumped into my daughter, Sheenagh, and told her he was coming round to see me. I knew then the police must have got to the bottom of it, so I challenged Fred and said, "Right, either you're going to tell me what's going on or the policeman is going to tell me." So Fred came clean and I got on the phone to this Watkin woman and told her to stay out of our lives.'

Although the Truemans knew the story was coming out, they didn't know when. The knock on the door came just after Christmas. 'First, we got the cub reporter from Malaga,' said Veronica. 'He was terribly nervous and I thought, it's not his fault, so I brought him in and made him a cup of tea. Then the paper sent this bloke round from Madrid and I gave him champagne. Eventually, the paper sent someone over from London – Stuart White. I knew I couldn't get round him with champagne and he ended up saying to me, "You're the hardest subject I've ever had to deal with," which I took as a compliment. But although it was a tough time and an unpleasant thing to deal with, I don't dislike dealing with people from the media because it's their job. Fred was in the business himself, after all, and it's the public who want the stories. It's the man in the street who creates the media.'

Veronica was determined to mend the marriage. 'I wanted us back where we were. It was actually better after that rift than it was before. It was five years out of thirty-seven – a splash in the bath, so to speak – and Fred was sorry about it for the rest of his life. To be honest, I didn't believe a lot of things in the paper anyway. Some of the things the article claimed Fred had said, I just couldn't imagine him saying. Apparently, she was the one who came on to him by approaching him on the train and asking for a light. I mean, even I could think of something more original than that.'

It wasn't the only tabloid story the Truemans had to contend with. In 2001, in a piece headlined 'FRED TRUEMAN'S FAMILY FEUD', Trueman's daughter Karen informed *Daily Mail* readers her father hadn't spoken to her for two years. According to Karen, they fell out after she talked to the press about the breakdown of her second marriage to musician Jon Slight. 'My father thinks you shouldn't air your dirty linen in public,' she told the *Mail*, thereby giving said linen a fresh airing for good measure.

The *Mail* article – a double-page spread that tipped over into a single column on a third page – was styled 'a telling saga of modern Britain' and revealed that Karen's sixteen-year-old daughter, Nicola, was a single mother with 'an uncertain future'. Nicola – fifteen when she fell pregnant – had a five-month-old daughter, Ellie, whom it was claimed Trueman hadn't bothered to visit. 'I don't know how he feels about Nicola being a teenage mum,' said Karen. 'I have heard from other family members that he is disappointed but I don't know because he doesn't speak to me.'

In some ways, the article was more embarrassing than the Diane Watkin story. It cited how broken families can have a devastating effect on future generations, implying Trueman was to blame for Karen's own marriage failures, along with Nicola's pregnancy, because his marriage to Enid collapsed in the sixties. 'I do hope Nicola one day meets someone special and is very happy but, as I know to my cost, if you come from a broken family you are more likely to be a statistic yourself,' said Karen.

The article described Nicola as a 'rebellious teenager' with 'little respect for marriage and a cynical view of relationships', adding: 'She describes her own father, musician Jon Slight, as "a waste of space" and refuses to have anything to do with him. She also has a similarly dim view of the man who fathered her own baby, a nineteen-year-old part-time nightclub worker from whom she separated shortly after Ellie's birth.' Nicola was quoted saying, 'You don't think "why am I having sex?" You just do it. Everyone does it. Girls of 12 round here are doing it these days . . . I liked my boyfriend at the time, but now he just gets on my nerves. When Ellie was born, he kept saying we'd get a house and a mortgage, but I said "How?" He can't afford to do that. He's just too laid back and unrealistic. He comes round to see Ellie, but he's not my boyfriend any more.'

If the Diane Watkin story and Karen article were humiliating in the extreme, at least one tabloid tale boosted Trueman's street cred. In June 1990, the *Daily Mirror* revealed his twin daughter, Rebecca, had secretly married Damon Welch, son of film star Raquel, during a ceremony in Los Angeles. The couple met in 1989 while Rebecca was working on marketing and PR for London night-club owner Peter Stringfellow's ex-wife, Coral, who was opening a club in the city. Naturally, the news Fred Trueman was related – however tenuously – to a Hollywood sex goddess prompted much choking on cornflakes and covetous comments.

Welch had shot to stardom in the 1966 film *One Million Years BC*. She'd emerged from behind a rock wearing a doeskin bikini, the poster taking pride of place on the bedroom walls of countless adolescent boys. Welch went on to appear in more than forty movies and dozens of television shows, sharing the screen with leading men such as Frank Sinatra and Richard Burton. But for all Trueman's sneaking satisfaction at being related to her, he was disappointed Rebecca hadn't told him about the marriage, hadn't involved him, hadn't given him the chance to give her the sort of magnificent wedding he'd given Karen and stepdaughter Sheenagh. For her part, Rebecca was sorry for eloping and disappointing her father, with whom she'd always had a good relationship. After flying back to England to explain her actions, she agreed with him the following statement:

We [Rebecca and Damon] decided it would be best to be married in England, probably in about a year's time. It was only later we realised that I could not stay in the USA simply as a fiancée if I wanted to work, as I did. That would require a work permit. We had, we felt, given our hearts to each other but legal technicalities were still in the way. The only thing to do was to get married now. We had both wanted to do this in our own time and with our families properly involved, but that would have taken a long time to arrange. So we went ahead with a small ceremony, with just a couple of witnesses, resolving to have a service later, in England, so that the marriage was solemnised in the eyes of God. It was difficult for both of us. I hadn't met Damon's parents and he did not know mine, so we hoped to keep the marriage secret until we had the chance to explain it all in our own way. We should have known it's difficult to keep that sort of secret when the bridegroom is Raquel Welch's son and the bride is the daughter of Freddie Trueman.

Rebecca and Damon followed through on their intention to have a service in England. In June 1991, their marriage was blessed at Bolton Abbey in the Yorkshire Dales. The occasion was not so much about two people affirming their commitment to each other, however, as the extraordinary media frenzy that enveloped Raquel Welch. Amid hype and hysteria hitherto unseen in North Yorkshire, Raquel dominated the day to the extent Rebecca and Damon felt superfluous.

The fun and games began several days earlier when Fleet Street reporters descended on the area. Tasked by their editors with finding Raquel, they were like the Frenchies in pursuit of the Scarlet Pimpernel. They sought her here, they sought her there, but still that 'demmed, elusive' Raquel was nowhere to be found. Amid rumours she was staying with a local aristocrat, Raquel had set up camp at the nearby Devonshire Arms, where she somehow avoided the media scrum. Unable to pin her down, journalists turned their attention to tailing Rebecca and anyone else they thought might give them a story. This led to circuitous car trips as Rebecca and co. cannily outwitted the Fourth Estate.

Although Rebecca didn't welcome the press intrusion, it has to be said she wasn't overly careful about protecting her anonymity. 'Rebecca was buying bridesmaid's dresses for my girls in a little boutique in Skipton,' said Karen. 'When we got to the shop, she said, "Right, I don't want anyone to know who I am. I don't want the press to find out I'm getting my dresses here. So keep your mouth shut, Karen. Don't speak. I'll do all the talking."

'So I said, "OK, Becky."

'So we get the dresses fitted and everything else and eventually the girl behind the counter said to her, "Can I take a name?"

'And Becky said, "Yes, it's Rebecca Trueman-Welch. That's Trueman as in Freddie and Welch as in Raquel."'

Considering she'd done her best to avoid the media in the build-up to the blessing, Raquel wasn't so coy on the big day itself. She upstaged Rebecca by arriving ten minutes late in a chauffeur-driven Mercedes with an entourage of beefy bodyguards in tow. 'I am afraid we are terribly late,' cooed Raquel from behind dark glasses as she stepped from the car to reveal a figure-hugging dress with a dramatically plunging neckline. 'Gosh, isn't Yorkshire beautiful,' she added. 'I've never seen anything like it. It's amazing. It's like a poem.'

Raquel's daring attire offended several members of the Trueman clan – notably Trueman's eighty-seven-year-old mother, Ethel, who had no hesitation telling her to her face. Flo Halifax remembered: 'When Raquel turned up wearing that low-cut dress, Mum kept saying, "It's not right, that, Flo. It's not right."

'Anyway, later on Raquel came over to speak to Mum and, straight out of the blue, Mum said, "You know, young lady, that's not the kind of outfit to be wearing at a wedding blessing."

'Raquel thought she was joking and said, "Now I know where Freddie gets his humour from." But Mum was deadly serious.'

Enid Trueman also took umbrage at Raquel's appearance. 'She completely ruined my daughter's wedding. Her boobs were showing and her skirt was up her bum. I don't think she ate a lettuce leaf at the reception. At one point, she dropped her purse and bent down to pick it up. Fred said, "Gerrup, we can see your knickers."'

Karen also thought Raquel's behaviour beyond the pale. 'I mean, she was something else. All day she was doing the whole Hollywood movie star thing. We had a three-and-a-half-hour photo shoot for *Hello!* magazine and Raquel was getting her lipstick touched up for every photograph. It was a nightmare.'

Rebecca, however, defends Raquel and believes she received unfair criticism. 'Raquel got a lot of flak for turning up late but it was more she didn't realise protocol than she was trying to steal the limelight. The press were quite cruel to her, in my opinion. Raquel certainly never did anything cruel to me. On the contrary, she was always very kind to me. I think everything got out of hand because the press took it out of hand. There was so much media attention around my dad and Raquel, it was ridiculous. Damon and I almost felt we were getting in the way.'

The blessing was the first time the famous in-laws had met. Raquel, then fifty, described Trueman as 'a lovely, lovely man', while he called her 'a little smasher'. More than a hundred people attended the ticket-only ceremony, including guests from the worlds of sport and showbusiness. The service lasted forty minutes, after which guests enjoyed a six-course meal at the Devonshire Arms, including lobster bisque, Dales lamb and crème brulée. Trueman footed the bill but brought his own wine. When asked by reporters what he thought of thirty-one-year-old Damon, an actor and personal trainer, Trueman said he was 'a great bloke' but knew nothing about cricket. 'It doesn't matter, though,' he added, 'because we will just get him on one of the Yorkshire committees.'

In an effort to interest Damon in the game, Trueman took him to Headingley to watch the Test between England and West Indies.

'Fred was on fine form that day,' recalled Sidney Fielden. 'He told us the police had accused him of breaking into Raquel Welch's bedroom the previous night and laying hands on her jewellery. He said he'd been found guilty – but insane.'

Within fifteen months, the marriage was over. In September 1992, reports emerged that Rebecca had walked out of their Los Angeles flat, Trueman confirming the couple were to divorce. 'It's tragic,' he told the *Sunday People*. Then, as if his own affair with Diane Watkin never happened, he added, 'It does seem that youngsters these days don't realise the responsibilities of being married.' Reflecting on that period, Rebecca believes her relationship was doomed from the start. 'The fact is Damon and I didn't even know each other. We basically eloped after just a few weeks. I regret that period and I regret disappointing my dad by not telling him I'd got married. I was young and crazy and didn't think any of it through.'

Rebecca's story had a happy ending. In 1998, she married Welborn Ferrene, a television and film editor from South Carolina. Trueman gave his daughter away at the ceremony at Welborn's parents' home on Hilton Head Island. Rebecca and Welborn live in Los Angeles and have two children – a son, Luke, and daughter, Tema. 'When Dad first heard I was dating someone called Welborn Ferrene, I think he got the impression I'd hooked up with a black southern Baptist,' said Rebecca. 'But Welborn is very much the blond, blue-eyed all-American type. I'm just so happy I got the opportunity to remarry and that Dad was involved. He and Welborn got on famously.'

With her first marriage well behind her, Rebecca is frustrated she is forever associated with 'the whole Raquel Welch thing'. She was extremely reluctant to talk about that part of her life because 'I've got a wonderful husband now and two great kids, so why would I want to drag it all up?'

'I'm just sick of it all,' she added. 'I don't want to be defined by that. The rest of my life has been lowered to an irrelevance almost. It was just a fraction of my life, a moment in time, and I feel I could go save a nation and all people would talk about is Raquel Welch.'

Raquel failed to respond to a request for an interview. Her agent said she would talk to her about it but, despite several follow-up calls and emails, her agent never replied. Perhaps, like Rebecca, it is a part of her life Raquel would rather not think about – a part that resulted in a lot of fuss over a fleeting relationship. As Fred Trueman put it, 'That marriage didn't last as long as my run-up.'

13

I Don't Know What's Going Off Out There

Cricket isn't what it was, cricketers aren't what they were, and the good old days are gone for ever – or so folk are forever telling me. It's a load of ruddy claptrap – and I'm reight fed up with it . . . If the England side of today were able to take on the best players of fifty years ago, I think we'd murder 'em . . . The game has advanced so much.

Fred Trueman wrote those words. They were published in his 1961 autobiography *Fast Fury*. Fast forward a couple of decades and Trueman was forever insisting, 'Cricket isn't what it was, cricketers aren't what they were, and the good old days are gone for ever.' The irony will be lost on no one acquainted with his work on *Test Match Special*.

Few former sportsmen have railed against their contemporary counterparts with a thunder akin to that shown by Trueman. A man who bemoaned as a player the tendency of ex-players to criticise all things modern became the embodiment of the individual he once despised. As time went by, Trueman came to believe cricket stopped sometime around 1968 – the year he left Yorkshire – and that everything thereafter was a pale imitation. This was summed up by his oft-repeated declaration, 'I don't know what's going off out there' – a catchphrase trotted out with such banal frequency it ultimately triggered his departure from the airwaves.

Trueman's *TMS* career nevertheless started well – albeit not without teething problems. As the late Bill Frindall recalled, Trueman's trademark badinage resulted in a hairy moment shortly after he was appointed summariser in 1974. Frindall, the *TMS* scorer, thought either Trueman's career or that of the programme would be short-lived – 'considering I'd had various conversations with him in the past when more or less every other word was the f-word.' And one particular incident did little to alleviate his anxieties. 'When Fred first came to *TMS*, we had a chap called Paddy Keaney, who was the producer of World Service sport. Now Paddy had a dangerous habit, if it was raining, of saying, "Well, we'll just go over to the *Test Match Special* commentary box to see what they're talking about," and they'd get the engineers to fade up the microphones.

'Now before FST, this policy was perfectly safe. They'd come over just as John Arlott was saying something like, "Oh, Reg Perks, he was a very fine bowler, but if only he'd got more sideways-on. He'd have moved it that much later and might have played many more times for England."

'Instead of which they came over just as Fred was saying, "Nah then, sunshine. Have you heard the one about the boy sat outside the brothel? Oh aye, he was sat outside the brothel, six o'clock in the evening, and this policeman comes along. He says, 'Hey, lad, what are you doing out there?'

' "The lad says, 'I want to go in.'

' "The policeman says, 'What do you want to go in there for?'

' "He says, 'I want to get a nasty, unsociable disease.'

' "The policeman says, 'Which one?'

' "The lad says, 'Well, the clap will do.'

' "The policeman says, 'What do you want to do that for?'

' "The lad says, 'Well, if I get it, I'll give it to the au pair, the au pair will give it to Daddy, Daddy will give it to Mummy, and Mummy will give it to the gardener, which serves him right 'cos he's just killed my f***ing tortoise." '

'So this went out on World Service. Of course, the BBC knew it wasn't Fred's fault because they shouldn't have been listening in the first place.'

Trueman first appeared on *Test Match Special* ten years earlier. He was invited to try his hand at commentating after taking his 300th Test wicket at the Oval. Trueman sat alongside Alan McGilvray, the legendary Australian broadcaster. The dialogue, on that occasion, was somewhat more prosaic:

Trueman: Change of bowling. Er, Tom Veivers is coming on at the bottom end. Bowling his off-spinners round the wicket to the left-handed Barber. And he pitches very wide of the off stick, and he plays no shot. (*Pause*) There's Grouty there, behind the wickets, as safe as usual. (*Pause*) Tom is getting his fingers wrapped round it again. Here he comes, just two or three little steps and bowls and that's wide of the off stick again, and Grout takes it. Plays no shot and throws it back to him. How we doing, Alan?

McGilvray: Very good. Do a couple more, will you?

Trueman (*laughing*): Oh dear, dear, dear, dear. I'll be writing for a contract soon. Tom moves in, bowls again and that one's on the wickets and he plays it out to Peter Burge, who's fielding at silly mid-off. He's fielding something like about ten yards away from the left-handed Barber on the off side of the wicket. (*Pause*) Tom just moves in, takes those three little steps and over he comes and delivers and that's on about the off stick and it's played out towards cover point where Norman O'Neill picks it up and throws it back to the bowler. (*Pause*) I think this wicket will turn a little bit, do you, Alan?

McGilvray: Agree, agree. Titmus was spinning yesterday, too.

Trueman: Yeah, he turned one or two, didn't he.

McGilvray: Yes.

Trueman: Tom bowls again – Tommy Veivers. And that's on the spot, and he pushes it back to the bowler. No runs. (*Pause*) Very casual and relaxed is Tom. He's always smiling, ya know.

McGilvray: A happy man, yes.

Trueman: I like playing against Tom. He's always laughing. (*Pause*)

Tommy Veivers moves in again and he bowls, and he pads that off, just outside the off stick, and Bobby Simpson catches it at slip. That's the end of the over, and it's a maiden.

McGilvray: Well, thank you Freddie Trueman.

Trueman even had a hand in the birth of *Test Match Special*. In August 1955, he was on a hat-trick against Nottinghamshire at Scarborough. The BBC's Robert Hudson was providing commentary on the game in a set half-hour slot. The transmission was about to rejoin the national Home Service (later to become Radio 4) and Hudson was getting increasingly anxious. With just forty-five seconds to go, Cyril Poole took guard for the hat-trick ball. Trueman charged in, Poole propped forward and was caught at short leg. 'It's a hat-trick. Back to the studio.'

Shattered, Hudson slumped back in his seat and decided there must be a better way of covering cricket. His solution was to suggest more use be made of the Third Network (later Radio 3) and that commentary be shared between that and the Light Programme (forerunner of Radio 2). Hitherto, cricket commentary had been confined to short periods on the Light Programme and the Home Service. Discussions continued through 1956, and in May 1957 Hudson got his wish. For the first Test against West Indies at Edgbaston (the match that effectively marked Trueman's 'reprieve' following his problems in the Caribbean in 53-54), a new ball-by-ball service was introduced. On Hudson's recommendation, this was aired on a combination of the Third Network and the Light Programme. The *Radio Times* for that week carried the programme title *Test Match Special* and the slogan, 'Don't miss a ball, we broadcast them all.'

Trueman already had radio experience when he joined *TMS*. Don Mosey produced programmes for the BBC in northern England and involved him in various regional projects. Trueman took part in *Sports Forum*, a topical debate show recorded before a live studio audience. He also undertook conversation pieces with fellow sports stars such as Yorkshire show-jumper Harvey Smith. At the turn of the seventies, Mosey, by then a *TMS* producer, advanced Trueman as a potential addition to the programme, only to encounter a lukewarm response. Only when former Wales rugby union international Cliff Morgan became Head of BBC Radio Outside Broadcasts did Mosey get his way and Trueman join the staff, making his debut at the 1974 Test between England and Pakistan at Headingley.

Morgan also adopted Mosey's suggestion that *TMS* should end its habit of slavishly returning to the studio for music whenever rain stopped play. From then on, the programme acquired a broader appeal as people tuned in as much to hear the dialogue when there was no cricket as when the games were in progress. Trueman came into his own during the weather breaks. Blessed with a formidable fund of stories (even radio-friendly ones that did not involve brothels and tortoises), he regaled listeners with a career's worth of anecdotes and an encyclopedic knowledge of the sport.

To this end, he was assisted by an extraordinarily gifted team of commentators who knew instinctively when to feed the bait ball or reel him in. Trueman walked into a commentary box that featured the poetic brilliance and soft Hampshire burr of John Arlott. Brian Johnston, a perpetual schoolboy who giggled his way through countless hours of larks and leg-pulling, was another broadcasting icon, while Christopher Martin-Jenkins, whose poise at the microphone was in direct contrast to the panic that invariably preceded him to the box, had not long joined the commentary staff. Amid the bedlam of life on the road, Martin-Jenkins was the voice of sanity (sort of) as he strove always to see the best in everything and everyone. In addition, there was Mosey – Yorkshire-born and nick-named The Alderman in recognition of his mayoral bearing. The other summariser was Trueman's former England team-mate Trevor Bailey, whose crisp, clear-thinking manner was underpinned by a mischievous sense of humour.

Completing the team was Henry 'my dear old thing' Blofeld, who also joined in 1974 and made celebrities of more pigeons and policemen than you could shake a *Wisden* at. Blofeld was taken with

Trueman's daily arrival in the box, which he described as like 'Laurence Olivier making a stage entrance at a rather anxious point during the Battle of Agincourt'.

'First, there was often a gruff word or two from without which was highly audible and then the commentary box door would burst open admitting Fred. He would be in full voice talking over his shoulder as he came in. Those of us who were there received a resounding yet cursory "morning all". There was usually a bit of clutter in his hands that needed to be put down. Sometimes there would be a friend with him who might be carrying a box or two of his latest book that he needed to autograph before flogging them somewhere during the lunch interval. Fred's arrival usually gave the box a bit of a shake-up. It would not be long before he turned to one of us and asked whoever it was if he had heard the one about . . .? When the answer came back in the negative, he bounded back on stage and unleashed what was always a splendid story, although at times he would have had the Lord Chamberlain reaching for his blue pencil.'

And then there was the pipe . . . Shaped not unlike an Indian hookah, Trueman would drop it on the commentators' desk and ram the tobacco in the bowl with all the finesse of a bull in a china shop. Then the first puffs of foul-smelling smoke would curl from his lips, much to the annoyance of fellow workers – notably Frindall. 'The only thing I found irritating about Fred was his pipe-smoking,' said the man Johnston nicknamed 'The Bearded Wonder'. 'It wasn't a normal-sized pipe, either; it was the size of a tea cup. I'm sure he had a mixture of rotting underwear and cordite in it. In enclosed boxes, it was an absolute nightmare and it got to the point where I had to get it stopped. I said to Peter Baxter, the producer, that unless he put a stop to Fred smoking in the box I wasn't doing the job any more. I felt quite seriously about my health and everybody else's. So Fred had to go outside after that, but, to be fair, he was very good about it.'

Trueman was a proud and prodigious puffer. In 1974, his services to nicotine were recognised by the British Pipesmokers' Council, which named him Pipesmoker of the Year. Thus Trueman followed in the footsteps of previous winners such as Harold Wilson, Peter Cushing, Frank Muir and Eric Morecambe. The coveted award was extinguished in 2004 because it fell foul of new laws on tobacco promotion, by which time Trueman had kicked the habit. 'The last time I saw Fred was at Trevor Bailey's eightieth birthday party in 2003,' added Frindall. 'Veronica came up and said, "Bill, you'll be interested to know that Fred has given up smoking." I said, "It's a pity the bugger didn't do it forty years ago."

'In fact, it used to get so bad in the *TMS* box I used to light joss sticks to cover the smell, only for the smell of the joss sticks to irritate Johnners. Fred's pipe also got on Johnners's nerves. On one occasion he said, "Oh, I think they're going to come off for bad light at any moment, I can't see the Tavern. Oh, it's Fred's pipe."'

Trueman's fondness for the briar lent his voice a smoky quality. His gruff contributions – delivered with British Rail slowness – contrasted with the erudite diction of Martin-Jenkins as he developed his own distinctive sound. Trueman had a habit of emphasising his words – for instance, 'I was the greatest fast bowler of *all* time', with the *all* extended for added effect. His unusual delivery, which sounded like it came from the bottom of his voice box, became a gift to impressionists from Manchester to Melbourne. 'Fred was born slightly short-tongued,' said his cousin Alan. 'His father was exactly the same. You'd hear it sometimes with Fred when he got tired but, generally, he'd been taught to lengthen his words in an effort to disguise it. That's where this totally unique voice came from.'

It was a voice that projected moderately at first. Although suitably critical when the occasion demanded, Trueman's work was more humorous than hostile. Back in the mid-seventies, Trueman still felt affinity with modern players, some of whom had been colleagues or opponents. His wit was sparkling, his analysis cogent; there was none of the bitterness that bedevilled later broadcasts. 'When Fred started he was a laugh a line,' said Tom Graveney. 'It was great stuff to listen to and invariably constructive, and it went down great with the general public.' Ray Illingworth agrees. 'Fred was very good when he first joined *TMS* and his knowledge of the game really shone through. But then he developed this "I don't know what's going off out there" business and you're not paid to do that as a commentator; you're paid to say what *is* going off out there.'

Nothing particularly triggered the transformation. Over time, Trueman simply couldn't understand what was happening on the field any more as the game underwent a series of changes. Fast bowlers, for instance, became increasingly chest-on, delivering the ball from inside rather than outside their leading shoulder in contrast to the way Trueman was taught. The sport became progressively influenced by one-day cricket, with consequent alterations to style and technique, and witnessed an invasion of coaching/backroom staff. Rather than ride with the times and adapt accordingly, Trueman became increasingly caustic. Sometimes his comments could be unbelievably funny; other times they carried a less appealing quality as objectivity was drowned in a vat of displeasure. In particular, Trueman raged against the modern pace bowler, whose principal crime was not to have been blessed with his own natural talent.

One of his most infamous outbursts came during the Headingley Test of 1992. Neil Mallender, Somerset's Yorkshire-born pace bowler, was making his debut in seaming conditions against Pakistan. After Mallender began with a couple of nervous overs, Trueman's opprobrium went into overdrive. 'There's plenty of good bowlers who've run in from that Kirkstall Lane end,' he thundered, 'and he's not one of them.' Then, of the man nicknamed 'Ghostie' on account of his near-albino complexion, he added, 'What's more, he doesn't look a well man to me.' Mallender recovered to take 3 for 72 and followed up with 5 for 50 in the second innings to help England to a six-wicket victory. His eight-wicket haul was the best by an England debutant at Headingley since Trueman captured seven wickets against the Indians in 1952.

Another Trueman target was Darren Gough. 'Quick? I could bowl quicker in me mac,' he bristled of his fellow Yorkshireman, thereby delivering perhaps the ultimate combination of humour, put-down and self-promotion that was a Trueman trademark. Trueman's attitude towards the cricket of the 1980s and 1990s was summed up when the Australian commentator Neville Oliver found him opening his mail at the end of an over when he should have been talking.

'Fred.'

'Yes?'

'You're supposed to be saying something.'

'Oh, I can't watch this rubbish.'

It wasn't just modern cricket to which Trueman objected. He railed against everything from modern spectators to modern life. This led to exchanges enshrined in broadcasting legend. Here he is with Christopher Martin-Jenkins talking about West Indian supporters:

Martin-Jenkins (*with horns blaring in the background*): Walsh bowls again, short outside the off stump and Capel pulls his head out of the way. But he hardly needed to though, really, because it didn't come back at him and just carried on its line outside the off stump and went fairly innocuously through to the wicketkeeper. (*The horns rise again*) It sounds as though the horns have had a drink, let alone their blowers.

Trueman: Ugh, they want throwing over the wall – with the horns after them. It's a terrible noise. Who wants to sit and listen to that all day? I wouldn't, would you?

Martin-Jenkins: No, you'd have a headache at the end, I think. In comes Walsh and bowls a ball of full length on the off stump and it's played by Capel up to mid-on, fielded by Hooper. (*Pause*) But it's, er, it's a different, er, culture, isn't it, Fred, because I notice Tony Cozier mentioning on the first day that there was an almost eerie silence around the Oval.

Trueman (*grunting*): Yes, well I'd rather put up with that eerie silence, me.

And here is Trueman getting mixed up between walkie-talkies and mobile phones:

Martin-Jenkins: The umpires are now using their walkie-talkies, which for some reason the ICC seem intent on abandoning, but it makes absolute sense for the umpires to be able to communicate verbally.

Trueman: Well, they use them everywhere else, so they might as well use them here.

Martin-Jenkins (*sounding nonplussed*): Well, they might as well.

Trueman: Every time I get on a train, they're ringing, carrying on. Ooh, it is annoying. One time you used to be able to get on the train, have a cup of coffee, read the paper, close your eyes, have a little nap. And now there's telephones ringing, people making bits for this and making bits for that. Ooh, it does annoy me on that train, and it's a shame, 'cos the trains on the east coast service are beautiful trains, they really are.

Martin-Jenkins: Quite.

Trueman: I mean, I don't want to know about people saying, 'Oh, I'm not going to pay more than two hundred odd thousand for that,' or, 'I offered them three hundred thousand pound a few weeks ago and I don't think it's worth that now.' I mean, I just don't want to know.

Martin-Jenkins: No, you've got a point there, I think. In comes Walsh and bowls to Capel . . .

Trueman's discontent with all things modern made him a butt of *TMS* wind-ups. His colleagues delighted not so much in feeding the bait ball as forcing it down his throat. It was rare that Trueman didn't bite, didn't launch into a tirade after being suitably stirred. Vic Marks, *TMS* summariser, journalist and former Somerset and England all-rounder, remembers Neville Oliver as particularly adept at drawing Fiery Fred's fire. 'It was always easy to wind Fred up and Neville used to pride himself on it. He'd say things like, "Well, Fred, this must be the best England fast bowler since Harold Larwood. I'll leave you with that thought as I hand over now to Christopher Martin-Jenkins . . ." Of course, steam would be coming out of Fred's ears and poor old CMJ would have to bear the brunt of his displeasure.'

Also guaranteed to draw gusts of disapproval was any mention of Geoffrey Boycott, the Yorkshire committee, Gubby Allen and/or Freddie Brown. But arguably the best Trueman send-up concerned a letter purportedly sent him by a Colonel Frobisher, a club cricketer of no especial repute:

> Dear Mr Trueman
>   I have taken your advice and started to stand sideways-on, but our first XI have had some real disasters. In fact, I got dropped to the second team and it didn't get much better there. In fact, I can't even get a game for the third team now. What shall I do?
>   PS: I'm a wicketkeeper.
>   Yours sincerely
>   Colonel Frobisher

An infuriated Trueman spluttered, 'Er, when I said cricket is a sideways game, I was not, I repeat *not* referring to wicketkeepers. If you turn front-on again, I'm sure you'll get back in the first team.' As the *TMS* box dissolved in mirth, Frindall playfully nudged Trueman in the ribs. 'Do you see that chap up there in the Grandstand, bending over the rails, convulsed with laughter?' he asked.

Trueman replied, 'Er, yes, what's the matter with him? Is he drunk?'

Frindall said, 'No, it's the chap who wrote you that letter.'

Trueman huffed, 'Er, I might have known it was a friend of yours.'

Occasionally, the tables were turned and Trueman played the part of practical joker. During the 1993 Edgbaston Ashes Test, the BBC's cricket correspondent Jonathan Agnew was asked to do a tea interval piece for *Grandstand*. Agnew's brief was to interview Bob Willis and former Warwickshire seamer Jack Bannister as to why England no longer had quality fast bowlers. Shortly before he was due on air, a little bird whispered in Agnew's earpiece, 'We've no Willis, I'm afraid. You'll have Fred Trueman instead.'

Agnew welcomed *Grandstand* viewers and put the pre-arranged question to Bannister, who answered, 'Well, I just don't know.'

Agnew turned to Trueman and received the same monosyllabic reply. Agnew tried desperately to inspire discourse on the subject as an angry voice ranted down his earpiece it was the worst interview *Grandstand* had carried. Trueman finished off pontificating on the merits of damp-proof courses before an exasperated Agnew concluded, 'Well, I don't think we've answered too many questions there, gentlemen.' Only later did he find out Brian Johnston had orchestrated the whole thing.

On another occasion, Trueman received a fax from Essex County Cricket Club that had all the makings of a classic wind-up but was, in fact, a pukka communication in response to Trueman's criticisms of their pace bowler, Mark Ilott.

Trueman: Er, I have a fax transmission here from James Davis, manipulative and sports physiotherapist of Essex County Cricket Club. He says, 'Having listened to your radio commentary this morning, I'd like to correct your solid belief that a fast bowler has to get side-on to deliver an outswinging delivery.' (*Long pause*) Well, I say that he *does* have to get sideways-on to be able to swing the ball, and that the left elbow should be pointing somewhere towards fine leg and the left shoulder pointing down the wicket towards the batsman. I have constantly said that I don't think he [Mark Ilott] can get sideways-on because the lad's had an operation. I've been saying that, haven't I? (*Pause*) Er, this James Davis goes on, 'I have spent many hours rehabilitating this potent left-arm swing bowler in the hope of eliminating the cause factors of back pain, which irresponsible short-sightedness from commentators such as yourself seem intent on introducing. When will you listen and learn and read the wealth of information available and thereby reduce the incidents of lower back pain in potential fast bowlers?' He says, '*I* would be only too happy to help *you*.' (*Very long pause*) Well, er, without blowing my own trumpet, James Davis, as one of the most successful fast bowlers of *all* time, I don't think you can give me much advice on how to bowl and swing the ball. Er, I'll talk about fast bowling, Mr Davis, and I will not be faxing you about physiotherapy. Well, what do you make of it?

Agnew (*laughing*): Well, fortunately it's not addressed to me, Fred. Emburey comes in and bowls to Mark Waugh, who flicks that firmly to mid-wicket.

Trueman (*indignantly*): Er, I think I might know a little bit about fast bowling.

Such marvellous moments – manufactured or otherwise – lay at the heart of *TMS*'s appeal. In the words of former *Daily Telegraph* cricket writer Martin Johnson: 'There was no better way of lifting your spirits in a 10-mile tail-back on the M25 than listening to Christopher Martin-Jenkins invite Fred to comment on the ever increasingly intolerable burdens of work placed upon modern fast bowlers, and then waiting for a sound that felt like the big end dropping off your engine, which was actually the noise of Fred biting through the stem of his pipe.'

TMS was a world of clowning and chocolate cakes, playfulness and puns. But it was also a world in which Trueman came to polarise opinion. For all those who considered his blunt offerings a breath of fresh air, as many – if not more – perceived them as drivel. An institution within an institution or the curmudgeon's curmudgeon? It depended on one's generation/outlook/sense of humour.

David Lloyd, the Sky television commentator and former Lancashire and England batsman, was firmly in the pro-Trueman camp. Lloyd says Trueman was his broadcasting hero – 'the first one who didn't speak like Mr Cholmondley-Warner'. 'I thought Fred was brilliant. I learnt so much about timing by listening to him speak on commentary and at dinners. On air, he could be outrageously funny and unbelievably cutting. He was an act, really. You had a suspicion he'd love to have been in the music halls of yesteryear, treading the boards. He just came out with brilliant one-liners. I remember he once came into the Sky box in South Africa and said, "I've been watching this guy. His front arm is all over the show. That's why the ball keeps going down leg side."

'I said, "Who, Fred?"

'He said, "Steve Harmison."

'I said, "But England are batting, Fred."

'He said, "Well, who's that, then?"

'I said, "Andre Nel."

'He said, "Well he's no f***ing good either."'

Don Wilson was another big fan. 'Was Fred telling the truth? That's the thing. He just gave it as he saw it, and you have to remember there were some very poor players around during the 1980s.' Martin-Jenkins believes Trueman was 'a very good judge of a cricketer who always spoke complete commonsense about the game', while Frindall said, 'Geoffrey Boycott is a lot more critical than Fred ever was – and nowhere near as funny.'

Others, however, were not so smitten. In 2001, *The Times*' chief sportswriter Simon Barnes penned a scathing article which described Trueman as 'that most crashing of malignant old bores, that most malicious of purblind glorifiers of his own past, that most resentful of all athletes whose day has gone'.

Barnes continued: 'Most people who follow sport would, when given a word-association test, respond to the word "Trueman" with the word "bore". Or perhaps with an involuntary impersonation of his radio commentaries: "Ah joost don't understand what's going off out there. Cricket is a sideways game." A few years ago, I invited readers of this newspaper to send in examples of the Truemanism, this being a piece of commentary that is immediately contradicted by events on the field. Trueman was the master; his resentment of aspiring England fast bowlers is so deep-seated that it blinded him to the events taking place before his eyes.

'"I'd be ashamed to draw my pay if I bowled like that in a Test," Trueman said of Bob Willis in 1981. "The worst bowling with a new ball I've seen." In the next six balls, Willis took three wickets. I spoke to Trueman a few years later and there was no fudging the matter. Cricketers were better in his day, cricket was a better game and fast bowlers of today really don't understand what they are doing. It was ungenerous, it was destructive, it was simple-minded, it was vicious, it was rubbish. So much for Trueman, t'greatest bloody cricketing bore that ever drew breath.'

Trueman's style was ripe for parody. On his seventieth birthday, Martin Johnson took him off in the *Daily Telegraph*: '"And after a word from Christopher Martin-Jenkins it will be Fred Trueman." "I, er, well, I mean, er, er, er, if someone would, er, er, care to tell me what, er, er, I mean, er, Michael Atherton, er, er, young man, er, good player, don't get me wrong, but, er, er, I mean, er, if, er, you can tell me Christopher, er, er, what, er, er, I mean, er, what's going off out there, er, I just, er, frankly, er, I just, er, don't know. Simple as that." "Well, thanks Fred, and now we welcome World Service listeners . . ."'

Trueman developed into a self-caricature and was widely labelled 'a professional Yorkshireman'. A once-great cricketer became a figure of fun, maligned by modern generations as he was prized by their predecessors. As former *Wisden* editor and *Guardian* writer Matthew Engel observed, 'Getting Trueman to comment on a modern cricket match is not unlike asking the late Lady Summerskill to do inter-round summaries on a world heavyweight fight. He is out of sympathy with the players and appears to have no respect for their abilities.' Modern players associated Trueman not with outstanding achievements on the field but with overt condemnation in the commentary box. They perceived him not as a once-great protagonist but as a grating antagonist, a man who never missed a chance to stick in the knife. 'Unfortunately, Fred couldn't recognise that anyone in modern cricket could play,' said John Hampshire. 'Because of that, he was thoroughly disliked by the modern player, who had the impression he was an arrogant man.'

One of Trueman's strongest critics was Darren Gough, who did not take the criticism lying down. In his autobiography, Gough claimed Trueman queried his bowling action at a book launch during the 1990s, ringing 'a certain person in authority' to relay his suspicions. 'I was furious,' he wrote. 'I used to turn up in a T-shirt that had Fred's face on the front. Not any more; that went straight in the bin. I could not believe it. I had heard stories about sad old cricketers living in the past, but I never expected someone like Fred to stoop so low. That was the end of Fred so far as I was concerned. From that day on, I no longer regarded him as a great Yorkshire or England player. In fact, I do not even think of him as a true Yorkshireman anymore.' Then, in a put-down of which the young Trueman might have been proud, Gough added he had better things to do than concern himself with 'the ramblings of a pensioner'.

According to Agnew, many of Trueman's criticisms were born out of frustration. 'Bowling fast came so naturally to him that sometimes he had difficulty realising just how challenging it could be for lesser mortals.' Agnew, who claimed Trueman once said 'I don't know what's going off out there' three times before the opening ball of a match had been delivered, added Trueman was 'deeply hurt that successive captains and managers had not called him in to talk to their bowlers'.

Few players, in fact, sought out Trueman, partly because he'd slagged them off, partly because they didn't have the good sense or humility to look beyond the bluster. Trueman helped the likes of Australian fast bowler Dennis Lillee but was never in demand for advice and assistance. However, as *Daily Telegraph* cricket correspondent and former Essex and England all-rounder Derek Pringle recalls, he didn't always help himself. 'Neil Foster and I were playing in a match between a Rest of the World team and an England XI at Durham in the 1980s. One day it pissed down and Fozzy and I found ourselves sitting next to Fred, who was there as a guest. He said, "I could improve both of you no end, ya know. Oh aye, half an hour in a net with me and I'd make you twice the bowlers." So Fozzy called his bluff and said, "All right then, Fred, what are you doing tomorrow morning?" Fred said, "Nothing," so Fozzy said, "Okay, we'll see you in the nets tomorrow morning," and Fred said, "It would be my pleasure, lads."

'Anyway, he didn't show up. Later in the week, he said in his newspaper column, "I don't know what it is about these young players today. I just don't know what they're all about. I was sitting next to Derek Pringle and Neil Foster the other day and they didn't

want to know." Fozzy, in particular, was apoplectic. I think he
wanted to sue him.'

Trueman's resentments cut deeper than frustration with lesser
mortals. He felt he hadn't had sufficient recognition from within or
without the cricketing community. When Trueman suggested in the
1960s his biography be entitled *T'Definitive Volume of T'Finest Bloody
Fast Bowler That Ever Drew Breath*, he was, as the prospective author
Michael Parkinson admitted, 'only half-joking'. Trueman considered
himself the crème de la crème and felt not enough people
acknowledged the fact.

'Fred never stopped short of telling you how good he was,' said
BBC Radio Leeds cricket correspondent Dave Callaghan. 'I spoke
with him at many functions and he would turn round and say,
without any qualms whatsoever, "I was the best." And, because he
was Fred, he used to get away with it. Some people would say, "Oh,
the arrogant so-and-so," but he put up a great argument, of course,
that he was the best.'

Not only did Trueman consider himself the finest, but also the
fastest. Callaghan added: 'Once, after a few drinks had gone down on
the after-dinner circuit, I said to him, "Fred, for me you were the
best English fast bowler, but I don't think you were quite as quick as
the West Indian Wes Hall." Well, that did it. Fred got very upset and
didn't speak to me for days. I did two dinners with him that week and
the second one was frosty.'

Trueman's *TMS* colleagues made a similar faux pas. 'One day it
was raining at Lord's and they were replaying television footage of
the 1963 series against the West Indies,' recalled Frindall. 'We were
remarking in the box that Fred didn't look particularly quick. All of
a sudden, there was a hush when we realised Fred was actually
standing at the back of the box. He walked up to the television
monitor, peered at the footage and said, "Er, isn't it amazing how
everything looks slower in black and white."'

No system can conclusively measure a bowler's pace. The modern speed gun is only a guide and was a distant concept in Trueman's time. Most good judges estimate he operated in the region of 90 mph, with the likes of Hall slightly faster. Plenty of bowlers, in fact, have been quicker than Trueman, whose skill was founded not so much on out-and-out speed as his ability to swing the ball late at devastating pace – a characteristic he shared with his hero, Ray Lindwall. Scientific studies have put the likes of Jeff Thomson, Andy Roberts, Harold Larwood and Dennis Lillee in the high 90s, while Shoaib Akhtar bowled the first officially recorded 100 mph ball for Pakistan against England in 2003, although Nick Knight, the batsman, claimed it felt 'about 78'. Neil Harvey says Trueman 'wasn't as quick as Ray Lindwall, Wes Hall or Frank Tyson but wasn't far behind'. He added: 'Fred's great talent was his ability to swing the ball *and* put it where he wanted; that's why he was such a difficult customer.'

Just as a speed gun is an unreliable barometer of a bowler's pace, so statistics are an undependable indicator of a bowler's worth. Statistics may paint a persuasive picture, but they can hardly provide a definitive one. All that can be said is Trueman's figures stand comparison with the very best. Of bowlers who have taken more than 300 Test wickets, only Malcolm Marshall (376 wickets at 20.94) and Curtly Ambrose (405 at 20.99) possessed superior averages. The only 300 club members to have eclipsed Trueman's strike rate of a wicket every 49.4 balls are Waqar Younis (43.4), Marshall (46.7) and Allan Donald (47.0). In addition, Trueman's total of 2304 first-class wickets at 18.29 is the most by a genuine fast bowler and, unless the Martians land and restore the systematically reduced first-class programme, will remain so for eternity.

Trueman's team-mates place him high in the pantheon. 'People often ask me how good Fred was. Well, he was as good as anyone there's been in my opinion,' said Ray Illingworth. 'Fred could bowl 90 mph, bowl leg-and-middle and turn a batsman round. You've seen medium-pacers do that, but not many quicks.' Geoffrey Boycott agrees. 'I would put Fred right at the top of the tree along with Malcolm Marshall and Dennis Lillee. They moved the ball, swung it and knew how to bowl on different surfaces. They also had an effect on the players around them, which is a really special gift. They had the ability to lift other players just by their presence, by the way they were.' Bob Platt goes further. 'I've heard people like Dickie Bird saying Dennis Lillee was the best fast bowler ever, but could Lillee play for twenty years, take over two thousand first-class wickets and never break down? Try and find me someone who's done that apart from Fred. Lillee was a great bowler, but Fred was better. All things considered, he has to be the best.'

Trueman's opponents were similarly complimentary. Denis Compton said batting against Trueman 'held some of the terrors of picking a path through a minefield . . . you dreaded the unexpected', while Trevor Bailey observed, 'on all pitches and in all conditions, it is doubtful whether there has ever been a more complete fast bowler'. Perhaps the greatest praise came from the game's greatest player. Asked in 2009 to name the best bowler he'd faced, Sir Garry Sobers replied: 'Freddie Trueman. He was very quick, improved with age and genuinely thought that he was going to take a wicket with every ball. He made things happen and made you, as a batsman, think things were going to happen. And he used to bowl all the time, by the way, throughout the season. There was none of this central contracts nonsense where fast bowlers like Harmison never do much bowling, so never get the right rhythm.'

Like Sobers, Trueman operated in an era where players struggled to reconcile the prestige of international cricket with relatively paltry financial rewards. In Trueman's case, this developed into out-and-out bitterness that less talented players nowadays earn significantly more than he did. When Trueman toured Australia and New Zealand in 1962–63, he earned around £800 – the equivalent of about £12,500 today. Nowadays, some players earn half that for one Test, while central contracts for England stars are worth £250,000–£400,000 per annum. In addition, the Indian Premier League, inaugurated in 2008, makes dollar millionaires of average players. One can only imagine how much Trueman would have fetched in

IPL – assuming, that is, he would have deigned to take part in it.

That is not to say Trueman didn't earn good money from the game. His 1962 Yorkshire benefit was worth around £150,000 today, but his earnings were meagre by contemporary standards. When Yorkshire swept all before them in the sixties, Trueman's basic salary was £1500 a year (around £20,000 today). He reckoned Brian Statham was on £2200 a year at Lancashire and that several counties paid their players £2000-plus. Trueman supplemented his income from endorsements, public appearances and speaking engagements and lived comfortably in retirement, but he was actually in debt when he died after lending a large sum of money to a family member. Veronica had to sell their property in Flasby to help pay the bills before moving to a cottage on the outskirts of Settle.

'I think Fred resented he never got the financial rewards players get now,' said Boycott. 'Unfortunately, that came across as curmudgeonly in his commentaries. In Fred's day, the money was poor for playing, the money was poor for endorsements, and I feel sorry for all the great sportsmen who never got their rewards – Fred Trueman, Stan Matthews, Tom Finney and so on. They just didn't get the money their talents deserved.' Trueman reckoned Yorkshire's decision to turn him down for a second benefit cost him around £15,000 (about £175,000 today), while the club even tried to cheat him out of money for representative games. When Trueman found out Yorkshire were withholding £34 of his £56 fee for Gents versus Players fixtures, so they could pay someone to take his place, he complained to MCC. They found Yorkshire guilty of 'malpractice regarding the payment of professional fees' and ordered them to pay Trueman all monies owed for representative matches.

Although Trueman was never swimming in money, he liked to show off the brass he possessed. 'Freddie once came round to Mum's in a Rolls Royce,' said his sister Flo. 'I'd popped round on my way home from work and Freddie said, "Come on, get in, I'll give you a lift round."

'I said, "I'm not getting in that. I'm not having everybody in Maltby staring at me."

'He said, "Why not? It's mine. I've bought it. I've earned it." And I said, "Ooh, I daren't go in there, Freddie. Everybody will think, "Who does she think she is?"

'Anyway, I got in the car eventually but I slunk right down in the seat, hoping no one would see me. Unfortunately, one or two folk did see me and said, "Hey, what were you doing in that Rolls Royce?" I said, "It was Freddie's idea, not mine. He insisted I got in." It was a lovely car, though – ice-blue-coloured and cream inside.'

Trueman had a weakness for attractive cars – pretty much his only financial extravagance – but was intrinsically gullible with money. Ted Corbett, who ghosted his newspaper column in the 1990s, recalled, 'He once rang me and said, "Do you want to join me in this scheme?" I said, "What sort of scheme, Fred?" He said, "Well, I've had this letter saying that if I send out five letters people will send me back £50. You want to get on that, you know. It sounds like a winner." I said it sounded like the sort of scam that's been going on for years and that I wanted nothing to do with it. I told him I hoped he made a million quid out of it, but I never heard him mention it again.'

Rebecca Ferrene believes people took advantage of her father's nature. 'Dad had this innocence about him – almost naivety. People could take him for a ride sometimes because he trusted them in business. If he gave them his hand and said, "We've got a deal," it was a deal. Sadly, not everyone possesses the same integrity.'

No amount of money could buy Trueman the thing he most craved – a knighthood. That would have been appropriate recognition, in his eyes, of an outstanding career. Instead, he had to content himself with an OBE, awarded in 1989 for services to charity as well as cricket. He accepted it with gratitude but felt short-changed, like a boy who expects a train set for Christmas but gets a pair of socks. The OBE came unconscionably late, and only after vigorous lobbying by friends. Brian Statham was awarded a CBE as far back as 1966, whereas Trueman got nothing. Whatever one's view on the merit of gongs, such inconsistency was manifestly unfair.

It was proof, were any needed, that Trueman's outspokenness cost him more than Test appearances.

Trueman went to his grave believing Harold Wilson had given him a knighthood but that Lord's blocked it. He heard this from Derek Jameson, the veteran journalist and broadcaster. 'I was told by a very good source that Fred was given a knighthood shortly after he'd retired from first-class cricket and that the toffee-nosed twits who run the MCC put a stop to it,' said Jameson. 'After that, Fred was known to us all on Fleet Street as "Sir Fred" in honour of the knighthood he never had.' To Brian Johnston, Trueman was always 'Sir Frederick' – a title that led to comical consequences. True to form, Johnston inscribed a copy of his latest book to Trueman with the words 'Sir Frederick'. Unbeknown to Johnston, his publishers addressed the envelope in exactly the same style. Trueman was thus not a little surprised to find an excitable postman coming up his garden path one morning offering profuse congratulations.

The lack of a knighthood, however, was no laughing matter to Trueman. He struggled to accept that contemporaries such as Frank Worrell, Everton Weekes and Clyde Walcott were honoured and he was overlooked. It was not that he disputed the right of the Three Ws to be recognised; he had enormous respect for the great West Indian batsmen. It was simply he felt at least their equal in terms of accomplishment. 'When Fred got his OBE I rang him and said, "Well done, son, on getting a medal for Other Buggers' Efforts,"' recalled Platt. 'Who knows, if you keep your nose clean, you might get a knighthood.' Fred said, 'A f***ing knighthood? If that King Arthur was alive today, he'd have to send his round table to f***ing Barbados.' Trueman was similarly piqued when New Zealand all-rounder Richard Hadlee – the first man to 400 Test wickets – was knighted. Although Trueman respected Hadlee's talent, he also felt that was missing the point.

Trueman's radio work became progressively sour. At the end of 1999, the BBC decided they wanted someone who did understand what was going off out there and dispensed with Trueman and

Trevor Bailey, the latter's style also thought too negative. According to Frindall, if Brian Johnston hadn't passed away in 1994, the BBC would probably have axed Trueman earlier. 'I'd heard Fred would have been moved out the door in the mid-nineties if Brian hadn't died. However, having lost Brian, it was felt they couldn't get rid of another major figure. But as we came towards the end of the nineties, we were in a battle with Talksport over a contract for the next five years and it was decided we needed a younger image. So Fred and Trevor were sent packing. It was sad, but you had to look at it from both sides. In later years, Fred tended to have one good session right at the beginning but then he'd just keep regurgitating the same things for the rest of the match. Of course, by getting rid of Fred and Trevor at the same time, we lost a tremendous archive of cricket history from the war onwards. Fred's recall, in particular, was second to none, and it was one of the highlights of my *TMS* career to see Fred and Ray Lindwall talking one day during a rain break, and seeing Fred in awe of the great Australian.'

Trueman and Bailey blamed their departures on Baxter, who they felt should have fought to defend their corner. Veronica Trueman believes Baxter behaved duplicitously. 'Fred and I went to Don Mosey's funeral in 1999 and Peter Baxter was there. I was talking to Peter and he said, "I've got to get back, Veronica, because I've got a very important meeting this evening."

'The next thing I know, I switch on the cricket next morning and Blowers was on saying we had a great *Test Match Special* dinner last night. Fred was still in the bedroom and I said, "Did you get an invite to the *TMS* dinner?" Of course, he knew nothing about it. I'll never forgive Peter Baxter for that. Why didn't he say they had a *TMS* dinner? Don Mosey had told Fred that as soon as anything happened to him, he'd be out the door. And he was right.'

Baxter stands by the decision to dump Trueman and Bailey. 'They held it against me, but it was the right decision at the right time. We were heading for a new era in terms of bidding rights and needed to have summarisers a bit more in tune with the modern game. In his heyday, Fred was a brilliant summariser. *TMS* without him was unthinkable to some, but, to others, it was unlistenable to with him.'

Trueman's colleagues were sorry to see him go. Vic Marks says Trueman was 'always very accommodating if I had some writing to do and would willingly juggle the rota around', while Shilpa Patel, *TMS* assistant producer, says Trueman was 'very charming, very professional – someone I'll always remember with a smile'.

A few weeks later, the *Sunday People* also pulled the plug, ending their forty-two-year association with Trueman via a telephone call to his villa in Spain. 'The *People* felt Fred was spouting repetitive stuff against the modern game and, to be fair, he was,' said Ted Corbett. 'The number of times, for instance, he'd say to me, "We've got to write that Courtney Walsh chucks it" and I would say, "Well, I don't think so, Fred, and we don't want to get ourselves involved in a bloody libel action."

'Fred would say, *"He* would never take a libel action out against *me*," and I would say, "Well, he might do, Fred, and I couldn't get what you're suggesting past the sub-editor." A lot of the stuff wasn't exactly useable. In his heyday, though, Fred was brilliant. He had a natural curiosity that made him want to get to the bottom of things, and no reporter can have a greater talent.'

Although he understood the paper's stance, Corbett stuck up for Trueman. 'I tried to put in a good word for him but they didn't want to know. They said he was too old and they would never get any younger readers while he was still around. When Fred left, I got floods of letters from pensioners in places like Bridlington and Rotherham who thought he was absolutely marvellous. At the same time, I know for a fact fifty per cent of the letters *TMS* received were complaints about Fred.'

Trueman's newspaper output was as opinionated as his radio work. As well as lampooning Boycott during the Yorkshire troubles, he had a public falling-out with Ian Botham. Trueman criticised Botham's bowling during the 1985 Trent Bridge Ashes Test, claiming he 'couldn't bowl a hoop downhill'. In his own column in the *Sun*, Botham hit back under a piece headlined 'Get Lost – You're Talking A Lot Of Twaddle' by declaring: 'Fred Trueman managed to put down his pint and his pipe for a few minutes to hammer me for wasting the second new ball.'

Trueman and Botham should have been made for each other. Both were charismatic cricketers and larger-than-life characters, but only in later years did they develop cordiality. 'I think that's probably why we used to bicker a bit,' reflected Botham. 'In some ways, we were running the same sort of treadmill. But I never took Fred that seriously, so it didn't bother me. I think a lot of it was for effect and a bit of an act. I'm pleased to say I got on better with him as I got older. He was an icon, one of the all-time greats and all-time characters. At times, he was a bit too hard on the modern players, but, once you got to know him, you understood where he was coming from. He became a bit of a caricature, unfortunately, and he was a much better person than that.'

Trueman continued to watch cricket on television in his post-media days but did so with the sound turned down, because 'a number of commentators who have no experience whatsoever of playing cricket at a decent level, never mind international level, talk a lot of drivel.' His opposition towards contemporary cricket – far from abating – further intensified. In 2005, after Andrew Flintoff spearheaded one of the finest summers of post-war fast bowling by an England side as they regained the Ashes after eighteen years, Trueman observed the Lancashire all-rounder 'would not have troubled anyone in my time'. With that single statement, the resentments and reproaches had reached full flowering.

Through his systematic chastisement of the modern game, Trueman became an object of ridicule, alienating himself from players and spectators. As Simon Barnes observed: 'Trueman's cricketing story is a great one . . . Why, then, did he have to spoil it? Why couldn't he leave us with the best of himself? His later career in broadcasting was the besmirching of his cricketing legend.' Trueman dwelt not on what he was – a cricketer to be ranked among the greatest of the great – but what he might have been. He focused not on becoming the first man to 300 Test wickets, but the fact he didn't take 400 – or even 500. He ruminated not on the universal esteem in which he was held, but the fact he didn't play more Test matches, get a knighthood, earn more money, and so on. As Rodney Trueman recalled: 'Dad would often say, late at night, I should have got more Test wickets, son. I should have got them.' Such frustrations – however justified – took precedence.

'I think that's the one real criticism people are able to level at Fred,' said Boycott. 'You can't get him as a legend, as a cricketer – fantastic. His record and everything was fantastic. You can't get him as a raconteur, as a character, as a humorist – fantastic. But, in that other respect, he left himself open. Fred never felt he got enough recognition when, in reality, he was universally regarded. Alec Bedser got a knighthood; Fred didn't. Richard Hadlee got a knighthood; Fred didn't, and so on. But it didn't make those who got knighthoods better bowlers. I think Fred dwelt on that sort of thing and it hurt him, but there's no point getting upset about it. It's like when I got cancer. Why me? I don't even drink. I don't smoke. I've lived a clean life. I've got no weight. So why did I get ill? There's no point going there, it does you no good.'

Trueman couldn't see through the fog of frustration. Although grateful for his talent and the life he enjoyed, he allowed himself to be blinded by bitterness. In doing so, he gave the impression of never having bowled a bad ball, of never falling short of the summit of excellence he alone scaled. Although there was an element of humour in his hubris, a sense of playing to the gallery, there was a greater sense of haughtiness that did him no credit. Far better Trueman had taken satisfaction in what he did achieve and was – a remarkable bowler whose feats will be feted as long as cricket is played. In the words of his great friend Don Wilson: 'At the end of the day, everyone's heard of Fred Trueman, and you can't buy that. He wasn't a here-today, gone-tomorrow sort of chap. He was hero-worshipped all over the world.'

14

The Birdman of Skipton

In 1960 Fred Trueman took part in a pre-season game in Settle, North Yorkshire. It was a match that changed the course of his life. As he neared the ground on his way from Scarborough, Trueman could scarcely believe his eyes. He'd never been near that part of Yorkshire and was struck by the beauty of the surrounding countryside. After the game, while relaxing in the club house, Trueman waxed lyrical about the location. 'You've seen nothing yet,' said one Settle player, who advised him to take 'the scenic route' home. Trueman drove back through Grassington and Gargrave, passing his future bungalow at Flasby. From that day on he promised himself he'd one day live in the picturesque Dales.

Trueman had always adored the countryside. From his earliest days as a child at Scotch Springs, he'd valued nature and the natural world. He treasured it more because of where he grew up and saw in the Dales reflections of his character. The Dales have many moods – and they were Trueman's moods: wild and stormy, soft and mellow. 'No matter where you are in the Dales, there's something different to see,' he said. 'Even after thirty years of living here, their magic is still unbelievable – and I still can't explain it. They have a power which keeps pulling me back when I'm away and I just thank God that He let me come and live here. I wouldn't exchange living in this part of England for any other.'

Trueman enjoyed the solitude of the Dales. Although extrovert in company, he was a loner at heart and liked to withdraw from the rush of the world. For Trueman, the Dales provided the perfect blend of privacy and practicality. He boasted he could see more traffic lights in one street in Leeds than in the whole of the Dales and yet was only three hours by train from the centre of London. The Dales also enabled him to indulge a passion for birds – of the feathered as opposed to skirted variety. Trueman liked watching them in his garden and claimed 136 species lived within nine miles of his bungalow – the result of a local study. Even this gentle hobby inspired fierce one-upmanship. Trueman had a running joke with Don Mosey – a fellow bird-lover – that Mosey always seemed to miss the nuthatch on his visits to Flasby, which would miraculously materialise as soon as he'd left.

Trueman said he preferred to hear his birds singing rather than coughing – as they might have done in the skies of Scotch Springs. It was a favourite saying – and a revealing one too. In later years, Trueman became synonymous with the Dales and increasingly distant from his South Yorkshire roots. It was a matter of self-perception as well as geographical circumstance. As time went by, Trueman disassociated himself from his humble background. It was as if it belonged to somebody else. He romanticised the realities of his past and interpreted them in suggestive style. This leaps from the pages of his autobiographies.

In *Fast Fury*, published in 1961, Trueman made his solitary reference to the 'shadow of the pit' and stated that 'facing the little bedroom where I was born early one February morning in 1931 is the Maltby Main Colliery.' But in *Ball Of Fire*, published in 1976, he announced: 'I grew up among fields and hedgerows and you wouldn't have known there was a colliery anywhere near because it was more than a mile away and behind a hill.' In *As It Was*, his 2004 memoirs, Trueman repeated the U-turn, insisting: 'Our home was a row of twelve terraced houses surrounded by open countryside. The houses were owned by a colliery, though when looking out from windows you would never know a colliery was nearby as it was situated over a mile away and out of sight behind a hill.' Tellingly, the Trueman memoirs made no mention of the proximity of the pit yard to Scotch Springs. Nor did they refer to the lonely landscape of slag heaps and slurry pits. Instead, Trueman painted a bucolic picture of a bleak locale.

Describing Scotch Springs and surrounding area, he told how 'tender wild mushrooms, their gills tickled pink, were strewn across the meadows like miniature white parasols'. He related how 'many was the time as a boy I saw purple and buttercup-yellow crocuses catching the first flakes of a snowfall in their orange hearts before closing, stiff and tight, imperishable and unearthly like plastic flowers'. He remembered fondly 'the clap of the wings of wood pigeon, the squawk of blackbirds and scuttling rabbits'. And he recalled long-lost Aprils when 'the petals of tulips were scattered across the still cold soil like colourful casino chips'. The impression created was more *Last of the Summer Wine* Yorkshire than a mining heartland. Trueman portrayed Scotch Springs as the sort of place where Compo, Clegg and Foggy might have stopped for a pint during their timeless meanderings through God's own county. Indeed, it is hard to believe Holmfirth – the idyllic West Yorkshire town where *Summer Wine* was set – is in the same county as Scotch Springs. Notwithstanding Trueman's tendency towards exaggeration and the artistic dash of his ghost-writer, Trueman's interpretation was highly revealing.

There were similar discrepancies in the way Trueman described his family's links with the mining industry. In his memoirs, he seemed at pains to point out mining did not run in his family as it did in many in the Stainton area. Trueman described his father as a 'countryman' who worked 'for a time' as a coal-face worker. Yet 'for a time' was no fewer than forty years, which made Dick Trueman a miner first and foremost and would have put him on the road to a second gold watch in some professions. In 2001, there was an illuminating moment when Trueman was interviewed on ITV programme *My Favourite Hymns*. When presenter John Stapleton asked what his father did for a living, Trueman shot an awkward glance. 'Well, er, Dad was in the jumping business,' he declared, referring to his father's brief stint as a stud groom. Not once did he mention his dad was a miner.

In *As It Was*, which might in parts have better been entitled *As It Wasn't*, Trueman described himself as a countryman and his family as country folk. The following sentences emphasise the fact. 'I love the country because I am, and always have been, a country person' ... 'Being country people, our lives were very much governed by the seasons' ... 'Being country folk who lived off the land, we enjoyed a good and varied diet of fresh meat, vegetables and fruit, which changed according to the seasons' ... Then, referring to the contents of his Christmas stocking, 'Being a country boy, I had the advantage of knowing the identity of the nuts I received, and of even knowing what an orange was.' And, just in case anyone still hadn't got the message, the opening chapter was entitled 'Mother Nature's Son'. The impression was of a man trying to convince himself as much as his readership.

The bleak reality of Trueman's birthplace puts his achievements into greater perspective. To think he rose from the edge of a pit yard is a profoundly affecting and precipitous climb. The Trueman story is rendered more powerful, more poignant by the fact he came from such conditions to conquer the world. But he preferred to play that side of it down, in effect repudiating his modest roots.

In Trueman's defence, there might have been an element of wanting to blot the truth from his mind. After all, who would wish to wax lyrical about slag heaps and slurry pits? At the same time, Trueman was not renowned for his reluctance to tell folk how good he was, so why not add weight to the story in every sense? Instead, he blocked out the shadow of the pit and remembered only 'the clap of the wings of wood pigeon, the squawk of blackbirds and scuttling rabbits'. Dennis Trueman believes his brother developed a lofty attitude. 'I think Fred perhaps got a little bit snobbish about it as he got older. He was immensely proud of Dad and loved him to bits – just as he loved the whole family to bits – but Fred moved into a different world as time went by. He also played cricket at a time when some folk looked down on people from the type of background we had, and I think that probably affected his outlook.'

Fred Trueman raged at suggestions he was a social inferior. There was a telling passage in his memoirs when he said: 'Snobbery was rife in my early days in cricket. Some of the so-called gentlemen players who had come straight out of Oxbridge into a county side would say to me, "I believe you're an ex-miner", with a sort of haughty disgust in their voices. I used to snap back at them, "Aye, and what are you? An ex-schoolboy?" because I never let anybody get away with anything when it came to a question of personal pride.' Instead of regarding his mining heritage as a badge of honour, Trueman perceived it as a disadvantage – a stick with which his critics could beat him. It was one of the reasons he distanced himself from Maltby, physically and psychologically.

'I don't think Fred was ever that keen on Maltby,' said his cousin Alan. 'It was as though he wanted to leave it behind. Over time, he moved into a different social sphere. To this day, there are people in Maltby who don't like Fred because of that.' When a statue was erected in Trueman's memory in 2010, it was significant it was sited in Skipton as opposed to Stainton or Maltby. The £80,000 bronze work, designed by Yorkshire sculptor Graham Ibbeson, is situated at the Canal Basin in Trueman's adopted home town. It captures his bowling action in full flow, complete with unfurled right sleeve and 'Gotcha' expression. Appropriately, given Trueman's ornithological predilection, it is something of a magnet for Skipton's pigeons.

Trueman saw no echoes of himself in the South Yorkshire coalfields. Not only did he like to be considered a countryman rather than a miner's son, his political complexion was anything but red. Trueman became a high-profile supporter of the Conservative party and counted among his friends the likes of former Prime Minister John Major. He even appeared on stage at Conservative rallies, including one at Wembley during the 1983 General Election when the British songwriter Lynsey de Paul sang a ditty unlikely to have been whistled at Maltby Main Colliery:

> *Vote Tory, Tory, Tory*
> *For election glory*
> *We don't want U-turns*
> *So we'll vote for Maggie T*
> *Vote Tory, Tory, Tory*
> *The only party for me*
> *Say No to Labour*
> *And No to SDP*

Sidney Fielden was among those shocked by Trueman's politics. 'I always found it quite incredible that Fred should be, in a sense, a high Tory. He was a fervent supporter of Margaret Thatcher, John Major and all the Tory governments, and in later life went to live in North Yorkshire in the Yorkshire Dales, with which he became associated. You would have expected a miner's son from South Yorkshire to have been a rampant, left-wing Labour man, like nearly all of them are down there, but he wasn't, he was a right-winger. Politically, Fred believed the Labour party would sell the country down the river and during Yorkshire committee meetings would often moan to me about what "that South Yorkshire lot" are doing to the country.'

In fact, only one member of Trueman's family was socialist – his brother Arthur. Otherwise, his parents and siblings were Conservative or Liberal. In an interview with the *Sheffield Morning Telegraph* in 1983, Trueman conceded his political outlook had possibly been coloured. 'Cricket did everything for me. It made my life. It took me round the world I don't know how many times. It moved me into a different class. I don't mean I'm no longer working class. It moved me into a different sphere of living. I don't know whether that's affected my outlook but, yes, I suppose I am a bit of a right-winger. Communism, Marxism, Trotskyism – all that sort of thing frightens me to death.'

Trueman was hugely vocal about his political views. He never missed a chance to tell socialists they were backing the wrong horse. 'Fred was always so aggressive about it,' said former Labour deputy leader Roy Hattersley. 'I'd meet him three times a year and we'd have a pint together and talk about cricket – particularly Len Hutton, my great hero. The conversation would always begin by him reminding me that he and I were of different political persuasions. It didn't matter a bugger to me, but it seemed to matter to him. But in my experience, very few sportsmen, footballers or cricketers, who start off as working-class lads remain that after they've got some money in their pockets. I'm not saying everyone, but it's certainly not unusual, and I suppose Fred had got on in life and thought everybody else could if they tried.'

In the 1980s, Trueman claimed to have repelled overtures to stand as a Conservative candidate in North Yorkshire. He said he was asked on a tentative basis, although did not say who by or where he would have stood. 'Apparently, someone floated the idea, but I don't know how seriously,' said Veronica. 'Fred thought about it, though, thought about it a lot. In the end, I don't think he believed he was really cut out for it. I remember Ken Livingstone saying to him at a dinner, "Don't even think about it, Fred. You're too honest for your own good. They would destroy you if you tried to become a politician."'

The thought of Trueman serving in Parliament is not unlike envisioning Ken Livingstone and Roy Hattersley opening the batting for England. It would also have offended those who once imagined marching behind Trueman's broad shoulders in the name of the proletariat. Trueman was the very definition of a working-class hero and yet had little spiritual affinity with the working class. The battle he fought was for personal acceptance; he was never on a wider crusade for the common man. 'Fred didn't like being ordered about and said so in no uncertain terms,' said Ted Corbett. 'He didn't like being treated as a servant and I don't think it went much deeper than that. I've seen him in the company of John Major and Ken Clarke and I think if they'd asked him to lick their shoes he might have done. He was a different person in that type of company.'

Sir Bernard Ingham, Thatcher's former chief press secretary, believes Trueman was conservative to the root of his being. 'I think

Fred was conservative both with a small and capital "c". He believed in conserving the past and he certainly didn't believe in change for change's sake. Once he'd got over the wildness of youth he found in himself, in his inner core, the conservatism I think had been born into him. He was a complex character and a man – once perceived as a rebel – who evolved into what might be termed a pillar of society.'

Bizarrely, some would say hysterically, Trueman protested he was never a rebel. It was a bit like Robin Hood proclaiming he was not an outlaw, or Dick Turpin insisting he was not a highwayman. It was emblematic, too, of the way Trueman developed a delusional self-image. He came to believe he was never 'Fiery Fred', that he never bowled purposely to hit a batsman. Trueman became something of an Establishment figure – although one never fully accepted by the Establishment. He was also an ardent royalist, one of his proudest moments coming at a British Achievers Luncheon in 2002 when the Queen caught sight of him in a crowded room. According to Trueman, the Queen made a beeline for him and said, 'Oh, I haven't seen you in such a long time, how are you?' It meant more to him than most of his wickets.

Enhancing the image of countrified respectability, Trueman became a regular churchgoer. He believed in God throughout his life, though did not attend church in his playing days. From the late eighties he worshipped at Bolton Abbey, where his daughter Rebecca held her wedding blessing and where his stepdaughter Sheenagh was married. 'Fred started going to church after Sheenagh's marriage in 1987,' said Veronica. 'I thought it was wrong people should only use Bolton Abbey for weddings, so Fred and I started attending the services. As a child, Fred went to church three times on a Sunday and was always a believer. Peter Parfitt used to joke that he was a God botherer, although Fred never shoved it down people's throats.'

Trueman attended the same church as Bob Appleyard. Much to the amusement of their former colleagues, this led to arguments as to which of them started going there first, echoing the Yorkshire cricket squabbles of the 1950s. In 1997, Trueman fulfilled a long-held ambition to visit the Holy Land. He walked in the footsteps of Jesus – an experience that deepened his Christian devotion. According to Reverend John Ward, former rector of Bolton Abbey, Trueman possessed a simple faith. 'Fred's greatest love outside his family and his sport was nature, and he thought a world so beautiful could only have been created by divine hand. He had the difficulty most people have in equating natural disasters with a God of love – a lot of people ask the "why?" question, and Fred was no different. But he didn't want to enter into discussions about the existence of God. As far as Fred was concerned, God was a given.'

Sidney Fielden, a practising lay preacher, believes Trueman's faith influenced his decision to make up with Geoffrey Boycott. 'Fred told me he used to say a prayer for Boycott in church every Sunday, which said a lot about Fred's kindness and generosity of spirit. Boycott, in contrast, didn't have much time for the church. He once asked me, "How much do you get paid for this preaching lark?" which was an absurd thing to say.'

Trueman was not content simply worshipping at Bolton Abbey. He also worked tirelessly to raise funds for the church. One day he approached Reverend Ward and offered to speak free of charge if they arranged a dinner. The event in Ilkley was supposed to be a one-off but was so successful it led to a series of annual dinners for which Trueman enlisted celebrity speakers. One year he invited Robert Runcie, then Archbishop of Canterbury, whom he'd met during a Lord's Test.

'I was sitting in Fred's house when he suddenly decided to ring Runcie's office,' said Reverend Ward. 'Runcie picked up the telephone, which threw Fred a bit because I think he'd been expecting Runcie's secretary to answer, and their conversation went something like this:

'"Oh, er, good afternoon, er, I'd like to speak to Robert Runcie, please."

'"Yes, this is Runcie speaking."

' "Oh, er, Lord Runcie. Er, Lord Runcie, gosh. Er, it's Freddie
Trueman, Lord Runcie."

' "Oh gosh, Freddie Trueman. Oh, my word, Freddie Trueman.
Gosh, how are you, Freddie, how are you?"

'Anyway, both were equally thrown by speaking to the other, and
it was obvious they had great mutual respect. It was a wonderful
evening, although Fred – supposedly the introductory speaker – got
up to speak at 10.30 p.m. and didn't pause for breath until 11.15 p.m.,
by which time Runcie was completely exhausted.'

The dinners raised thousands for the upkeep of the priory church.
Trueman brought along cricket bats he'd had signed on his travels
and also provided gifts and raffle prizes. 'I'd speak for a bit, Fred
would speak for a bit, and then the celebrity speaker would do his
bit,' said Reverend Ward. 'Fred's speeches were terrific – and he
never swore once. Sometimes he came out with something that was
a little bit risqué, but, being Fred, he had the ability to get away with
it. His sense of timing was incredible and he was very instinctive.'

Reverend Ward became a good friend of Trueman and says one
of his greatest qualities was loyalty. 'Fred was very loyal – whether
to a cause close to his heart such as Bolton Abbey, or if you happened
to be a friend. He would always treat you as an equal and valued
companion, and if he felt you were being left out of a conversation
would make a point of bringing you in. He used to take his doctor
and me to Headingley to watch the Tests, joking he was looking after
his body and soul at the same time, and it was noticeable how he
treated everyone properly, from the menial worker to the
programme seller, and always paid attention to them. Some people
don't do that when they get to a high level, but Fred did, and I really
admired him for it.'

For all his faults, Trueman possessed a generous nature. He
displayed it through actions that spoke louder than words or political
beliefs. 'I always remember an incident at the Oval,' said David Frith.
'A disabled man was driving his car through the Hobbs Gates and
up towards the stone steps of the old pavilion. He was easing his way
around – it was very crowded, the match was starting in half an hour

or so – and I was with Fred. This bloke accidentally pressed the accelerator instead of the brake, just missed Fred and me and crashed into the old stone steps. A couple of people suffered minor grazes – just hit up the bum or something, although no one was seriously hurt. This poor old fella sat there, dazed and embarrassed, and people were abusing him, saying things like, "You stupid old sod." It was only Fred who said, "Oh, poor old bugger, don't condemn him, he didn't do it on purpose, he hasn't got two good legs like the rest of us." That really impressed me. While others were shouting and screaming at this disabled chap, Fred was the first to defend him and make sure he was all right.'

Trueman's stepdaughter Sheenagh recalls a time he gave money to a total stranger on Christmas Day. 'Fred was just about to cut into the turkey and we were all there with our Christmas hats on, pulling the crackers. Suddenly, the doorbell rang. This bloke explained he couldn't afford any Christmas dinner for his family, so Fred went straight to his wallet and gave him some money. He helped him out without a second thought.'

Trueman was no less generous to family members. He lent them money if they needed help and never complained if he wasn't paid back. In 2003, Trueman bailed out daughter Karen to the tune of £3200 after she was found guilty of benefit fraud. A court ruled she'd fiddled housing and council tax relief and made her the subject of a twelve-month community rehabilitation order after she'd admitted eight offences of making false claims. 'Nothing was too much trouble for Fred,' added Sheenagh. 'If he had the capacity to help you, he'd do so immediately.'

Never was Trueman's kindness more manifest than when he arranged a tribute dinner for Brian Statham in 1989. Statham had fallen on hard times – he'd lost his job as a Guinness representative and developed osteoporosis – and Trueman pulled out all the stops to alleviate the burden. With boundless energy, he sought out practically everyone who'd played with or against Statham and helped sell around a hundred tables at London's Grosvenor House Hotel at £1000 a time. He enlisted the Minister of Sport to chair the occasion and Leslie Crowther and Rory Bremner to run an auction. 'It meant the world to Brian,' said his widow, Audrey. 'It meant he didn't feel deserted or alienated by his peers. Brian had suffered a great deal of mental stress through work; a new hierarchy had come in and all the work had changed, and he was working incredibly hard. I can remember him doing party nights in Cheshire, being there until the end of the night in a public house and then reporting to Leeds for a breakfast consultation the following morning. It meant he was getting about three hours' sleep at the time and eventually it took its toll. The dinner raised a significant five-figure sum and Fred also bought Brian a car – a Subaru. It was typical of Fred to help him like that. He was an extremely kind and generous man.'

It wasn't just friends and the church for whom Trueman raised funds. He was a prodigious supporter of good causes, with children's charities close to his heart. Trueman's support of disadvantaged youngsters stemmed from his playing days. One year, Yorkshire coach Maurice Leyland bet him a stone of humbugs he couldn't score a half-century and take six wickets in the same game. When Trueman achieved the feat, Leyland brought the humbugs to Yorkshire's next match.

The story was widely publicised and Trueman was inundated with confectionery from Yorkshire manufacturers who saw it as a chance to gain favourable PR. After he and his team-mates had taken their fill, Trueman took the rest of the goodies to a home for disabled children near Harrogate. He was deeply moved by what he saw. Trueman was particularly touched by the plight of a small boy encased in a frame of tubular steel.

'How are you, son?' he asked.

'I'm fine,' came the reply. 'I'm going to win the Brighton–London road race next year.'

It was too much for Trueman. His eyes welled with tears and he had to leave the room. From that day, he vowed to do everything he could to help children's charities.

'It would break Fred's heart to go into children's hospitals,' said

Veronica. 'Adult suffering he could cope with, but children's got to him every time. He used to say, "When you're a sportsman, you're so physically fit you take it for granted. These kids will never have the health and opportunities I had." Very often, Fred had to take time to compose himself before going into a children's hospital.'

Trueman also raised cash for the Stepping Stones Appeal at Wakefield's Pinderfield Hospital, which helps those with spinal injuries. He raised money for Yorkshire Air Ambulance, for the Scanner Appeal at Keighley's Airedale General Hospital, and for various charities through the annual Fred Trueman Golf Classic at Harrogate. Having had little time for golf in his playing days, Trueman developed a keen interest in retirement and took part in celebrity and charity tournaments. He played off a single-figure handicap and was characteristically competitive.

Trueman also helped several animal charities. He raised money for Canine Helpers, which assists disabled people by training and placing dogs, and supported Jerry Green Dog Rescue at Thirsk in North Yorkshire, from where he and Veronica sometimes got strays. The Truemans always kept dogs – starting from the time Veronica brought Simba, her Alsatian, to live with them at Flasby. When Simba died, the Truemans got William, an Old English sheepdog. They then found William a friend – Tara, another Old English. Whenever one dog passed away, they replaced it with another and usually had two at any one time. There were two more sheepdogs, Digby and Alfie, as well as Cassie, a bearded collie cross, and Tessa, a Samoyed. Trueman once took William into the *Test Match Special* box at Headingley. Unfortunately, the dog caused chaos. 'The bugger ate two microphones,' remembered Bill Frindall. 'It wasn't what you'd call a fluffy sort of dog.'

Trueman grew extremely attached to his dogs. He'd be utterly devastated if one passed away. When Tara died, Trueman had to pull out of a television interview because he feared he might break down on air. He was proudly protective and caring of his pets. 'Fred and Veronica once came to stay with us and brought William with them,' said their friend, Morag Brownlow. 'Unfortunately, our dog and William had a scrap and William came off worse, and we had to take him to the vet to get him stitched up. That evening, Fred insisted on bringing his mattress down to the drawing room where William was and slept next to him all night to make sure he was all right. Fred loved animals and cared for them deeply.'

Revealingly, Trueman also cared what animals thought about him. Veronica recalls their journey to collect Alfie in 2003. 'We were driving to Jerry Green's rescue kennels and Fred's conversation suddenly dried up. I thought, "What on earth is wrong with him?" So after a while, I said, "Fred, what is it?" and he didn't answer.

'A few minutes later, I tried again, "Fred, what is it?" and again he said nothing.

'A few more minutes passed and then he suddenly piped up, "I wonder if he'll like me, Veronica," and I said "Who?" and Fred said "The dog."

'I looked at him to see if he was serious – saw that he was deadly serious – and said, "Fred, it's a dog, of course it'll like you. Dogs like people – even you." But he was absolutely terrified this dog wouldn't like him.

'When we arrived at the kennels, Fred started pacing around the office while the staff went off to fetch the dog, then he went to the toilet, then he came back out again, then he started fidgeting around in his chair, that sort of thing, and basically carried on like a nervous wreck. Eventually they brought this dog through and of course the first thing it did was bound straight over to Fred and lick him all over his face, and the relief on Fred's face just had to be seen. He started grinning from ear to ear just because this dog so obviously liked him, and from that moment on, Fred and Alfie were inseparable until Fred passed away.'

Despite his outward self-confidence, Trueman was not nearly so confident within. A streak of insecurity lay beneath the surface. 'Fred could go on a cricket field in front of thousands of people and he was fine,' said Veronica. 'Likewise, he could go on stage in front of a thousand people and it wouldn't bother him one bit. But if someone invited him to a party, a small gathering, he didn't like it. I would nearly always have to go into the room first because he was nervous. Similarly, when he was at home, he never liked people invading his space. If someone came and sat next to him in the house, he'd go into himself a bit.'

As befitted the archetypal Englishman, home was very much Trueman's castle. Once he'd kicked off his shoes and lit his pipe, he was as happy as the proverbial pig in muck. 'Television was invariably tuned into sport,' said Veronica. 'Fred liked snooker, he liked football, but he was particularly fond of rugby league. He'd also sit up watching westerns and war films. Basically, anything with a gun in it. Late at night, I'd hear the guns and bombs going off and I'd say, "Fred, turn the television down." Unfortunately, he'd go a bit deaf on such occasions.'

Rebecca Ferrene says the best way to spend time with him was to watch dreadful TV. 'He was usually the last up and he'd be sat there watching his sport and his films. Then he'd always expect a kiss goodnight. If you got up to go to bed without giving him a kiss, he wouldn't say anything but would give you a look.' Rebecca says he also loved cartoons. 'He absolutely adored *Tom and Jerry*. Someone once came round to outfit him for a suit and *Tom and Jerry* was on TV. We were saying, "Dad, someone's waiting for you," and he was going, "Oh, sorry mate, I'm just watching *Tom and Jerry*. Do you like the show? Do you want to watch it?" He would have had this guy watching *Tom and Jerry* if he could have done.'

Trueman often watched television while reading a book. 'He'd be sat there watching a film and you'd suddenly see him walk across to the bookshelf, pick up a *Wisden*, find the appropriate page and start reading it,' said his stepson, Patrick. 'His mind was active all the time. He'd do the same if he didn't recognise a bird in the garden. He'd go straight to the bookcase to find out what it was.'

Trueman also enjoyed listening to music and, in 1978, revealed an eclectic selection on *Desert Island Discs*:

The closing passage of Tchaikovsky's '1812' Overture

'Tables and Chairs' by the players of Yorkshire County Cricket Club

'Blue Hawaii' by the Ray Conniff Orchestra

'White Christmas' by Bing Crosby

Bizet's 'Carmen Suite'

'And I Love You So' by Shirley Bassey

'Unforgettable' by Nat King Cole

The Largo from Dvorak's 'New World Symphony' (popularised by the Negro spiritual song 'Goin' Home')

Trueman's luxury item was a pair of high-powered binoculars, so 'I can study the island's wildlife', while his chosen book was the memoirs of Harold Macmillan – 'the last statesman that this wonderful country had'.

In reality, Trueman wasn't still long enough to listen to music or watch TV. He was forever on the go, dashing around in later life as much as he did in his playing days. His energy was boundless, his stamina phenomenal. Trueman spread himself thinner than water and sometimes undertook two engagements in a night. 'I once ghosted a piece with him on fast bowling,' said the writer David Foot. 'We met in a London hotel, where he was making a speech at a dinner that evening. "But I can do better than that," announced Fred, "'cos I'm walking straight out of this place and into another dinner."'

Trueman once flew to South Australia, spoke at two dinners on consecutive evenings and flew straight back again. During his time on *Test Match Special*, he thought nothing of doing a day's commentary stint, driving 100 miles to speak at a charity function and then returning to the cricket. 'Fred once came up from London to play in a charity match I'd organised in Leeds,' said his former Yorkshire Federation team-mate Eric Fisk. 'It was for a friend of my son's at school who'd broken his neck on a trampoline. The game took place on the rest day of a Test match in which Fred was summarising. He came up, played for nothing and went straight back afterwards.'

Trueman tore around like a twenty-something until May 2006, when he was diagnosed with lung cancer. He was given six weeks to live without treatment. 'It was a terrible shock,' said Veronica. 'Fred had a cough and couldn't get rid of it. He had X-rays and nothing showed. Then he was diagnosed – and our world fell apart. Fred asked the doctors, "How long have I got if I have treatment?" They said, "You might have a couple of years, you might have a couple of months." In the end, he only had a couple of months.'

Trueman had chemotherapy but the cancer was aggressive. It rapidly spread to his bowel. Veronica and the family issued a statement through Bob Platt saying doctors were confident they had caught the disease early and that Trueman would make a full recovery. In reality, they didn't want the press and public to know how seriously ill he was. In 1983, Trueman contracted legionnaire's disease – the illness that tragically killed Bill Frindall in 2009 – and there was a media frenzy. The family even had to put a guard outside Trueman's hospital ward. It turned out he'd caught the disease from a shower head in an Adelaide hotel. Trueman fell ill on the flight home from Australia and, for ten days, four pints of antibiotic solution were pumped into his body every eight hours. 'He very nearly died,' said Veronica. 'I remember him saying he could hear beautiful music. No one else could.'

Trueman made a speedy recovery but there was no way back from the cancer. Typically, the man who fought for everything in life did not go gentle into that good night. 'The last time I spoke to Freddie he was very poorly,' said his sister Flo. 'They'd brought him home from a chemotherapy session and when I rang he was sat in his garden, watching the birds. He said, "Flo, I'm going to fight this, I'm going to beat it." I said, "With your determination, duck, I'm sure you will." Then he went right quiet before saying, "You know, Flo, I've had a good life. I've been around the world more than most people. I'm looking down my garden now and I'm thinking of all those children who will never have the opportunities I've had. Some poor kids will never have a life, and I've had a wonderful life. I don't think I've got too much to complain about." '

In late June, Trueman was admitted to Airedale General Hospital. To protect his anonymity, he was registered on the hospital noticeboard as 'Mr Thrower' – a moniker that appealed to his sense of humour. 'They'll never guess it's me with that name,' quipped the man with a bowling action made in heaven. Family and friends kept a constant vigil – including daughter Rebecca, who flew back from America. 'I was pregnant with Tema when Dad was in hospital. As he was lying there, incubated and practically unconscious, I put his hand on my tummy and told him I was going to put Sewards in her name. I was also so grateful that my son got to meet him before he fell ill. In fact, the last time I took Luke to see Dad we'd gone for a little walk just behind Dad's house, where there's a beck. He said, "Let's do Pooh sticks." I thought, "What? Freddie Trueman playing Pooh sticks? I'd never heard Dad talk like that. He had this big grin on his face and he wanted to be the winner, of course, and it was just such a sweet moment.'

Reverend Ward also kept watch by the hospital bed. 'It was so sad to see Fred lying there. He was full of tubes and the thing that came into my mind was the story of *Gulliver's Travels*. Gulliver, this great giant, had been tied down by the Lilliputians with all these cords and pegs and now there was Fred, this great giant of a man, no longer able to exercise control of a life he'd always had control over. In fact, there was something particularly not right about this whole bundle of energy just dying.'

In his last hours, Trueman was fortified by those he loved and his faith in God. The man who couldn't face the death of his own relatives, who couldn't physically place his Yorkshire cap on top of his father's coffin because he was too upset, himself passed away with dignity and courage. 'Fred knew he was dying, his family knew he was dying and I knew he was dying,' said Reverend Ward. 'But he was prepared to accept that the God who'd been good to him in life wouldn't desert him in his hour of need. In his final hours, Fred was brave and didn't go to pieces as some people do. He held himself together extremely well.'

Shortly after noon on Saturday 1 July 2006, Fred Trueman passed away. Veronica rang Ted Corbett, whom she knew would be covering the one-day international between England and Sri Lanka at – of all places – Headingley cricket ground. Corbett rose to his feet in a crowded press box and solemnly announced the death of a legend. Minutes later, the news was conveyed on the giant replay screen above the West Stand. Without prompting, the crowd broke into sustained, moving applause that sent a shiver down the spine. During the break between innings, the teams observed a minute's silence, while flags at the ground were lowered to half-mast.

Across the Pennines, Flo Halifax learned of her brother's passing in poignant circumstances. 'My husband Des and I had gone to Blackpool for the day on a coach trip from Maltby. We'd all had a wonderful time and were boarding the bus to go home. I was one of the last on and said to everyone as I walked past, "Hasn't it been a wonderful day." They all said nothing and I thought, "Well, aren't they a miserable lot." Des was at the back of the bus and he beckoned me over. He put his arm around my shoulder and said, "Flo, I'm sorry to tell you that Freddie's gone." Well, I shouted and screamed and said, "How could he have gone?" I cried all the way back to Maltby. It turned out the news had been on the coach radio.'

At Headingley, Sri Lanka beat England by eight wickets. Steve Harmison conceded 97 runs from ten overs – England's most expensive one-day analysis. As *Wisden* would observe, 'it was just as well he [Trueman] wasn't on the radio.' The cricket, however, was rendered insignificant as tributes poured in from far and wide. 'Fred was not only a great fast bowler, but a great person,' proclaimed Sir Everton Weekes. 'He never failed to remind you he was a great fast bowler either.' Michael Parkinson reflected: 'I can hardly believe it. I mean, Fred's not the sort to die, is he? He was a huge character – full-blooded, Shakespearean almost, and a funny man. The gap he leaves is massive.' And former Prime Minister Sir John Major proclaimed: 'England has lost a national treasure – and history has gained a legend.'

Among the dozens of eulogies and appreciations, none extolled

Trueman more passionately than Brian Close, Ray Illingworth and Geoffrey Boycott, who'd gone to watch a cricket match only to find themselves at the centre of a uniquely poignant day. How bitter-sweet now seemed the memories – and how trivial all the bitter years of infighting at Yorkshire County Cricket Club – as the three remaining 'Greatest Living Yorkshiremen' remembered their former colleague. 'I captained many cricketers in my time, but none finer,' said Close, while absent-mindedly flicking cigarette ash on to the press box carpet. 'He was a tremendous wit and a lovely fellow.' Illingworth, too, cut a picture of melancholy as he told reporters: 'Fred, Brian and myself were together with the Yorkshire boys in 1948 – and it went on for twenty more wonderful years after that. We always had a smile on our faces when we played with Fred.'

And then there was Boycott, his eyes strangely distant, his voice unusually hushed, as though all the years of enmity with Trueman were turning in his mind. 'Fred and I falling out should never have happened,' he said. 'We were both, I think, wonderful cricketers for Yorkshire and England, and it should never have happened in a million years. I was just glad that in the last few years of his life things were different; he came to my house for lunch, I went to his house for lunch, and I got on great with him. It's like it should have been all our lives.'

15

Goodbye, My Friend

It was the sort of midsummer's morning Fred Trueman would have loved. The air was heavy after early-morning rain; the overcast conditions were tailor-made for swing bowling. Just after 11 a.m. – around the time he would have been running in to bowl from the Kirkstall Lane end – Trueman's coffin was shouldered into the Priory Church of St Mary and St Cuthbert at Bolton Abbey as Elgar's 'Nimrod' faded to echo. Right on cue, a pair of RAF aircraft flew directly above the twelfth-century church, their engines roaring in deafening salute. Inside the weathered walls of grey and orange sandstone, some three hundred mourners watched in silence. The coffin was laid beside the altar, where an inscription on a bouquet of red roses said it all. 'From Lancastrian friends', read the touching dedication. Fred Trueman transcended the usual rivalries.

I was among those privileged to be at Bolton Abbey for the funeral on 6 July 2006. It was exactly one year to the day since the only time I'd met Fred Trueman, when he'd revelled in the company of Brian Close, Ray Illingworth and Geoffrey Boycott at their touching reunion at the Sawley Arms. Now I'd been sent by the *Yorkshire Post* to cover the final journey of England's greatest fast bowler. I felt honoured and unworthy to be among the congregation. Alas, there was no public memorial service – and on Trueman's orders. 'When I'm dead and gone, I don't want those two-faced bastards from Yorkshire and MCC who I didn't get on with standing up and saying nice things about me,' was the gist of his instruction to family and friends. Although one could admire his principled stance, one wondered how many of those 'two-faced bastards' were still around, and whether that was sufficient cause to deprive his admirers of the chance to give him a rousing send-off. In death, as in life, the rebel was rebelling, making his exit with all guns blazing.

It would be difficult to imagine a more beautiful farewell than the one afforded Trueman, or a more breathtaking final resting place than the grounds of Bolton Abbey on the banks of the Wharfe. The evocative scenery attracts a quarter of a million visitors a year, a good number of whom come to venerate him. The stunning setting has fired the imagination of some of the world's greatest artists: Edwin Landseer and J.M.W. Turner were moved to paint by its pastoral beauty, while William Wordsworth's poem *The White Doe of Rylstone* was inspired by a visit in 1807. On the day we said farewell to Trueman, that beauty was in glorious evidence. Swallows and martins wheeled and dived. A heron landed lazily on the barely moving Wharfe, like an autumn leaf tumbling gently to ground. Calves and sheep grazed contentedly in the paddock, while oaks and chestnuts stood as sentinels. High above the West Tower, the flag of St George fluttered in the breeze.

The mourners began arriving from 7 a.m. – or, to be precise, a certain Dickie Bird arrived at 7 a.m. Invited by Veronica Trueman to deliver the tribute, the former Yorkshire batsman and legendary umpire – who once turned up at the Oval at 6 a.m. in readiness for a county game – admitted he'd been anxious to leave nothing to chance. 'When I arrived there was no one around, so I just sat in the Devonshire Arms down the road chatting to the night porters,' he said. 'They thought it a bit odd I'd turned up four hours before the service, but I've never been one for arriving late – unlike Fred.'

As morning unfolded, the trickle became a steady procession. Close rolled up in a Vauxhall Vectra, taking unusual care as he navigated the Priory's narrow bends, while there was no mistaking Illingworth in his black Jaguar with number plate 'ILLY'. Other Yorkshire team-mates included Bob Platt, John Hampshire, Richard

Hutton, Bob Appleyard, Philip Sharpe, Bryan Stott, Doug Padgett and Vic Wilson. One notable, however, was not in attendance. Four days earlier, Geoffrey Boycott had paid glowing tribute to Trueman at Headingley. Now the former opening batsman was conspicuous by his absence. 'Boycott didn't dare go to the funeral because he knew he'd have been ostracised by the former Yorkshire players,' claimed Platt. 'He knows he's not acceptable and that the players would have turned their backs on him.'

Boycott, however, gave the following reason. 'I'm not a big one for funerals – never have been. I think the funeral should be for the family, personally, but that's only my view. A memorial service is different, but Fred didn't want that. And you have to respect his wishes.'

The service began with an introduction by Reverend John Ward. He described Trueman as 'a cricketing colossus – a man capable of crossing all boundaries, be it four runs, six runs or social class'. Referring to the defeat of England's footballers in a World Cup quarter-final against Portugal in Gelsenkirchen on the day Trueman died, Ward added: 'England lost more than a football match on Saturday; it lost a genuine sporting hero . . . Frederick Sewards Trueman by name and true man by nature.' The congregation sang 'Dear Lord and Father of Mankind' – one of Trueman's favourites – before Bird performed the tribute. It is by no means unusual for Bird to cry in public – Platt jokes his statue in his native Barnsley has rusted around the eye sockets in honour of its lachrymose subject – but Bird held himself together as he declared: 'People ask how great Fred was. Well, he was higher than great; he was a genius. He was up there with the likes of Muhammad Ali and Pele.' Then, turning to the coffin, his voice thick with emotion, Bird trembled, 'Goodbye, my friend.'

The service continued with a rousing rendition of 'Lord of All Hopefulness' before Canon Ward gave the address. His own voice shook as he declared: 'It used both to amuse and irritate Fred when people expressed surprise at his ecclesiastical associations. But it may also come as a surprise to many of them that the man who was rarely reluctant to pass an opinion on any subject, let alone cricket, was, when it came to faith, possessed of a great humility in a thankful heart. "God's been good to me," he would say time and time again . . .

'The words were sometimes harsh and uncompromising, but the heart was tender and generous. He couldn't stand insincerity, or cruelty or abuse of any kind – especially when it related to children or animals, and he genuinely cared for those who were in trouble not of their own making . . .

'Fred was my boyhood hero, and though sometimes your heroes fade or disappoint when you meet them face to face, that was not so for me with Fred. Quite the reverse . . .

'Little did I think that I would find myself where I stand today. Nor where I stood last Friday night as I said prayers by his hospital bedside and talked to him about the God who promises an end to pain and the drying of tears, a God who makes all things new. A God whom Fred recognised as good, and who would not let him down in his hour of need. A God who has a safer pair of hands than did David Sheppard. And when I said that, I'd like to think I saw him smile.'

Platt read Henry Scott Holland's 'Death is Nothing at All', his smoky voice refusing to crack, before the service concluded with 'Thine Be the Glory' and a reading of G.D. Martineau's 'The Pitch at Night':

> The sunset brings the twilight chill
> That steals, all noiseless, on the air.
> The wind-freed world is standing still,
> The smoothed, worn ground looks strangely bare.
>
> The bowler's run has blurred the crease,
> Which glints, a dim and spectral white,
> Half sad, half comforting, this peace
> That settled o'er the ground at night.

Steps give a faintly eerie hiss
On less tried turf towards the rough
(Was I too hard on Jones's miss,
Or was I not quite hard enough?)

Here is an ancient, useless pad.
The score-board stares, a square of ink.
Some of this outfield's rather bad. . .
It's colder now; to bed, I think.

The grave is cut on a soft slope to the east of the Priory, wending down to the Wharfe. It is a quantum leap from Scotch Springs, where Trueman was born on the edge of a pit yard. There is no greater measure of how far he came in life than to contemplate his birthplace and final resting place. As his body was committed, children played and splashed by the river, while a flock of birds appeared from nowhere.

'Curlews flew over at the burial,' said Veronica. 'That got to a lot of people. Fred loved curlews. They call on the wing, and they were there, calling at his graveside. It was symbolic, as though they were paying their own special tribute. What with the river, the children, the wildlife and everything, it was just so beautiful, so moving.'

When asked what epitaph he wanted on his headstone, Trueman always quipped, 'It wasn't Fred, 'cos he's here.' Instead the inscription carved in black letters beneath a Tudor rose reads:

FREDERICK SEWARDS TRUEMAN OBE
CRICKETER
YORKSHIRE COUNTY CRICKET CLUB & ENGLAND
BORN 6TH FEB 1931 DIED 1ST JULY 2006

It is a simple dedication to a singular individual, a man of sweeping contrasts and stark contradictions. Some called him the 'Greatest Living Yorkshireman'; others – himself included – 'T'Finest Bloody Fast Bowler That Ever Drew Breath'.

But John Arlott put it best:

'He could be harsh and gentle; witty and crude; unbelievably funny and very boring; selfish and wonderfully kind . . . and he was, when the fire burnt, as fine a fast bowler as any.'

Acknowledgements

It isn't every day that someone you've never met emails out of the blue to ask whether you'd be interested in writing a book about one of the great sporting figures of the twentieth century. That was the position I found myself in when Graham Coster, publisher at Aurum Press, proposed this biography of Fred Trueman. I would like to thank Graham and Aurum for giving me the opportunity and also the Australian cricket writer Gideon Haigh for pointing them in my direction. Gideon has written several titles for Aurum and thought I would be well placed in my capacity as *Yorkshire Post* cricket correspondent to give it a go.

I owe an enormous debt to the Trueman family, who have been unfailingly helpful and supportive. In particular, I am grateful to Fred's widow, Veronica and sister, Flo, for their insights and encouragement. I came to appreciate during my investigations what a loving family Trueman had around him, and my thanks go also to his brothers, John and Dennis; children, Karen, Rebecca, Rodney, Sheenagh and Patrick; first wife, Enid; cousin, Alan; and niece, Pauline. It has been a pleasure and privilege to meet you all.

Every writer needs a shoulder to lean on (in my case, several shoulders), and I have been fortunate to have some stellar support. For his sage advice on this project, as well as his assistance throughout my journalistic career and, above all, his friendship, I would like to thank Duncan Hamilton, author of a superlative biography of another great English fast bowler, Harold Larwood.

No one could have a more talented tutor than Duncan, formerly my assistant editor at the *Nottingham Evening Post* and my deputy editor at the *Yorkshire Post*. Hopefully he can now get back to writing his own books instead of being constantly pestered for his thoughts on this one.

I am also very grateful for the guidance of my friends and fellow cricket writers Brian Halford, Paul Edwards and Bruce Talbot, who cast perspicacious eyes over the manuscript, as well as the assistance of another friend, Peter Wynne-Thomas, the venerable Nottinghamshire County Cricket Club librarian. A constant source of support during my previous life as *Nottingham Evening Post* cricket correspondent, Peter diligently checked for factual errors. Stephen Chalke was also a perceptive sounding board in the project's early stages.

I have made much use of the 1964 BBC documentary of Fred Trueman's life, which is so rare that not even the BBC possess a copy. However, where conventional channels fail there is invariably David Frith, who unsurprisingly had a recording of it in his voluminous cricket archive. I am grateful not only for David's help with the documentary but also his observations on Trueman and his generous encouragement to a first-time author. Having experienced the agonies of writing only one book, I cannot begin to imagine how David must feel having written over thirty.

For help with Fred Trueman's family history, I am obliged to Anthony Adolph, one of Britain's leading genealogists, while military researcher Jonathan Collins was invaluable in helping me shed light on Dick Trueman's war service. Former *Test Match Special* producer Peter Baxter assisted my efforts to track down several recordings, while the BBC's Guy Worsick and Gareth Jones helped out with general radio recordings. Douglas Miller kindly provided details of MCC minutes and shared his memories of collaborating with former England player/manager Charles Palmer. Thanks also to staff at the British Library, British Newspaper Library, Leeds Central Library, Lincoln Central Library, National Archives, National Coal Mining Museum for England, Royal Air Forces Association (Lincoln Branch) and the *Yorkshire Post*, along with Aurum's Steve Gove, Barbara Phelan, Melissa Smith and Catherine Bailey.

The book draws heavily on interviews with those who came across Trueman at various stages. From his earliest days/schooldays: Frank Anderton, Brian Beardsall, Les Bowden, Colin Brierley, Betty Buck, Ron Buck, John Gibson, Phillip Gibson, Chris Hunt, Terry Hunt, Tom Layden, Brian Pickering, Ken Pickering and Walter Smith. From his RAF days: Colin Blower, Colin Fisher, Norman Maxwell, Brian Smith, Ray Upson and John Whitehead. Thanks also to Geoff Hastings and Glynis Sievwright for enabling interviews with former RAF colleagues.

Many former cricketers offered their support, the extent of their contributions mainly evident in the text. Almost everyone had a Fred story – often more than one – to the extent that it was difficult to determine what to leave out. Other press-box colleagues provided help and encouragement, while a number of people facilitated interviews. Space precludes everyone an individual eulogy, but my heartfelt thanks go to: Qamar Ahmed, David Allan, Bob Appleyard, the late Trevor Bailey, Alec Bedser, Scyld Berry, Alan Biggs, Jimmy Binks, Dickie Bird, Paul Bolton, Lawrence Booth, Sir Ian Botham, Geoffrey Boycott, Stephen Brenkley, Bill Bridge, Simon Briggs, Claude Brownlow, Morag Brownlow, Eric Burgin, Jim Cadman, Dave Callaghan, Brian Close, Andrew Collomosse, Geoff Cope, Ted Corbett, Mike Cowan, Tony Cozier, Carol Crabtree, Jon Culley, Ron Deaton, Ted Dexter, Maureen Fielden, Sidney Fielden, Eric Fisk, David Foot, Angus Fraser, the late Bill Frindall, Anshuman Gaekwad, Datta Gaekwad, Pat Gibson, Robert Gledhill, Harry Gration, Tom Graveney, Andy Graver, Hugh Griffiths, Julian Guyer, John Hampshire, Neil Harvey, Roy Hattersley, June Hawes, John Helm, Derek Hodgson, Richard Hutton, Ray Illingworth, Sir Bernard Ingham, Doug Insole, Derek Jameson, Martin Johnson, Cecil Kippins, Ted Lester, David Lloyd, Revd Malcolm Lorimer, Vic Marks, Christopher Martin-Jenkins, Geoff Miller, Alan Moss, Donald Nannestad, Chandresh Narayanan, Chris Old, Peter Parfitt, Shilpa Patel, Bob Platt, Derek Pringle, Tom Richmond, Helen Riley, Neil

Robinson, Mike Selvey, Philip Sharpe, Audrey Statham, John Stern, Bryan Stott, Richard Sutcliffe, Richard Sydenham, Bob Taylor, Ken Taylor, Frank Tyson, Sid Waddell, Mike Walters, Revd John Ward, David Warner, Sir Everton Weekes, John Westerby, Simon Wilde, Roy Wilkinson, Bob Willis, Don Wilson, the late Vic Wilson and John Woodcock.

Apologies to anyone I've stupidly forgotten.

I began this book with an account of the only time I met Fred Trueman; I'll end it with an anecdote from the last occasion I spoke to him on the telephone. It was the spring of 2006, and I'd just written a series of articles for the *Yorkshire Post* inviting readers to select their greatest-ever Yorkshire XI. The competition attracted more than 5,000 entries, and Trueman received the most votes of any player, with 99 per cent of readers picking him in their side. For the record, the XI chosen was Len Hutton, Herbert Sutcliffe, Maurice Leyland, Darren Lehmann, Brian Close, George Hirst, Wilfred Rhodes, Jimmy Binks, Fred Trueman, Bill Bowes and Hedley Verity. When I rang Trueman to relay the news, he expressed suitable delight before pointing out at some length that it was impossible to pick a definitive XI because different pitch conditions, and so on, had to be taken into account. Then, with the sort of delayed reaction that put one in mind of Cyril Heslop, the character played by Brian Glover in the television series *Porridge*, the significance of the vote suddenly dawned. 'Er, you said 99 per cent of readers voted for me?' he said, sounding indignant. 'Er, only 99 per cent? I tell you what, I'd like to catch up with the bastards who didn't vote for me . . .'

C. W.
Headingley, Leeds
September, 2011

Bibliography

Agnew, Jonathan, *Over to You, Aggers*, Gollancz, 1997

Alston, Rex, *Test Commentary*, Stanley Paul, 1956

Arlott, John, *Test Match Diary 1953*, James Barrie, 1953

Arlott, John, *The Australian Challenge*, Heinemann, 1961

Arlott, John, *The Great Bowlers*, Pelham, 1968

Arlott, John, *Fred: Portrait of a Fast Bowler*, Eyre & Spottiswoode, 1971

Arlott, John; Trueman, Fred, *Arlott and Trueman on Cricket* (ed. Gilbert Phelps), British Broadcasting Corporation, 1977

Arlott, John, *A Word from Arlott* (selected by David Rayvern-Allen), Pelham, 1983

Arlott, John, *Arlott on Cricket* (ed. David Rayvern-Allen), Willow, 1984

Arlott, John, *Another Word from Arlott* (selected by David Rayvern-Allen), Pelham, 1985

Arlott, John, *Basingstoke Boy*, Willow, 1990

Bailey, Philip; Thorn, Philip; Wynne-Thomas, Peter, *Who's Who of Cricketers*, Newnes Books, 1984

Bailey, Trevor, *Championship Cricket*, Frederick Muller, 1961

Bailey, Trevor; Trueman, Fred, *From Larwood to Lillee*, Queen Anne Press, 1983

Bailey, Trevor, *Wickets, Catches and the Odd Run*, Collins Willow, 1986

Bailey, Trevor; Trueman, Fred, *The Spinner's Web*, Willow, 1988

Bannister, Alex, *Cricket Cauldron*, Stanley Paul, 1954

Barker, J. S., *Summer Spectacular*, Collins, 1963

Barrett, Norman, (ed.), *The Daily Telegraph Chronicle of Cricket*, Guinness, 1994

Batchelor, Denzil, *The Test Matches of 1964*, Epworth Press, 1964

Baxter, Peter, (ed.), *Test Match Special*, Queen Anne Press, 1981

Baxter, Peter, (ed.), *Test Match Special 2*, Queen Anne Press, 1983

Baxter, Peter, (ed.), *Test Match Special 3*, Queen Anne Press, 1985

Baxter, Peter, (ed.), *From Brisbane to Karachi with the Test Match Special Team*, Macdonald, 1988

Baxter, Peter, (ed.), *From Arlott to Aggers: 40 Years of Test Match Special*, Andre Deutsch, 1997

Baxter, Peter, (ed.), *Test Match Special: 50 Not Out*, BBC, 2007

Baxter, Peter, *Inside the Box: My Life with Test Match Special*, Quiller, 2009

Bedser, Alec, *May's Men in Australia*, Stanley Paul, 1959

Benaud, Richie, *Way of Cricket*, Hodder & Stoughton, 1961

Benaud, Richie, *Spin Me a Spinner*, Hodder & Stoughton, 1963

Benaud, Richie, *Anything But: An Autobiography*, Hodder & Stoughton, 1998

Benaud, Richie, *My Spin on Cricket*, Hodder & Stoughton, 2005

Benaud, Richie, *Over But Not Out: My Life So Far*, Hodder & Stoughton, 2010

Berry, Scyld, (ed.), *The Observer on Cricket: An Anthology of the Best Cricket Writing*, Unwin Hyman, 1987

Bird, Dickie, *From the Pavilion End*, Barker, 1988

Bird, Dickie, *My Autobiography*, Hodder & Stoughton, 1997

Bird, Dickie, *White Cap and Bails*, Hodder & Stoughton, 1999

Birley, Derek, *A Social History of English Cricket*, Aurum, 1999

Blofeld, Henry, *Cakes and Bails*, Simon & Schuster, 1998

Blofeld, Henry, *A Thirst for Life*, Hodder & Stoughton, 2000

Boothroyd, Derrick, *Half a Century of Yorkshire Cricket*, Kennedy Brothers Ltd, 1981

Bowes, Bill, *Aussies and Ashes*, Stanley Paul, 1961

Boycott, Geoffrey, *Put to the Test*, Arthur Barker, 1979

Boycott, Geoffrey, *Opening Up*, Arthur Barker, 1980

Boycott, Geoffrey, *In the Fast Lane*, Arthur Barker, 1981

Boycott, Geoffrey, *Boycott: The Autobiography*, Macmillan, 1987

Boycott, Geoffrey, *Boycott on Cricket*, Bantam, 1990

Boycott, Geoffrey, *The Best XI*, Michael Joseph, 2008

Callaghan, John, *Boycott: A Cricketing Legend*, Pelham, 1982

Callaghan, John, *Yorkshire Cricket Greats*, Sportsprint, 1990

Cardus, Neville, *Cardus in the Covers*, Souvenir Press, 1978

Chalke, Stephen, *Runs in the Memory: County Cricket in the 1950s*, Fairfield Books, 1997

Chalke, Stephen, *Caught in the Memory: County Cricket in the 1960s*, Fairfield Books, 1999

Chalke, Stephen, *One More Run*, Fairfield Books, 2000

Chalke, Stephen, *At the Heart of English Cricket: The Life and Memories of Geoffrey Howard*, Fairfield Books, 2001

Chalke, Stephen; Hodgson, Derek, *No Coward Soul: The Remarkable Story of Bob Appleyard*, Fairfield Books, 2003

Chalke, Stephen, *Ken Taylor: Drawn to Sport*, Fairfield Books, 2006

Chalke, Stephen, *Tom Cartwright: The Flame Still Burns*, Fairfield Books, 2007,

Chalke, Stephen, *The Way It Was*, Fairfield Books, 2008

Clark, C, D., *The Test Match Career of Freddie Trueman*, David & Charles, 1980

Clarke, John, *Challenge Renewed: The MCC tour of Australia 1962–63*, Stanley Paul, 1963

Clarke, John, *Cricket With a Swing*, Stanley Paul, 1963

Close, Brian, *I Don't Bruise Easily*, Macdonald & Jane's, 1978

Collomosse, Andrew, *Magnificent Seven*, Great Northern Books, 2010

Compton, Denis, *End of an Innings*, Oldbourne, 1958

Compton, Denis, *Compton on Cricketers Past and Present*, Cassell, 1980

Cowdrey, Colin, *MCC: The Autobiography of a Cricketer*, Coronet, 1977

Cozier, Tony, *The West Indies: Fifty Years of Test Cricket*, Angus & Robertson, 1978

Derlien, Tony, *Bowled Statham*, Breedon Books, 1990

Dexter, Ted, *Ted Dexter Declares*, Stanley Paul, 1966

D'Oliveira, Basil, *Time to Declare*, W. H. Allen, 1980

Engel, Matthew, (ed.), *The Guardian Book of Cricket*, Pavilion, 1986

Evans, Godfrey, *The Gloves are Off*, Hodder & Stoughton, 1960

Farnsworth, Keith, *Before and After Bramall Lane: Sheffield United Cricket Club and Yorkshire Cricket in Sheffield*, K. Farnsworth, 1988

Fingleton, Jack, *The Ashes Crown the Year*, Collins, 1954

Fingleton, Jack, *Four Chukkas to Australia*, Heinemann, 1959

Frindall, Bill, (ed.), *The Wisden Book of Test Cricket 1876–77 to 1977–78*, Macdonald & Jane's, 1980

Frindall, Bill, *Bearders: My Life in Cricket*, Orion, 2006

Frith, David, *The Fast Men*, Corgi, 1977

Frith, David, *Caught England, Bowled Australia*, Eva, 1997

Gough, Darren, *Dazzler*, Michael Joseph, 2001

Green, Benny, (ed.), *Wisden Anthology 1900–1940*, Queen Anne Press, 1980

Green, Benny, (ed.), *Wisden Anthology 1940–1963*, Queen Anne Press, 1982

Green, Benny, (ed.), *Wisden Anthology 1963–1982*, Queen Anne Press, 1983

Green, Benny, (ed.), *The Wisden Papers of Neville Cardus*, Stanley Paul, 1989

Gregory, Ken, (ed.), *In Celebration of Cricket*, Hart-Davis MacGibbon, 1978

Gregory, Ken, (ed.), *From Grace to Botham: Fifty Master Cricketers from The Times*, Times Books, 1989

Halford, Brian, *Past Imperfect: The Story of Lincoln City F.C.*, Parrs Wood Press, 2000

Hall, Wes, *Pace Like Fire*, Pelham, 1965

Hamilton, Duncan, (ed.), *Sweet Summers: The Classic Cricket Writing of JM Kilburn*, Great Northern Books, 2008

Hamilton, Duncan, *Harold Larwood*, Quercus, 2009

Hamilton, Duncan, (ed.), *Wisden on Yorkshire*, John Wisden, 2011

Hampshire, John, *Family Argument: My 20 Years in Yorkshire Cricket*, Allen & Unwin, 1983

Harris, Bruce, *Defending the Ashes*, Hutchinson, 1956

Heald, Tim, *Brian Johnston: The Authorised Biography*, Methuen, 1995

Hill, Alan, *Johnny Wardle: Cricket Conjurer*, David & Charles, 1988

Hill, Alan, *Brian Close: Cricket's Lionheart*, Methuen, 2002

Hill, Alan, *Daring Young Men*, Methuen, 2005

Hodgson, Derek, *The Official History of Yorkshire County Cricket Club*, The Crowood Press, 1989

Hoult, Nick, (ed.), *The Daily Telegraph Book of Cricket*, Aurum, 2007

Howat, Gerald, *Len Hutton*, Heinemann Kingswood, 1988

Hutton, Len, *Cricket is My Life*, Hutchinson, 1949

Hutton, Len, *Just My Story*, Hutchinson, 1956

Hutton, Len, *Fifty Years in Cricket*, Stanley Paul, 1984

Illingworth, Ray, *Yorkshire and Back*, Queen Anne Press, 1980

Illingworth, Ray, *The Tempestuous Years 1979–83*, Sidgwick & Jackson, 1987

James, C. L. R., *Beyond a Boundary*, Hutchinson, 1963

Johnson, Martin, *Can't Bat, Can't Bowl, Can't Field: The Best Cricket Writing of Martin Johnson* (compiled and edited by Andrew Green), Collins Willow, 1997

Johnston, Barry, *The Life of Brian*, Hodder & Stoughton, 2003

Johnston, Brian, *It's a Funny Game*, W. H. Allen, 1978

Johnston, Brian, *Chatterbox: My Friends the Commentators*, Methuen, 1983

Johnston, Brian, *It's Been a Piece of Cake*, Methuen, 1989

Johnston, Brian, *Down Your Way*, Methuen, 1990

Johnston, Brian, *An Evening With Johnners* (ed. Barry Johnston), Partridge, 1996

Johnston, Brian, *A Delicious Slice of Johnners* (ed. Barry Johnston), Virgin, 2000

Johnston, Brian, *Another Slice of Johnners* (ed. Barry Johnston), Virgin, 2001

Johnston, Brian, *A Further Slice of Johnners* (ed. Barry Johnston), Virgin, 2002

Kay, John, *England Down Under: The MCC tour of Australia 1958–59*, Sporting Handbooks, 1959

Kilburn, J. M., *Cricket Decade*, Heinemann, 1959

Kilburn, J. M., *A History of Yorkshire Cricket*, Stanley Paul, 1970

Kilburn, J. M., *Thanks to Cricket*, The Sportsman's Book Club, 1973

Kilburn, J. M., *Overthrows*, Stanley Paul, 1975

Laker, Jim, *Spinning Round the World*, Frederick Muller, 1957

Laker, Jim, *Over to Me*, Frederick Muller, 1960

Laker, Jim, *The Australian Tour of 1961*, Frederick Muller, 1961

Lee, Alan, *Lord Ted: The Dexter Enigma*, Gollancz/Witherby, 1995

Lemmon, David, (ed.), *Cricket Heroes*, Queen Anne Press, 1984

Lemmon, David, *Cricket's Champion Counties*, Breedon Books, 1991

Lewis, Tony, *Double Century: The Story of MCC and Cricket*, Hodder & Stoughton, 1987

Lindwall, Ray, *Flying Stumps*, Stanley Paul, 1954

Lorimer, Rev Malcolm, (ed.), *Glory Lightly Worn: A Tribute to Brian Statham*, Parrs Wood Press, 1990

Marshall, John, *Headingley*, Pelham Books, 1970

Martin-Jenkins, Christopher, *Ball by Ball: The Story of Cricket Broadcasting*, Grafton, 1990

May, Peter, *A Game Enjoyed*, Stanley Paul, 1985

McKinstry, Leo, *Boycs: The True Story*, Partridge, 2003

Miller, Douglas, *Charles Palmer: More Than Just a Gentleman*, Fairfield Books, 2005

Morgan, John; Joy, David, *Trueman's Tales: Fiery Fred – Yorkshire's Cricketing Giant*, Great Northern Books, 2007

Mosey, Don, *The Best Job in the World*, Pelham, 1985

Mosey, Don, *Boycott*, Methuen, 1985

Mosey, Don, *Botham*, Methuen, 1986

Mosey, Don, *We Don't Play it for Fun*, Sphere, 1988

Mosey, Don, *Jim Laker: Portrait of a Legend*, Macdonald/Queen Anne, 1989

Mosey, Don, *Fred: Then and Now*, Kingswood, 1991

Mosey, Don, *The Alderman's Tale*, Weidenfeld & Nicolson, 1991

Moyes, Alban, *The Story of the Tests*, Angus & Robertson, 1959

Moyes, Alban; Goodman, Thomas, *With the MCC in Australia*, Angus & Robertson, 1963

Nannestad, Donald & Ian, *Who's Who of Lincoln City 1892–1994*, Yore Publications, 1994

Nannestad, Donald & Ian, *Lincoln City F.C.: The Official History*, Yore Publications, 1997

Parkinson, Michael, *Selected Interviews from the Television Series*, Elm Tree Books, 1975

Parkinson, Michael, *Michael Parkinson on Cricket*, Hodder & Stoughton, 2002

Parkinson, Michael, *Parky: My Autobiography*, Hodder & Stoughton, 2008

Peebles, Ian, *The Fight for the Ashes*, George G. Harrap & Co, 1959

Pope, Mick; Dyson, Paul, *100 Greats: Yorkshire County Cricket Club*, Tempus, 2001

Rae, Simon, *It's Not Cricket*, Faber and Faber, 2001

Rayvern-Allen, David, (ed.), *Cricket Through the Pages*, Andre Deutsch, 2000

Rayvern-Allen, David, *Jim: The Life of E. W. Swanton*, Aurum, 2004

Rayvern-Allen, David, *Arlott: The Authorised Biography*, Aurum, 2004

Rice, Jonathan, *The Presidents of M.C.C.*, Methuen, 2006

Ross, Alan, *Australia 55*, Michael Joseph, 1955

Ross, Alan, *Cape Summer and the Australians in England*, Hamish Hamilton, 1957

Ross, Alan, *Through the Caribbean*, Hamish Hamilton, 1960

Ross, Alan, *Australia 63*, Eyre & Spottiswoode, 1963

Ross, Alan, *West Indies at Lord's*, Eyre & Spottiswoode, 1963

Ross, Alan, *The Cricketers' Companion*, Eyre Methuen, 1979

Ross, Gordon, *The Testing Years*, Stanley Paul, 1958

Ross, Gordon, *Cricket's Great Characters*, G. Ross, 1977

Sheppard, David, *Parson's Pitch*, Hodder & Stoughton, 1964

Sheppard, John, (ed.), *Cricket: More Than a Game*, Angus & Robertson, 1975

Snow, John, *Cricket Rebel*, Hamlyn, 1976

Sobers, Garry, *Twenty Years at the Top*, Macmillan, 1988

Sobers, Garry, *My Autobiography*, Headline, 2002

Statham, Brian, *Cricket Merry-go-Round*, Stanley Paul, 1956

Statham, Brian, *Flying Bails*, Stanley Paul, 1961

Statham, Brian, *A Spell at the Top*, Souvenir Press, 1969

Stern, John, (ed.), *My Favourite Cricketer*, A & C Black, 2010

Stollmeyer, Jeff, *Everything Under the Sun*, Stanley Paul, 1983

Swanton, E. W., *West Indian Adventure*, Museum Press, 1954

Swanton, E. W., *West Indies Revisited*, Heinemann, 1960

Swanton, E. W., *The Ashes in Suspense*, Daily Telegraph, 1963

Swanton, E. W., *Sort of a Cricket Person*, Collins, 1972

Swanton, E. W., *As I Said at the Time* (ed. George Plumptre), Collins, 1983

Swanton, E. W., *Gubby Allen: Man of Cricket*, Stanley Paul, 1985

Trelford, Donald, *Len Hutton Remembered*, H. F. & G. Witherby, 1992

Trueman, Fred, *Fast Fury*, Stanley Paul, 1961

Trueman, Fred, *Freddie Trueman's Book of Cricket*, Pelham, 1964

Trueman, Fred, *The Freddie Trueman Story*, Stanley Paul, 1965

Trueman, Fred, *Ball of Fire: An Autobiography*, Dent, 1976

Trueman, Fred; Hardy, Frank, *You Nearly Had Him That Time – and Other Cricket Stories*, Stanley Paul, 1978

Trueman, Fred; Morecambe, Eric; Rushton, Willie; Rumsey, Fred, *The Thoughts of Trueman Now: Every Cricket Maniac's Anthology*, Macdonald & Jane's, 1978

Trueman, Fred; Mosey, Don, *My Most Memorable Matches*, Stanley Paul, 1982

Trueman Fred; Mosey, Don, *Fred Trueman's Yorkshire*, Stanley Paul, 1984

Trueman, Fred, *Fred Trueman's Dales Journey*, Dalesman, 1988

Trueman, Fred; Mosey, Don, *Cricket Statistics Year-by-Year 1946–1987*, Stanley Paul, 1988

Trueman, Fred; Grosvenor, Peter, *Fred Trueman's Cricket Masterpieces: Classic Tales from the Pavilion*, Sidgwick & Jackson, 1990

Trueman, Fred; Mosey, Don, *Champion Times: Yorkshire CCC 1959–1968*, Dalesman, 1994

Trueman, Fred; Mosey, Don, *Fred Trueman Talking Cricket with Friends Past and Present*, Hodder & Stoughton, 1997

Trueman, Fred, *As it Was: The Memoirs of Fred Trueman*, Macmillan, 2004

Turbervill, Huw, *The Toughest Tour*, Aurum, 2010

Tyson, Frank, *A Typhoon Called Tyson*, Heinemann, 1961

Tyson, Frank, *The Test Within*, Hutchinson, 1987

Vaughan, Michael, *Time to Declare*, Hodder & Stoughton, 2009

Walcott, Clyde, *Island Cricketers*, Hodder & Stoughton, 1958

Walcott, Clyde, *Sixty Years on the Back Foot*, Gollancz, 1999

Wardle, Johnny, *Happy Go Johnny*, Robert Hale, 1957

Watson, Willie, *Double International*, Stanley Paul, 1956

Wellings, E. M., *The Ashes Thrown Away*, Bailey Bros & Swinfen, 1959

Wellings, E. M., *Dexter versus Benaud*, Bailey Bros & Swinfen, 1963

West, Peter, *The Fight for the Ashes 1956*, George G. Harrap & Co, 1956

White, Crawford, *The Ashes Go Home*, News Chronicle Book Department, 1959

Wilde, Simon, *Letting Rip: The Fast Bowling Threat from Lillee to Waqar*, Gollancz/Witherby, 1995

Wilde, Simon, *Number One: The World's Best Batsmen and Bowlers*, Gollancz, 1998

Williams, Marcus, (ed.), *Double Century: 200 Years of Cricket in The Times*, Collins, 1985

Wilson, Don, *Mad Jack*, Kingswood Press, 1992

Wisden Cricketers' Almanack, various editions

Woodcock, John, *The Times One Hundred Greatest Cricketers*, Macmillan, 1998

Woodhouse, Anthony, *The History of Yorkshire County Cricket Club*, Christopher Helm, 1989

Wooldridge, Ian, *Cricket Lovely Cricket*, Robert Hale, 1963

Worrell, Frank, *Cricket Punch*, Stanley Paul, 1957

Yardley, Norman, *Cricket Campaigns*, Stanley Paul, 1950

Yorkshire County Cricket Club Yearbook, various editions

Index